A great "you are there" memoir of the Women's Music Era. Jamie puts you on the ground, in the air and backstage so vividly you'll believe you toured with her.

> \- **Suzanne Westenhoefer**, candid, bold and
> brazen lesbian comic

Singer/songwriter Jamie Anderson's road memoir, *Drive All Night* is a spot-on peek into the life of a traveling comic musician. A lesbian folk comic musician, at that. Her recollections of grungy lodging, shady producers, half-deaf sound engineers and miles of highway weariness are juxtaposed with her road warrior's wit and the magical, musical friendships she has made over the years. It's a funny, crazy, complicated journey, and she leads with her sense of humor and heart. I have shared many stages with Jamie over the years, and she is constantly in motion—writing, gigging, networking, recording, booking. And always laughing. This book gives you an inside look into the not-so-glamorous daily grind and tremendous joys of a career as a working musician.

> \- **Lisa Koch**, singer-songwriter-comedian-actor-raconteur

Curious about the nitty-gritty of life on the folk road? Then these stories, told by a fearless, good-natured minstrel in the tradition of the second oldest profession, are for you. My own experiences confirm the truth of what sister Jamie describes in this series of intimate, revealing and humorous vignettes.

> \- **Alix Dobkin**, groundbreaking musician, composer,
> *Lavender Jane Loves Women*

She is singing some wonderful songs.

> \- **Holly Near**

Despite the stressful conditions, terrible hours, and worse pay, there are times of kindness and love, exhilarating performances, standing ovations, transcendent improvisation with the likes of Holly Near, and brilliant jamming musicians. These rewarding exper path of her huge talent and heart f

> \- **Nancy Manahan**, autho
> *On My Honor: Lesbians Re*

…Solid songwriting and engaging stage presence.

- Billboard

Jamie Anderson's *Drive All Night* captures her peripatetic musical career. She brings alive the experiences of so many of us who have (to lesser degrees) been on the road as Public Lesbians. She depicts not only our celebrities, but her very endearing interactions with them and with her fans. Our beloved troubadour chronicles her own ups and downs and decades of women's music and lesbian culture. Always warm, real, a little self-deprecating, and proudly sexy, in *Drive All Night*, Jamie's as endlessly funny an entertainer on the page as on the stage.

- **Lee Lynch**, author of *The Amazon Trail* and *Beggar of Love*

She's one of our best writers.

- **Jennifer Layton**, *Indie-Music.com*

DRIVE ALL NIGHT

•Jamie Anderson•

Bella
BOOKS

2014

Bella Books, Inc.
P.O. Box 10543
Tallahassee, FL 32302

First Bella Books Edition 2014

Editor: Katherine V. Forrest
Cover Designer: Sandy Knowles
Photo credit: Woodland Willow Photography

ISBN: 978-1-59493-399-8

About the Author

Jamie Anderson is a singer-songwriter with ten albums. Since 1987, she's toured nationally in the U.S. and Canada. Her articles and book chapters have appeared in *Acoustic Guitar*, *Curve*, *Minor7th*, *SingOut!*, *Songwriting and the Guitar*, and *On My Honor: Lesbians Reflect on their Scouting Experience*. Jamie lives in Ottawa, Ontario with her wife, Pat.

Acknowledgments

Thanks to Mosa Baczewska, Galia Goodman, Janice Rickert and Kaia Skaggs for slogging through my first draft and offering great suggestions. Deepest thanks to Pat Laberge, my sweetie-honey-baby-darlin', who not only read several versions of this book and gave solid feedback, but also puts up with a wife who drags her sorry ass all over to perform, and who doesn't come home from her own demanding job and ask, "You *only* wrote today?"

I offer a special thanks to my fans that make the music and the stories possible. Blessings to all of you.

For my mom, Joy Anderson, who was always in the front row, and for my dad, Gary Anderson, one of the best singers I've ever heard.

FOREWORD

I've been a touring solo singer-songwriter for over twenty years, playing in hundreds of venues, from women's music festivals to tiny folk coffeehouses to the '93 March on Washington for several hundred thousand people. I've roomed with a pig, taken my shirt off for Amy Ray, met Melissa Etheridge and shared the stage with exotic dancers. It was either get these stories down or take up heavy drinking.

Before all that, for a brief period I worked as a paralegal for a state attorney general's office. The cases were confidential and it was really hard to keep my mouth shut for some of the more notorious lawbreakers. I found ways to get around it and still satisfy my need to vent. There was one case where a slimeball who owned several stores was sexually harassing his female employees. From the way he swaggered into the office, gold chains draped on his hairy puffed-out chest, dressed in sports shirt and shorts when everyone around him was in suits, I knew the guy did it. One day while driving past one of his stores with my girlfriend, I blurted out, "Don't shop at that store! Don't ask me why."

This book is a little like those cases. Some of these stories probably should remain private since playing music is one of the ways I put bread on the table. Burn too many bridges and I'll find myself back at a temp agency answering phones. However, I can't help but blurt out a few facts. Some minor details, like names and locations, have been changed in several of the stories to protect the near-innocent. None of the major details have been altered. If I use a first and last name, it's a real name.

Most of these stories take place over my performing career. I started touring in the late eighties before the advent of modern cell phones and the Internet. I continue to perform today and am grateful for the technology available to me—especially for Marcia, my GPS with the sexy voice—although the lack of a cell phone really made for some interesting times on those early tours. And I can't imagine writing this book on a Smith-Corona. I'd surely suffer brain damage from the correction fluid fumes.

For the first forty-one years of my life I lived in Arizona. A move to North Carolina was next and now I reside in Ottawa, Canada. (I keep moving north. If I end up at the Arctic Circle, please slap me.) I mention all this just to put the stories in perspective. It makes the Alaska story more poignant when you know that I was living in Arizona at the time.

I owe thanks to the couple from Vermont that I met in 2003 at the Highlands Inn in New Hampshire. They commented, after hearing one of my road stories, "You should write a book." They aren't the first folks to urge me to write, but they had the best timing. I was between gigs and without a steady net connection or good cell phone service. It was a freezing November with icy roads and a chilly wind. I was snuggled under a warm afghan, with an even warmer computer sitting on my lap, and writing was my best option. More stories were written in the following years, whenever I had time and a place to plug in the laptop.

My apologies to anyone who thinks I've written about them here. I believe that almost everyone in this book acted with good intentions—sometimes their mamas just didn't teach 'em about putting on a show or having guests. For most of the people I met on my journey, your mama taught you right. I mention some of you here, but for most, the cool happy things just didn't make for as good a story. The carefully packed lunches, tirelessly promoted shows and comfortable beds were appreciated more than you know. As for the rest of you, please don't bother suing me. I don't own much and you'll never be able to pry my guitar out of my cold, dead hands. Besides, you don't want to piss off a songwriter. Ask my exes.

I like how the steering wheel is firm under my hand
I like how the headlights cut across the shadow land
I like how your voice is low and breathless in my ear
I like that it's cold outside but warm in here

Surrounded by this highway, we're at the speed of light
Baby, let's drive all night

CHAPTER ONE

Let's Pretend We're Booking Agents!
My First Tour.

In 1987 I did my first tour. It wasn't part of a grand plan—I just wanted to get to the Michigan Womyn's Music Festival. However, money from a part-time clerical job in Tucson, Arizona, wasn't going to buy enough gas to get across the street. Fueled by the new women's music network, my friend and fellow singer-songwriter Martie van der Voort and I decided we'd gig our way to the festival. No one told us we couldn't do it.

We had booked local performances for ourselves, but we didn't have the faintest idea how to book a tour that spanned hundreds of miles. We found a woman who wanted to learn to be a booking agent so we hired her to get us gigs in folk and women's music venues. Martie and I set about working out harmonies and lead guitar parts on each other's songs. Although my main instrument is the acoustic guitar, I think I even played banjo on one or two numbers. I hope someone got a picture of that, because I haven't been seen in public with one since. Next thing ya know, I'll be taking up the accordion and offending an even greater part of the population…you know I'm kidding, right? I love both instruments. I just happen to be a lousy banjo player. I'd have to go to a gym for a year to even lift an accordion. Besides, injured animal sounds aren't in high demand at concerts.

I managed to save enough money for a festival ticket and it had already arrived in my mailbox. With the money from gigs we should be all right…if only we had some gigs. A few weeks before we were to leave, our esteemed booking agent called us and said she couldn't get anything for us. We could only wonder: What did she do? Call her second cousin in Cat Litter, Wyoming, and then give up?

Martie, ever the positive one, happily exclaimed, "Let's pretend we're booking agents!" We needed shows so we started making phone calls to friends, friends of friends and strangers we randomly dialed who might be connected to a coffeehouse, bar, women's center or church. This was before email, before cell phones and even before many people had answering machines. A lot of times the phone rang and rang…and rang. Sometimes I'd get an answering machine. If I was really lucky, I'd get a five-year-old telling me that Mommy was in the bathroom. I'm great with kids and sometimes I managed to get the little guy to give Mommy the phone.

If they didn't answer or get back to me in a week, I called again. And again. I called until I got a yes or a no. Even a no was as good, because that meant I could cross them off my list. (Another musician once told me that "no" was his second favorite answer. I concur.)

Martie and I knew we could play at our local lesbian bar a few weeks before we left. While our friends generously showed up to cheer us on, my portion of the one-dollar bills in the tip jar left me $110 short. That was a couple of weeks' salary for me. I had no money left after rent, food and school expenses. The out-of-town gigs, if we were able to get them, were a crapshoot—we could make $500 or $5. I told a few friends that I might have to cancel our trip and eat the money I'd spent on the ticket.

About three weeks before we were supposed to leave, an envelope arrived in the mail. My address was scrawled on the front and there was no return address. Inside was a postal money order for $110. The signature was unreadable. I did not intend to be a charity case. I angrily confronted Martie. Surely, she had convinced a friend to send me the money. She swore she had nothing to do with it. I talked to everyone I knew and they all shrugged. I went back to Martie, and she said in her oh-so-sage way, "Maybe you should just say thank you."

We ended up booking a half-dozen gigs, all played to people who'd never heard us live. It helped that we were making use of the women's music circuit. Only in existence a few years, there was still a lot of enthusiasm for any women performers, whether you'd just learned how to change from G to C without stopping or had recorded a few LPs. (Back before DIY recordings, albums were very expensive, so not many had produced them.)

We set off in Martie's van. A few years old and a little beat up around the edges, it would only stop if I stood on the brake pedal with both feet. As long as no one pulled out in front of us, we were golden.

We had some wonderful shows, from a small theater in Albuquerque to a YMCA basement in Kansas City. We had some interesting gigs also, including one at a small bar where the van refused to start. A tow truck driver helped us by shoving a small twig in a hole in the carburetor, enabling us to continue on our way. There's much more to that story, including a night's stay in a kid's bed with sandy sheets, a dog that peed on my foot and a drunk bar owner who didn't want to pay us, but I'll refrain from whining.

We had a great time at the festival. After hearing all those strong women who could most definitely change chords without stopping, we felt like Amazons. We played at open mike and at the jam tent. I dreamed of playing onstage there and finally did, in 2004.

With no gigs, the drive home took a lot less time. The brakes kept working, resulting in great new calf muscles, and the twig stayed in place. Plus, it started a dream of touring, something I ended up doing for twenty-plus years, thanks to someone who scrawled an illegible signature on a money order for $110. I hope they know now what a tremendous impact they had on my life.

CHAPTER TWO

Bunny Boots and Square Tires

I got a call from an Alaska producer who wanted me for a concert…in January.

"Uh," I stammered, "you know you called Arizona?"

She explained that in the summer she couldn't get anyone to come indoors for shows. I reluctantly agreed to the gig after she guaranteed they'd keep me warm. I didn't ask for details and envisioned a steaming hot tub, peeled grapes and…oops, wrong fantasy.

I borrowed my girlfriend's down jacket and headed toward the frozen north. My friendly producer met me at the Anchorage airport. It was below freezing, but with the sun shining there was the illusion that it was warm enough that my nostrils wouldn't freeze shut if I took a big breath.

In the two days before my show a couple of different women showed me around the area. I saw a lot of beautiful snow-covered forestland and visited an ice-blue glacier frozen in a bay. It wasn't until I got out to that huge chunk of ice that I saw the signs warning KEEP AWAY. Apparently those things are still moving, even in subzero temperatures. Still, I have a photo of me with a big ol' goofy grin, standing in front of it. Jamie defies death!

We also went sledding not far from my housing. To the people in the neighborhood, this was an everyday thing, but to this folksinger who lived most of her life in the desert, it was like a really fun roller coaster inside a giant freezer. The adults stood around and talked about big, grown-up things while the kids and I screamed down the hills. Everyone politely ignored me, like New Yorkers overlooking that guy on the subway who's arguing with the voices in his head.

My show was in a nice theater with a wonderful crowd in attendance. They'd made up a set just for me, with big plywood cactuses and a howling coyote against the backdrop of a beautiful orange and red desert sunset.

Next I flew north to Fairbanks. A wiry, weathered woman with an easy smile greeted me. After her enthusiastic welcome she helped me out to her pickup truck in the below zero weather. We hefted my guitar and suitcase into the back of the open truck. I wondered what effect the cold would have on my guitar, but there was no room in the cab. I winced as I plopped down on the unexpectedly hard seats.

"Cab's not warmed up yet, the seats are frozen," said my companion.

Frozen seats? I thought she was pulling my leg until she went on to explain that the weather was so cold that things like seats and tires froze. There was such a thing as "square tire" and that's why the ride would be rough for a few minutes. She put the heater on its highest setting and we blazed away through streets with so much snow piled on the sides that I couldn't read most of the street signs. It was like driving through a tunnel with a small opening on the top.

At my housing I was greeted by a barefoot woman in shorts and T-shirt. I joked that she must be a native to be dressed that way in winter. "No," she cheerfully answered, "I'm from South Africa."

The house was warm, due to triple-paned windows and a good furnace, but still, I'll wear jeans, sweatshirt and heavy socks thank you very much.

Getting ready to go out for the gig I pulled out my beloved purple snow boots that were a gift from my girlfriend. A smile played around the corners of my host's mouth as she cracked, "You'll need something much sturdier for our weather. We've gotta find you some bunny boots."

Bunny boots? Was this a joke played on naïve tourists?

No, there really was such a thing and fortunately, some were found that I could borrow. They were huge white rubber boots that looked like a cartoon character's feet. The soles were a couple inches thick to keep out the cold underneath and they laced up to protect your ankles from frostbite. They were so heavy I felt like I had a Volkswagen tied to each leg. However, they kept my feet fairly warm with only one pair of socks.

I would definitely need snow pants, too. They were sure I could borrow some, but it seemed every woman I met was smaller than I was, so I opted for thick jeans over a pair of long johns.

My glasses wouldn't be good either since they were metal and sat directly on my nose. "They'll freeze to your face," my host thoughtfully pointed out.

With my lousy eyesight and poorly insulated leg wear I wouldn't survive a walk from a parking space to the front door of our destinations, so everywhere we went I was dropped off right in front. The princess arrives.

Almost everyone I met regaled me with stories of frostbite. One woman showed me some purplish spots on her leg where leaky snow pants had let in the cold and killed the tissue. After a few more tales, most involving body parts dropping off, I wanted to check my clothing for leaks. But how could I do that? Ask my hosts to blow air up my leg? I wondered would that line work in a crowded bar? "Hey honey, wanna check me for frostbite?"

My gig that night was in a tourist bar used mostly in the summer. In the winter, it was sort of a women's bar open only on weekends. As women arrived, I noticed how adept they were at greeting buddies and removing protective clothing. Hug, remove snow boots. Wave hello to your friend across the room then hug someone else while removing scarf. Briefly wrap your arms around a friend while telling her about your new job, take off snow pants. If this were an Olympic event, Alaskan women would take all the gold. They came in looking like well-padded Michelin Tire guys and ended up looking like any audience, some even wore dresses.

Just before I was to go onstage my producer once again reminded me to perform not longer than forty-five minutes, then take a break and go on to do my second set. She'd seemed so easygoing about everything else that I wondered why she was so adamant about my set lengths. Until I finished my first set and saw half the women rush out the door.

At first I wondered if I sucked and they couldn't wait to escape. It was then that it was explained to me that the bar didn't have hookups. "What are hookups?" I innocently asked. Those are the electrical outlets you see outside most businesses, they told me. Before you go inside you plug in a special car heater to keep your engine warm. Because this was a bar used mostly in warmer weather there wasn't such a convenience and they needed to start their cars. I joked that it was the butch women who rushed out there, but frankly, all the women in Alaska looked butch to me except for the few wearing dresses inside the bar. While I waited I could hear lots of cars starting up outside. They ran for a few minutes, then everyone came back in and I finished the show. There was a great dance afterward. Alaska women know how to party.

I got a couple of wonderful offers to go dog sledding and to go up in a bush plane, but unfortunately didn't have time to do either. However, there was one day to go sightseeing. I visited a museum at the university. That only took an hour or two. My hosts talked about taking me to some hot springs, but decided that the short drive out of town was too dangerous. "Why?" I naïvely asked.

I was patiently told that there weren't many cars on the road or any open gas stations. If the car broke down you can die, especially when you have a princess on board who can't walk more than a few feet. Then they asked if I wanted to see the pipeline. Even though it was a bit out of town it wasn't as far as the hot springs and should be safe. I have a photo of me in front of the huge snow-covered pipe. I know I'm smiling by the way my eyes crinkle, but the rest of my face is covered in a bulky scarf. The remainder of my body is thickly layered with down, wool and nylon, and ending with those ridiculously enormous boots. In town, later that day, I took a photo of the temperature sign outside a bank building. It said minus fifty-five.

The next day as I got ready to leave I heard the weather report on the radio. It was fifty-eight below! I commented to my hosts that my flight would surely be delayed. "Oh no," they responded, "the airport is open, schools are open, everything is normal for Fairbanks."

As I sat on the plane, the flight attendant spoke over the loudspeaker and apologized for the lack of coffee. "The water lines are frozen," she explained.

They deiced the wings. I couldn't get coffee, but the plane could fly—just another day at the Fairbanks airport. Takeoff was smooth. Over the next hour I was transfixed by the view outside the window, a vivid orange sun rising over blue-white snow-covered peaks. That same day I arrived in Tucson to seventy-degree weather and within a couple of days had one of the worst colds of my life.

It was all worth it, funny boots or no.

CHAPTER THREE

She's Shorter in Person

I was a little nervous about this gig because it was in a fourteen-hundred seat theater in Los Angeles, a city that's used to huge, slick touring acts, not folksingers from North Carolina. Fortunately, I was opening for the fabulous comic Kate Clinton. After sweating through my own set, I knew I'd get to relax and laugh my way through her portion of the show.

It was a hard gig to get, requiring many phone calls. The promoter booked me because a well-known booking agent for someone else recommended me. We decided on the details and signed a contract. I knew something was awry when she sent me a short email asking me about the kind of piano I needed.

I play guitar.

When I phoned her, she told me that the show was being taped for a documentary about funny lesbians.

"Great!" I exclaimed, "I'd love to have a good recording of one of my performances."

There was a pause on the other end of the line, a sigh, and then she responded, "We're only filming comics."

Okay, so I don't do comedy clubs, and I've never been on HBO. However, with songs like "Menstrual Tango" and "I Miss the Dog

(More Than I Miss You)" it's pretty clear I'm not a folksinger who warbles about unicorns.

It could be that the promoter had never heard my music. Ah well. A gig's a gig and I was getting the chance to play for several hundred people. It couldn't be bad.

I arrived at the venue dog-tired from that day's plane ride from North Carolina. I did a quick sound check, and then wandered around the huge backstage area. I had my own dressing room that included a wall of mirrors ringed with bright lights. Beats the hell out of the dingy, smelly bathrooms I've been offered in other venues.

Kate and a few of her friends were hanging out as a woman with a camera filmed them. I introduced myself. Kate thanked me for opening the show. Hey, twist my arm.

Strolling out front, I saw rows and rows of chairs. I'd made plans to meet an old friend, Oshara, so I wandered out to the lobby. There she was, smiling and waving at me. We sat and caught up until I realized it was getting close to concert time. She followed me backstage.

Walking down the long hallway to my dressing room, I saw a large group of women. All I wanted was a quiet space and a little more conversation with my friend, not a mob of people I didn't know. I was just working myself up to a good grumble when I realized that one of the women in the group was Melissa Etheridge.

Okay, she can stay.

The promoter had hinted in an earlier phone call that she'd be there. Oh *sure*, Melissa Etheridge…lives in LA…friend of Kate's.

I told a few friends and they joked that I should do "Bring Me Melissa," my parody of her "Bring Me Some Water." I pooh-poohed that idea, but now I was thinking, hmmm, does she have a sense of humor? Evil lawyers? Will I have to hand over my house, my car and my cats before it's all over?

I didn't give myself too much time to think. I strolled up to her and the group like it was something I do every day. I thought I'd casually smile and say, "Oh, hi, Melissa."

Not quite. Instead, I stood like a stone statue on the periphery of the group until the promoter extended her hand toward me, turned to Melissa and said, "Melissa, this is Jamie Anderson. She's opening the show."

Melissa grinned broadly, shook my hand and said, "Well hello, Jamie Anderson."

I have no idea what I replied. It might have been something grown-up like, "Nice to meet you" or I might have babbled incoherently. Next, I think I was introduced to her girlfriend. I couldn't tell you her name, because she was wearing a tight, low-cut T-shirt and I turned into Ed Bundy. I don't even have a thing for breasts—hell, if I want to see them, I'll just strip and stand in front of a mirror—but there were those breasts like a pulsing sign blinking look…look…look.

I'm five-nine in heels, and I towered over Melissa. I know it's a cliché, but she was so short. With stage presence like hers, I expected her to be forty-seven feet tall.

I stood there for a while, trying to remember to blink. I couldn't find a way to slip into their conversation about how to get Melissa and her girlfriend safely to their seats. I have no superhero alter ego who can save a Big Star from hundreds of adoring lesbians.

See, when a big-name performer wants to come to another entertainer's show, they usually have their people call the entertainer's people to get free tickets. They get seated in a VIP section in front where no one bothers them. Not only was there not a VIP section, but Melissa bought tickets to the show. My opinion of her immediately rose.

The discussion continued. The promoter thought she could put them in the fourth row instead of the seats they bought that were further back. They could be escorted in just before the show started.

Instead of standing there like a department store dummy, I elected to step into my dressing room, located immediately behind the group. Oshara followed me. I shut the door, turned to her and calmly asked, "Did I just meet Melissa Etheridge?"

She replied that I had.

"Oh my God!" I screamed, before I realized the group we'd just left was right on the other side of the flimsy door.

I willed myself to breathe, then carefully went over my set list. Before I knew it, I was alone onstage in front of several hundred people. The stage lights prevented me from seeing any farther than the first two rows, so fortunately I couldn't see Melissa and consequently forget how to form a G chord. However, I was keenly aware of her presence, especially when I did my faux rock song "Potato Chips." Between two verses, I leaned forward rock-star-like, whipped my hair around and quipped, "I look just like Melissa Etheridge, don't I?"

The crowd roared with laughter.

Also in my set was one of my most popular songs, "Dark Chocolate," a sensuous bluesy ballad about loving women.

The way to a woman's heart is through her lips
Through the shudder of her sighs and the motion of her hips
Through the softness of her thighs to that place between her...
shoulders
And if a woman wants her, do you want to hold her back?

I had fantasies of Melissa meeting me backstage and asking to cover the song or to open her shows. I was already planning the tour schedule when I stepped off the stage.

The audience loved me. Not that I was chopped liver, but they loved Kate even more and rightly so. She gave a wonderful performance.

I slipped in the stage door to congratulate Kate. I expected mobs of people doing the same, but I found her alone. As I shook her hand and opened my mouth, a woman with a movie camera came in the same door and pointed it at us. I paid my compliments. Kate grinned, hugged me and exclaimed, "We did it!"

"Yes we did…but let's not tell our girlfriends."

Well, *I* thought it was funny. Kate looked at me with a half grin and turned down the hall, trailing the camerawoman. Several smiling people waited for her at the end, so I held back to give her time with her friends.

Melissa never did come backstage.

I knew my performance wasn't filmed. I hoped that a clip or two of me backstage would make it into the movie. Nope. All that exists is the movie in my head and the feeling of Melissa's warm palm pressing into my right hand. Somebody bring me some water.

CHAPTER FOUR

The Acorn Didn't Fall Far from the Tree

My career didn't start with meeting Melissa Etheridge. In the beginning no one screamed "Oh my God," except maybe my mother, Joy.

I can't remember a time when I wasn't surrounded by music. My dad, Gary, learned to play ukulele when he was a kid. He joined the air force at seventeen, taking that ukulele to entertain his buddies on base. Later, he graduated to the guitar.

My parents are cousins. That explains a lot, right? Dad was stationed in Yuma, a small town on the border between Arizona and California. His mother told him he had relatives in Phoenix, so when he had leave, he hitchhiked the two hundred miles to meet them. They were distant cousins by marriage—I know, that ruins the story—and Mom was engaged to someone else at the time. It didn't stop her from falling in love with this skinny and charming private. Months later, when they decided to marry, Mom's parents offered to pay for a wedding or for a new TV. Mom chose the TV and they were married in her parents' living room.

The babies came quickly. I was born in 1957, almost exactly nine months after they married. Yes, I've done the math. Two more, my brothers Kelly and Todd, arrived in quick succession. At one point, my poor mother had a three-year-old (me) and two in diapers. My brother Cris popped into the world nine years after me.

Not long after Kelly was born, our little family moved to the Phoenix area to be closer to my mother's parents and because my recently discharged father could more easily find work. My mother worked outside the home in a variety of jobs, from an inspector at an electronics manufacturer to the cafeteria at a bank operations center. She always chose jobs that allowed her as much time as possible with us kids, often working a grueling overnight shift so she could see us off for school in the morning. Dad went through a succession of jobs and finally settled in as an insurance agent. With his easy smile and hearty laugh, he could sell ice cream during a blizzard. In his heart of hearts, though, I think he would've preferred making music for a living. He often had a guitar in his hands, playing pop standards like "Tammy," a song that was a hit the same year I was born. He used to sing it to me, his booming voice singing "Jamie" instead of "Tammy."

Dad loved to entertain. It wasn't a party until Gary showed up with his guitar. Over the years, he expanded his repertoire to include country tunes and an array of funny lines and songs, many of them dirty. He even had a blue version of "Puff the Magic Dragon." (No, you don't want to hear it. No one can remember it, anyway. It's better, trust me.) It wasn't until years later that I found out he wrote some of that funny stuff himself.

In addition to the live music, our little kitchen radio was tuned to KOY, playing pop hits of the sixties. In the car, it was often the country music station, with Dad singing along and tapping out the rhythm on the steering wheel. He loved the pop-country of Jim Reeves and the story songs from country singer Marty Robbins. Sometimes the radio wasn't on and we all sang in the car, on songs like "You Are My Sunshine." My mother joined us, although she claims she can't sing. Funny, since our speaking voices are so similar that people mistake us for each other on the phone. We look a lot alike too, so many times we've been asked if we're sisters. Mom deadpans that she was five when she had me.

Dad always had guitars lying around the house and when I was fifteen, I absconded with his Harmony classical and never gave it back. Sequestered in my room, I memorized every chord in a book of pop music and learned the songs, including Joni Mitchell's "Both Sides Now." I also learned a bunch of the folk songs that I'd been singing in Girl Scouts since the age of seven. Most only had three or four chords, perfect for a determined teen focused on becoming John Denver or something akin to that. I loved his music and saw him in concert a couple of times. At one show, I joyfully added the harmony part to every song until the lady next to me sternly informed me that she'd come to hear him. I also discovered seventies singer-songwriters like Carly Simon, Karla Bonoff and Dan Fogelberg, and learned as many of their songs as I could.

I lovingly named the guitar Baby because I had no case for it and had to wrap it in a blanket. I dragged it to every Girl Scout camping trip and talent show. When I wasn't playing, I was trading words and chords with the other musicians. We had no Internet and we couldn't afford a lot of songbooks so we hand-copied lyrics and chords from each other. Sometimes we taught each other songs. I had an enormous crush on a guitar-playing camp counselor who taught me to play "Photographs and Memories" just like Jim Croce.

A lot of people think Dad taught me to play, but we didn't like the same kind of music so I never asked him. He did, however, take the guitar and insist on tuning it once in a while when his seasoned ear couldn't take it anymore. One day he came into my room and asked to hear a song. I proudly played Neil Young's "Needle and the Damage Done." I had recently learned to play it by dropping the phonograph needle down on the LP over and over again, learning it a few seconds at a time. My musician friend Peter said I played it just like Young. Dad wouldn't know him from a slap upside the head, but after I was done, he thoughtfully commented, "You're pretty good at those hippie songs."

At a high school talent show, I met several other musicians. We formed an acoustic band and played at a local coffeehouse. I sang one of our big numbers, a Mason Williams tune, "You Done Stomped on My Heart," where he rhymed "sorta" and "aorta." Hearing an audience laugh was better than sex. (Uh, not that I was having any, Mom.) I was hooked.

In 1972 I met Lois. She was an "older woman" in my senior Girl Scout troop, seventeen to my fifteen, drove an orange Model

A that she restored with her father, and wrote poetry and never wore shoes. How could I not fall in love? We wrote syrupy songs together—she on the lyrics, and me on the music—and planned to move in together as soon as I graduated from high school. We snuggled together on overnights.

I had male friends and even went out on a date or two. One New Year's Eve I went to dinner with an attractive guy I knew from high school. Before midnight, though, I had him drop me off at Lois's house. Her parents were having a party. I knew I'd have a great time there and really, she was a lot more fun to kiss at midnight, even if we had to do it in the privacy of her room.

Lois took me to my first gay bar. The Habit was the only lesbian watering hole in the Phoenix area in the mid-seventies. I was terrified that the cops would haul my seventeen-year-old butt from there and call my folks because I was two years from the legal drinking age of nineteen. It was only a year or two earlier that the police had stopped regularly raiding gay bars. They still strolled in from time to time, checking everyone's IDs, whether you looked sixteen or sixty. Fortunately, those cops never asked me for mine. Good thing, because I didn't have one. The first time, I got in the bar using Lois's battered driver's license. She's six inches shorter than me and we looked nothing alike, but when you put that piece of plastic through the laundry a few times, it turned into something that sort of looked like me, if you'd had a few drinks. After that first visit, I simply signed the book at the door. It said that you'd forgotten your ID and realized the consequences of that, should the cops decide to get picky one night. It also didn't hurt that I'd give the doorwoman a big sloppy kiss.

Three weeks after turning eighteen, I moved with Lois into a beaten-down one-bedroom apartment that cost $125 a month. Switching on the lights in the kitchen at night illuminated an army of roaches, some of whom just stood and looked at me, squinting their little beady roach eyes—good training for some of the housing I was to get later on in my touring life. After about a year our teenage angst-ridden relationship ran its course and we went our separate ways. We stayed friends for a while until we lost contact in 1984.

The Habit certainly was. You could find me there almost every night of the week, despite the half-hour drive each way. I was comforted by the familiar cast of characters—feminists in thrift store flannel shirts, old-style butch-femme couples, and young lesbians like me. A free buffet was offered on Sundays after a local softball game, a solo acoustic musician performed on Tuesday nights, beer bust was Thursday, and the Indavana Blues Band played on Friday and Saturday nights. I idolized the band. Before them, I'd never seen a woman play drums or an electric guitar. They played disco covers like Donna Summer's "Love to Love You Baby," as a sweaty mass of very happy women writhed around the dance floor. I was a little shy so I used to bring cookies that I'd baked and share them. Some called me Cookie Lady, not even knowing my real name. The rumor was that I put an extra ingredient in them, but that wasn't something I could afford on a part-time salary from Jack-in-the-Box. (Not that I'd do that anyway. I wasn't much into mind-altering substances, choosing to drink water when everyone around me was downing gallons of beer.) Indavana's harmonica player, Rochelle, loved cookies so she sometimes had a stack of mine sitting on the table next to her onstage. When I found out the lead guitar player, Jeanine (aka Nee-nee), didn't like cookies, I brought her an avocado.

It was around this time that I discovered women's music in a tiny corner rack at the local women's bookstore. I ignored the LPs for a while—why would I be interested in anyone who wasn't Carole King or Carly Simon? But during one visit, an LP picturing a shiny orange juice can caught my eye. I bought the Olivia compilation *Lesbian Concentrate* and it was love at first listen. That same year, in 1977, I attended my first women's music concert, Therese Edell. Oh, that silky alto voice, those charming stories and those beautiful songs! I learned to play her music, as well as Meg Christian's and Cris Williamson's. I especially loved the funny tunes, like Edell's "Mama Let Your Children Go" and Christian's "Ode to a Gym Teacher."

Outside of The Habit, I started hanging out with a friendly group of women who ran a women's center. I played at some of their coffeehouses, as well as a few showcases in the local gay bars. In 1979, I played my first big gig, a fundraiser for the women's center, held at a community college. I was one of five acts on the bill. The sound guy had to show me how to use a microphone. My big ending number was "Albino Roach Blues," a tune I'd written with a local singer that had a great punch line toward the end. People were laughing so hard, I had to stop the song. Don't encourage me—I'll only keep doing it.

And I have. Bolstered by the burgeoning women's music circuit, I played many local fundraising concerts, lesbian bars and women's coffeehouses. For a couple of years, I also performed as part of a guitar and flute duo that did parties and weddings.

I lost contact with my first girlfriend Lois for many years, but found her again in 2010. I asked if she was still writing poetry and she replied, "No." A few months later, though, I opened my email and found a poem from her. I wrote music for it and performed our song at the 2012 National Women's Music Festival and there she was, sitting in the front row, positively beaming.

CHAPTER FIVE

Streetwalking

I sped through the early morning streets of the tiny tourist town yelling, "Fuck you Provincetown! Fuck you!"

My visit didn't start out that way.

I first came to this charming New England town on Cape Cod in October of 1990, during a break on tour. I loved the quaint buildings and quiet streets scattered with lesbian couples holding hands and young families pushing strollers. I saw large old houses with neatly trimmed lawns and gardens bursting with bright flowers. I noticed the plethora of gay clubs and thought maybe there would be some good work in this town.

It took several months to track down the phone numbers of the venue bookers since they don't publish their home numbers, and many don't live in town year round. (This was before the Internet so no websites or emails, either.) After I bugged the booker for a couple of years, a small bar on the far side of town agreed to hire me for a few days in the summer of 1993. He assured me that even though it was several blocks from the center of town people would walk there. As my pay I'd get a room and a percentage of the admission. It was up to me to promote the shows by handing out little fliers in the streets.

I arrived to find a town much different than the one I'd seen on my leisurely fall visit. As I drove slowly down the main street looking for the venue, I marveled at the mass of humanity clogging the streets and sidewalks. After much searching, I managed to squeeze into a parking spot, and then struggled several blocks with my bags to the small inn and bar where I would play.

As I opened the door to my tiny room the scent of mildew blasted back at me. The furniture was new...in the sixties. A swaybacked bed squatted in one corner. A worn dresser slumped against the opposite wall. A carpet too tired to have any color graced the floor. Dusty faded curtains that once featured a cheery beach scene hung limply across the only window. A cacophony of grumbling cars, clinking glasses and giddy laughter seeped in through the cracks, providing the soundtrack for most of my stay.

I quickly unpacked, then met the owner in the bar. A middle-aged man with slightly unfocused eyes, he leaned forward, the ice clinking in his drink, and exclaimed that I was much prettier in person than I was in my photos. As he talked about P-town and its vagaries, I scanned walls that were crowded with eight-by-ten glossies of drag queens with huge hair and breasts. Four or five tiny tables crowded the room. A bar stretched along one side. A pop diva moaned a ballad over the small stereo speakers.

"You'll stand over there," said the owner, pointing to a small clearing. "We'll set up the PA when you come in tomorrow. Meanwhile, you need to start handing these out." He placed a short stack of fliers in my hand. A small photo of me graced the corner of each one, along with information about my show.

I stepped onto the street. A manufactured grin on my face, I thrust fliers at a few people and mumbled something about the show. As I made my way toward the center of town, it got easier. To some I was invisible, like a homeless person asking for spare change. I forged on until most of the stack was gone.

The next morning, bathing suit on and fliers packed, I headed for the queer beach. Another performer cautioned that advertising on the beach was illegal, although all the entertainers did it. Someone would yell out "Ranger!" and we'd drop onto the nearest beach towel, smiling broadly at whoever was already seated there. Everyone was in on the game. Complete strangers treated me like a long-lost friend for the couple of minutes the ranger drove by on his ATV. You could be fined or asked to leave the beach, so I was careful never to be caught.

Seven people came for my show that night. I was disappointed but pushed on, convinced that if I just handed out enough fliers I'd fill the place. It could only hold twenty-five or so, if they liked each other a lot, so I figured that wouldn't be too hard. I discovered that handing out fliers right after an afternoon dance at a bar at the other end of town was good. As throngs of happy drunk people poured out, I could approach them with a joke and that little piece of paper.

One night I made the mistake of handing them out to women leaving Suzanne Westenhoefer's show at another venue and had a bar employee come charging out like a mad bull. I didn't wait for her stern reprimand. I simply turned around and sauntered down the street, waiting a few minutes before I handed out more fliers.

If I drove to the beach too late the parking lot would fill up and close. There was no other place to park and I couldn't walk the several miles from my room. One afternoon I rented a bicycle. As I pumped the pedals, burned by the sun and sweat pouring down my face, I wondered if I loved performing that much. I resolved that from then on I'd get to the beach early enough to park. I'd just have to hang out for an hour or two and wait for the beach to fill up.

When it was time, I'd trudge up and down the hot sand making jokes about calling a taxi as I handed out fliers. Many of the women were friendly, asking me where I was from and offering me cold drinks and cookies. If I played it right, I could get a sandwich and chips. I sat with a few women for a while, hoping that if I made friends with them they'd come to my show. Sometimes it worked, more often than not it didn't.

In front of city hall was also a good place to distribute fliers. With plenty of park benches, I could sit down every few minutes. Also, there was often a group of women I could chat up. Again, I thought that if I acted friendly enough, they might come to my concert.

I never did fill up that tiny bar, although Suzanne Westenhoefer came to my show one night. She sat at the bar by herself, mouthing the words to my song "Dark Chocolate" and smiling at the jokes.

Undaunted by the small crowds, I tried again the next summer, this time snagging a gig at a bar closer to the center of town, but still one block from the main street. They didn't offer housing, so I called a few inns and discovered that a room would eat up all of my pay. Zoe Lewis, a performer who lived in Provincetown year round, told me about a rooming house on the far east end where rooms were reasonably priced. My spartan room there was the size of my bedroom at home, with an ancient dresser against the wall and a double bed in the center. The sloping wood floor was once a pretty dark-stained pine, but a patina of scratches gave it a lighter color. None of the rooms had TVs or phones. At each end of the hall was a bathroom shared by all the guests on that floor and in the middle, a telephone and a small refrigerator. There was no central heat or cooling. In hot weather, a window could be opened. Once I was there during Women's Week in October when it was a little chilly. They thoughtfully gave me a space heater. Every time it came on, the lights dimmed. The inn rooms weren't much, but they were clean and I didn't have to sell my car to pay for one. I usually stayed there after that.

I hit the streets immediately with fliers I'd made myself extolling the virtues of my show. Feeling like an old hand, I hit the tea dance after it ended, a smile plastered on my face. I had a shtick to make them remember me—"Hi, come to my show, I'm dating k.d. lang!" "Come to my show and I'll sleep with you!" (I didn't use that one on anyone who was so drunk they might ignite if near an open flame, just in case they wanted to take me up on the faux offer.) Another favorite line was to approach a group of women and inquire politely, "Excuse me, I'm looking for the lesbians." I posted on the three legal bulletin boards and did my best to avoid town officials (since I heard they didn't like you to roam the streets with those fliers). The next day, I went to the gay beach.

That night, I drove to my show. The only parking lot would take a large chunk of my income, after circling the block and finding nothing, I surrendered to it.

I fiddled with the unfamiliar sound equipment and got everything to work. Two tired audience members trudged into the bar. Better than empty, I guess. I unplugged my guitar, sat at their table and asked what they wanted to hear. Fortunately, they were big fans and knew my music well enough to suggest tunes. I was sure to end ten minutes before the hour to give myself time to pack up before the next act.

After that evening, I learned that if I strapped my guitar to my back and carried my gig bag, I could easily make the half-hour walk to the venue, saving me parking fees.

The second night I had four people, and the third, twelve. Things were looking up.

One night I cut it a little close for the next act. As I was setting up CDs she pushed her way through the door yelling, "It's time for me!" Her crowd followed her like baby ducks as she told my audience they better drink up or pay for the next show. I learned to be precise about my ending time.

One of the bars had a showcase where they brought in acts from other venues. Even though I wouldn't get paid, I was told it was a good way to advertise my gig. Getting sandwiched between two drag queens, one in bright pink feathers who lipsynched to a *Dreamgirls* song pumping through the speakers, didn't do me any favors. During my performance, a very drunk woman jumped onstage with me. I joked, "Hey! It's my show!" No one laughed. I didn't even do the second song I'd planned.

Most clubs there feature more than one act per night, usually comics. I can do a whole evening of funny songs, so I fit in. At one venue, the act after me consisted of hideous Muppet-like creatures with huge red lips that mouthed the words to dance numbers like "It's Raining Men," made tacky jokes about freshening up with Febreze, and faked sexual acts with their microphones. It was hard to associate the sweet men I'd met offstage with the performance I saw them do.

No matter how you felt about the other performers, there was a nice camaraderie between most of the entertainers in town. We all had to worry about attendance at our shows and most of us had to hand out those hated fliers. (A few made enough money to hire someone to do the fliers and I envied them.) One time a couple of the comics where I worked made up a big banner that they paraded up and down the gay beach, yelling out jokes to get folks to come to the shows. I joined them. We stopped a couple of times—my cue to crank up some John Phillip Sousa on my boom box and twirl the baton. Whether we were entertaining or just looked desperate, I'm not sure.

Another time I put on my bellydance costume and did a shimmy each time I handed out a flier. I wasn't the only one out there in sequins and fringe. I had to jiggle the cup of my beaded bra to assure some of the flier recipients that my breasts were, indeed, real.

I was supposed to receive a free meal on the nights I entertained. I eagerly arrived in the venue's dining room after my first performance. After waiting over an hour for overcooked roast and tasteless vegetables, I opted for a dinner at the coffee shop where most of the entertainers went. It cut into my budget, but it was fast, hot and edible. The rest of the time, I ate food I'd stashed in the tiny refrigerator in the rooming house hallway. I'm sure the other guests weren't happy about fitting their beer in amongst my juice, milk and lunchmeat. I began to shop by size. Watermelon, no. Tiny containers of yogurt, yes.

Many of the entertainers would offer you the courtesy of attending their shows for free. Over several years of playing in Provincetown, I had the pleasure of hearing comic Suzanne Westenhoefer, impressionist Jimmy James, rock band The Fabulous Dyketones, singer-songwriter Zoe Lewis and others. They came to my shows too.

Every day that first summer—as it was for all my gigs there—was filled with handing out those damn pieces of paper. After a while, I felt like a ten-dollar hooker. "Hey, come to my show, baby." A couple of times I took the day off, relieved to just sit on the beach and read.

If the weather was nasty, the crowds were sparse, so either the show was canceled or I played for five drenched people who looked like they'd rather be scooping up dog poo. Getting back to housing on those nights was hard, since I walked to work. One night, unable to wait the storm out any longer, I took a cab, killing my earnings for that evening. My guitar would've been an expensive boat.

When I wasn't working, I could sometimes find another entertainer or townie to spend time with. Suzanne was fun to hang out with, but she wasn't always in town when I was. I spent a lot of my off-work time alone. Usually that was okay, but there were times when I craved company. If I didn't know any of the other performers, I was at a loss—almost everyone else in town was a tourist just there for a few days. One night I was so lonely I asked my audience if anyone would like to go out to dinner with me. A small group of very nice women from Rhode Island said yes. We chatted politely over meatloaf and mashed potatoes. One of them insisted on paying for my dinner.

Most nights I played for a smattering of ten or fifteen sunburned people slurping overpriced drinks. Thank God for that one night where a rowdy group of women from Cleveland helped to fill the room and gave me two standing ovations or I would've tossed my guitar in the trash and told people I used to play. The audience stayed for the next performer, singer/guitarist Mary Day. When she heard me singing harmony from the audience, she invited me up for a rowdy version of "Closer to Fine." Big fun.

After paying for restaurant meals, my housing, the fliers, and transportation, there wasn't much left. A couple of other entertainers told me that if I played at one of the more centrally located bars, I would do better. One graciously gave me the name and home number of the booker of the best-known club. It took me a few calls from a pay phone (there were no cell phones then) to realize that if I called her before noon, she was still sleeping. Later in the afternoon, she'd be too drunk. Finally, my timing was right and with the recommendation of that same performer, the bar owner agreed to book me for one night as a live audition.

Because I was currently booked at another club, I couldn't advertise my show with her until I'd finished my run the night before. I quickly designed another flier using a borrowed computer, and then used the only copy machine in town for rent. Right after my show at the old place, I hit the streets with a blinding smile and bad jokes about sleeping with celebrities. The next day I took my baton to the beach, spending two hours twirling and handing out those little pieces of paper.

The bar where I was to audition had housing for entertainers and I was grateful to save on room rental for the night. The old house was disdainfully called the crack house by the performers because of the huge crack that ran across the ceiling and down one wall. My guess is that it was sliding down the hill. In most cities, it would have been condemned. My room had a bare mattress on the floor and no other furniture. One of the comics staying there thoughtfully loaned me an extra set of her clean sheets. I made up the bed then hurriedly put on my makeup in the hot, tiny bathroom as sweat dripped off my nose.

Minutes before the show I got a quick sound check. It was a club designed more for stand-up comics and lipsynching drag queens. It wasn't really set up for an acoustic guitar and someone who did her own singing. We settled on a balance where you could hear my voice clearly, even if the guitar sounded like something I'd bought at Walmart.

I ducked out and distributed a few more fliers just before heaving my exhausted body onstage. Even though I felt like I was moving through mud, the thirty or so people there were gracious with their applause, even when the microphone quit working during "Wedding Song." It wasn't a full house, although it still looked pretty crowded. They laughed loudly throughout the show and gave me a standing ovation when I was done. I found the owner in the back of the room. Smiling broadly, she slurred, "I like your crowd. They ordered mixed drinks. I don't like Lucie Blue's audience, they only order Perrier. I can't make money with Perrier." No mention of the standing ovation or the thirty people I'd drawn with only twenty-four hours' notice.

She wanted to hire me again, hinting that Women's Week in October would be possible. I called her several times in the next two months, but she always had someone with a bigger name who was almost booked, could I call next week? After talking to her voice mail a few times that year and the next year, I gave up. She never booked me again.

The following year, I played at the smaller bar again, this time for Women's Week, and the following year for Labor Day weekend. I never made enough to justify the expenses. The morning after my last gig, I got up early and got the hell out of Dodge.

I've thought about vacationing there—hey, a town full of lesbians and a beautiful ocean are pretty seductive—but I'd probably bump my head and wake up on the beach in my bellydance costume, wondering why I was begging sandwiches from strangers.

CHAPTER SIX

Snow in Snoqualmie

Too bad there wasn't a warm beach at a 1991 gig in Spokane. As I played, I looked out the huge window to my right where I could see snow falling steadily. It looked so pretty. Almost spring, I didn't think there'd be that much of it, but on the drive back to my housing I noticed several inches.

The next morning, after brushing the snow off my truck, I set off for my next gig in Seattle, normally a five-hour drive. The streets hadn't been plowed, but my little truck maneuvered the snowy roadway easily. Even though I'd spent most of my life in the desert, I felt confident driving in this weather. Besides, how bad could it be in March?

As I drove west, the white landscape cleared to reveal asphalt. A sprinkling of snow still blew across the roadway, but it was considerably less than what I'd seen in Spokane. I stopped for a leisurely lunch, and then guided my truck back to the interstate.

The light snow turned heavier as I drove toward the mountains. It looked awfully white up in the pass, but still I felt sure of what I was doing. As the roadway rose in elevation, ice crystals started sticking to the windshield wipers. The unplowed highway gathered more and more snow. Visibility faded as icy white fog swirled around me. I gripped the steering wheel and turned up the stereo to bolster my confidence. Still more snow fell as I climbed the mountains until I couldn't see where the roadway ended and the cliffs began, one dropping off sharply to the left side, then the right. If it weren't for the big semi in front of me, I wouldn't have known where to drive. I prayed that the driver could see better than I could. I would've pulled over, but was afraid that someone would run into me. At least I wasn't one of the many cars I saw nose-end in a ditch after spinning out.

Lightly tapping on the brakes made the rear of my truck slide, so I avoided the brake pedal, downshifting when I needed to slow down. I hoped no one ahead of me would need to make a complete stop. In my head, I ran back things I'd learned twenty years ago in driver's ed—do you turn the wheel in the direction of a spin or against it?

Along the way were signs warning folks to put on chains. I had a set, but had never used them. I figured as long as there were cars around me that were making their way without them, I was okay. Finally, near the three-thousand-foot-high summit of Snoqualmie Pass was a huge sign commanding everyone to pull over *now* and put on chains. I dutifully pulled off and parked behind a VW van, crawled into the back of my truck and pulled out the chains. In the short time it took for me to do that the guy in the van ahead of me had almost finished putting on his chains. I pulled a tangled mess out of the plastic box and tried to read the directions, most of which had rubbed off. I had no idea what to do with this puzzle. Approaching the van driver with the pile of metal in my hand, I asked if he could help me. He smiled warmly and said sure, trotting to the back end of my truck. Looking at my Arizona license plate, he did a cartoon double take. "What are *you* doing here?" he questioned.

"I'm a musician with a gig in Seattle," I replied, as if the explanation made complete sense. He quickly applied the chains as I watched. I was certain I'd know how to do it next time.

I pulled out, driving slowly, but still avoiding the brakes. After I crossed over the pass and elevation dropped, the snow turned to rain. I pulled over to remove the chains. I unhooked them, and then backed up the truck slightly so I could pull them out. One of the ends wrapped itself around the axle. After a very frustrating few minutes I threw up my hands and pulled out my portable CB. I found nothing but static on the emergency channel. No luck with the others, either. I lifted the hood of the truck and waited for a Good Samaritan. And waited…and waited. Everyone sped by me, including a cop. I tried standing outside the truck in the freezing rain, in a bright pink Windbreaker looking mournful, and still no one stopped. After an hour that seemed like years, a hippie guy in an old VW bug (must've been my day for kind VW drivers) stopped and asked if I needed help. It took me longer to explain the problem than it took for him to fix it. As I thanked him I burst into tears, feeling like a big, tired, stupid broad…who was late to a gig. I zipped down the mountain, quickly found my housing, called my girlfriend and cried some more, changed clothes, then jumped into the truck.

I swear Seattle lies over a vortex of confusion. I've gotten lost there more times than most other cities, and this time was no exception. Driving up and down the confusing streets I squinted at the tiny street signs to find the bar where I was supposed to play. I stopped at a convenience market for directions, but the young guy behind the counter just shrugged and said "I dunno." I drove around some more, convinced I was close, and after more searching, found the venue, only two blocks away from that market.

I had just enough time to set up the club's ancient PA and start the show. My conversation between songs dwelled on my precarious trip that day. At least my trials were worth a few laughs. Really tired from my day, I said I was cutting my set short. I did the last song, and as I left the stage someone yelled out, "Is that all?"

CHAPTER SEVEN

Flight Delayed

There's a kind of bonding done between parents watching their kids at a playground or between players on a sports field. While the action may not be as exciting, a similar thing happens with travelers at an airport, especially when you've been tossed by the weather and delayed by mechanical problems on a holiday weekend.

In 2001, I flew on the Monday after Thanksgiving from Phoenix, and after two hours in the air, was returned to where I started. When the door covering your landing gear won't close you can't turn right around. You have to fly for two hours to burn off fuel, taking an unplanned tour over northern Arizona (I've seen the meteor crater in photos, did I need to see it from the air?) before returning to Phoenix. I finally escaped out of Phoenix, but landed in Charlotte too late to make my connecting flight to Chicago. Add hundreds of other passengers delayed by rain and fog, and you've got a lot of bored and angry people staring down one haggard-looking airline gate clerk.

I sat next to three well-dressed African Americans, the women in shiny pointy heels and the guy in a neatly pressed gray suit. They laughed lightly at their long day of missed flights and airport scenery. Across from me, a young white guy was slumped in his chair and mumbling about getting a substitute teacher for his grade school class. Next to him was a young woman who, like a battery-powered toy with extra juice, rattled on about being a youth minister and made a phone call every ten minutes to give updates to her parents. "Now they've announced that the flight is coming in at 10:05. That's the fourth delay. Where are you? Stop and get some coffee." At the end of the row sat a frowning older guy who'd obviously had a worse day than I had.

I glanced at the mandolin beside me. No, I thought, they'll all stare at me if I pull it out, but what else was I going to do? I'd finished my book, I couldn't get a net connection, and I'd done nothing but lose miserably at solitaire since I fired up the computer.

I slipped the instrument out of the case, at first thinking I'd sneak away to some quiet corner to work on a few tunes, but there's that performer gene from my country musician dad that screamed, "Hey! An audience! And they can't go anywhere!" I started strumming. The cranky guy stared at his shoes, but one of the well-dressed ladies beside me smiled. She likes me! My tiny musician's brain rejoiced. I hit a G chord, found a funky rhythm, moved to a D chord and started "Wild Thing."

"Sing along!" I encouraged. I could see a few mouths move and heard a little hum under their breaths, as I sang more. Miss I-must-report-every-breath-to-my-parents across from me reached for her phone, changed her mind, smiled broadly and started singing. I segued into "Born to be Wild"—what mandolin rock medley would be complete without it?—then whatever snatches of rock songs I could remember—"Gloria," "La Bamba" and "Louie Louie." Folks sang along or just listened, a quiet grin on their faces. One little guy, about three, jumped up and wiggled his butt to the music, egged on by applause. And, because I'm a songwriter and couldn't resist, I started making up a song about being stuck in the airport with this fine group of people. Louder, I sang "And we're all beeeeautiful and we'd like to leeeeave this airport."

The woman with the cell fired it up, and exclaimed "Dad, you've gotta hear this," holding her phone up.

I was building up to a big finish, the chords getting faster (where was the drummer for my big rock ending?) when a passenger, at the counter trying to negotiate his way home, threw his head back and belted, "I just wanna go hoooooome!"

I ended with a flourish and jumped out of my chair in a rock-star finale. Applause ricocheted off the walls. I heard, "You should put out a tip jar" and "Hey, you're good at that."

I continued to play, more quietly this time, running through some fiddle tunes, an original song and a few random chords, just to keep myself busy. When the incoming flight finally arrived, I put the instrument away and nervously awaited my fate with the other twenty standby passengers.

There was no room on that plane, the last one of the day, so the airline put me up in a nearby hotel. Arriving early for my flight the next morning, I didn't see any familiar faces from the day before. All of the seats in the waiting area were taken so I plopped on the floor, settled into a cross-legged position and pulled out my little mandolin. I tinked through a few tunes but no one noticed. Maybe they couldn't hear me or maybe, so sure they were getting home, they didn't need to add their own "I just wanna go hoooome."

CHAPTER EIGHT

I Was Always Cold and There Was Little to Eat

I'm not sure why I first visited the Shaker community in Canterbury, New Hampshire, in 1991. I'm not a particularly spiritual person and I knew nothing about the Shakers except that they made beautiful furniture. Maybe I was there because I had a day off from touring and I love going through old buildings. At any rate, there I was on a beautiful spring day, following behind a young tour guide. That was my introduction to one of the few major religions started by a woman. Her name was Ann Lee. Followers called her Mother Ann. Her little band of supporters sailed from Britain in 1774, almost perishing in a storm on the way, but Mother Ann saw an angel above the ship's mast and assured the captain they'd make it safely.

That was one of the issues with Mother Ann. Not only was she a strong woman, but she had visions, and that didn't make her well-received in her new country; neither did her habit of breaking into a church during a service, giving an impassioned sermon, and then leaving with the parishioners. For this, she was beaten and thrown into jail. Later, after she passed away, her followers continued to grow a religion based on her doctrines. They lived communally and thrived in the eighteen hundreds and early nineteen hundreds, from Kentucky to Florida to Maine. Most are gone now, but they left behind these beautiful buildings and a record of their fascinating way of life.

I was captivated by this group of people who lived together in a place where men and women were treated equally. They also welcomed people of all races (although most were white). Some of the larger buildings were used as sleeping quarters, the men separated from the women. The wood structures were beautiful, but simple, because the early Shakers believed that ornamentation was prideful and therefore sinful. Every community had a meeting house where they would hold services. Their name came from the dancing they did during worship. The townspeople were shocked, and used to gather at the windows of the meeting house to watch. I wish there'd been film in those days because all we have are a few drawings and some writing describing the movements as frantic and high energy.

The Shakers also loved music and have written thousands of songs. The most well-known is probably "Simple Gifts," because Aaron Copland used it in "Appalachian Spring."

How could I not be attracted to a group of people led by a woman, and who embraced dancing and music?

The buildings in Canterbury were not restored completely. Even the meeting house, built in 1792, hadn't been painted for decades. The paint wasn't peeling though, because it was a special paint created by the Shakers. They were known for inventing many things, but for many years didn't believe in patents. It's said that a Shaker sister invented the circular saw. How utterly cool is that?

If I closed my eyes, I could almost hear the bustle of the busy community kitchen or the laughter of the women out in the orchard as they picked apples. The schoolhouse still seemed to hold the sound of children and featured a list of names on the blackboards, from a reunion of Shakers that had happened years ago.

At the end of the tour, I eagerly visited the gift shop and bought a couple of books. In the next few years, I devoured every book I could find about the Shakers. Odd, when you know that I hadn't stepped into a church for years, except when it was rented for one of my concerts.

I returned to Canterbury a year or two after that, during another break from touring. I was especially interested in a photo exhibit. The pictures from the late eighteen hundreds and early nineteen hundreds were standard group shots of Shakers, posed in formal portraits or informally at work, the women in long dresses and bonnets, the men in overalls or black suits. Early Shakers were rarely photographed alone because to single out the individual was thought to be against God. Everything Shakers did was for the good of the community. But there was one photo of a single woman. Dressed in a dark dress and bonnet, she was descending a short flight of stairs and looking up, like the photographer had just called her name. Her luminous eyes looked frankly at the photographer and directly at me. I stood for several minutes, transfixed by her. Why was she photographed alone? Who was she? I made my way around the rest of the room, looked at the other photos, and came back to her one more time before I left.

I went through all of my books and couldn't find that photo. On my next visit, I looked for it, but the exhibit was gone. One of the docents said it was a temporary display and the picture was probably loaned from a private collector. No one I asked knew anything about it.

I don't believe in reincarnation. If I did, though, I'd think I'd met her before. Or maybe the photographer was just really good at capturing the moment and who she was.

Whenever I had the time, I visited other Shaker communities. I went to one in Hancock, Massachusetts that included a unique round barn. There are still Shakers in Sabbathday Lake, Maine. You can't tour many of the buildings, but the countryside is beautiful and they have a gift shop where you can purchase books and handcrafts. The community in Pleasant Hill, Kentucky was distinctive in some ways, but ultimately, I was disappointed. Their woodworking talents are famous and it's easy to see why, especially on the circular double staircase featured in the trustee's house. However, their brochure called the Shakers "zealots," which to me is pejorative, and the tour guide knew less about the Shakers than did I, telling us that followers were celibate because they thought the end of the world was near. If that was true, why did Mother Ann have a premonition that Shakers would decline in membership, but would be revitalized when their number reached the same as the number of fingers on one hand?

I was excited to stay in one of the buildings, but horrified at the updates, including ugly acoustic ceiling tiles. The other buildings had been restored also, and that ruined it for me. I don't need the pretty tourist version of their lives.

Mother Ann is buried in Watervilet, near Albany, NY. There's also a museum, located in the former meeting house. I parked in front of it and on a blustery early winter day, I walked to the cemetery to see the rows of simple headstones. My memory is fuzzy, but I don't remember those listing individual names—maybe they had no inscription at all. One headstone was higher than the others, with "Mother Ann Lee" engraved on it. She never wanted to be thought of as more special than the others, so I'm sure that the bigger stone was not her idea. I stood at the grave for a while, remembering all that I had read about that amazing woman.

I headed back to the museum as dry leaves swirled around my feet. I pulled my jacket in a little closer and these words came me, "I was always cold and there was little to eat." It wasn't like I heard the words, they were just there. I hurried to the museum where I knew it would be warmer.

Standing on the scratched wood floor of the meeting house, I swore I could feel the vibrations of a hundred dancing feet. I stood for a moment and wondered what it would be like to be one of those joyful Shakers. I wandered into an adjoining room where I found displays about early life there, including one featuring a newspaper account of a visit to the community. I read that the first group of Shakers were so poor that sometimes the only food they'd get in a day was a bowl of porridge. Another line was a quote from a Shaker sister, saying that she was always cold.

In a room full of people who are comfortable, I'll be the only one who's chilly. (The fact that I now live in Canada is nothing short of amazing.) Reading the words in that museum made me think of the other parallels between my life and theirs. I am rich in many ways, in music and in dance, just like they were.

Not long after that, I wrote "Ann Lee:"

A vision brought me here, she said, with the angels by my side
Hands to work and hearts to God, those words are mine
And they'll never die

Canterbury remains my favorite community. On one of my last visits there, I sat by myself at the edge of their mill pond. It was a quiet day, the beginning of fall, with a few trees on the other side showing a dull red with a few bright spots of yellow that reflected in the gray-blue water. I thought about how that view might have looked in 1850, at the height of the existence of this community. One of the docents walked on the path near me, turned and softly commented, "This is one of my favorite views, too." In that peaceful moment, I think I saw one of Mother Ann's angels in a ray of sun.

CHAPTER NINE

If It's Snowing in Atlanta

In March of 1993, I was playing in a nice hotel in Atlanta for a women's conference. A gathering of women in psychology, I'd never had so many people ask me how I was doing. Not only were they kind, they were also an attentive crowd and afterward, I had a comfortable hotel room in which to sleep. Snow was forecast for the next day, but how much could it snow there, especially in March? I tried to find The Weather Channel on the TV, but like many luxury hotels where I've stayed, there weren't many channels, including that one. (Why is it I can stay at a Super Eight and find thirty channels, but at a Hilton, only seven? Do moneyed people not watch TV?) I found nothing on the local news except Chicken Little-type statements about snow. Shoot, I was headed south the next day. Even if the cold stuff fell here, chances are I wouldn't find much as I journeyed away.

I called the next evening's concert producer in Florida on the phone in my room. Her phone just rang. I thought it was odd that I didn't get her voice mail, but figured I'd just phone her the following day. I didn't have any other method of reaching her since this was also in the days before the Internet.

The next morning was quiet with snow. Most residents had stayed home which was fine with me. I didn't want to share the interstate with crazed Southerners without a clue about driving in winter weather. Not that I was the experienced traveler, growing up in southern Arizona, but I felt confident that if I took it slow, I'd soon be safely out of the bad weather. Just before leaving my room, I tried my Florida contact again. Still, no answer.

One of the bellhops helped me load my truck, asking, with eyebrows raised, where I was going in that weather. Not even the cab companies are running he said, except for one that had snow tires, and there was a long wait for one of those. In a slightly uppity tone I answered, "Oh, I'll be fine. I'm headed to Florida."

As I pulled away from the hotel, I rejoiced in the near empty streets. Noting that there were only a couple inches of snow on the ground, I was even more sure I'd be fine.

Out on the interstate, I switched on the radio, looking for a report on the weather and road conditions, but only found bored DJs reciting an endless list of canceled events and closed businesses and schools. When there was news about the weather it was, "Spalding County will get four more inches of snow! All the roads in Locust Grove are closed."

Where the hell was Spalding County? And how close was I to Locust Grove? My map didn't tell me and this was way before GPS's were available.

I inched along the roadway, carefully staying in the double row of ruts made by earlier motorists. Outside the divots, it was too slippery. I only saw a couple other cars and a lot of semis, most passing me. Snow was steadily falling, clumping to my wipers in a big icy mass. The high drifts on the right side of the roadway prevented me from pulling over to remove the ice so I peered out the little clear space the wipers left, hoping there'd be somewhere to pull off. I squinted at the road signs, wishing for one that would say I could exit soon, but snow obscured most of the lettering, leaving me to guess what was coming up ahead. Most of the exits hadn't been plowed anyway.

A blue sign appeared through the snowy mist. I couldn't read it, but it looked like one of those signs announcing a rest area up ahead. I slowed down even more, to be sure not to miss the road leading off the interstate. It hadn't been plowed, but enough vehicles had been there before me that I could see where the roadway was and as I got further along, I saw that indeed I had found a rest area! After parking, I fiddled with the radio some more. I still couldn't find a good weather station and just ended up screaming at some inane DJ as he informed me of yet another important event, probably a bingo game, that had been canceled.

My little truck and a brown sedan were the only ones there. I don't usually talk to strangers at rest areas, but we were two compatriots stranded in the weather and I thought he might know about the roads up ahead. As he headed from the restroom back to his car, I smiled and asked if he knew anything. He gave me a look of annoyance and moved his right hand up toward his face, signing, "I'm deaf."

I'd taken enough sign language to talk to a deaf toddler, but certainly not an adult. I racked my brain for long-forgotten signs, finally remembering how to say "snow." I pointed down the road, made the sign, and hoped the questioning look on my face was enough to ask him what I needed.

He furrowed his brows, turned down the corners of his mouth, angrily shrugged and ducked into his car. He didn't have to sign anything for me to know he was thinking, "Dumb broad, of course it's snowing."

I thought about waiting in the rest area until the snow let up. With few snowplows out and about, though, I knew I could be there all night. The bathrooms were heated and I suppose I could start up the truck now and then to keep warm, but I had my gig in Florida that night. When we musicians book a gig, we get there. We don't spend months planning a tour only to have Mother Nature screw it up.

At the rest area pay phone, I tried to call my Florida producer again, only to hear it ring and ring. I chipped the ice off the wipers and crept back onto the snowy highway.

The three lanes normally found on my side of the road had become a pair of icy ruts surrounded by high drifts of snow. I continued to drive slowly. At one point, the interstate divided. I'd planned to take the choice that was straight ahead, but the ruts went to the left so that was the direction I took. On the map, it looked like a slightly longer way, but would still get me to my next gig.

With a death grip on the steering wheel, leaning forward to gaze in the little spot left free on the windshield, I listened to tapes of Bonnie Raitt, singing loudly along to bolster my courage. That wasn't going to help me, though, when the gas tank's needle inched to empty. Still unable to read the signs to find out when an exit with a gas station would be available, I took a chance and left the highway on an exit that, while unplowed, looked safe enough to drive on. The snow and fog were too thick to see anything until I got to the top of a rise where the road met another one. My spirits fell when I saw no buildings. What might have been a road, but was thick with snow, stretched to my right. To my left, on a bridge going over the interstate, were the imprints of several sets of tires. I chose the left. My truck barely moved as I drove over the interstate. All I needed now was to skid on ice and dive over the edge into the traffic below. It wasn't busy, but none of those people could use their brakes without spinning out of control.

I'm not a religious person—however, when I saw that familiar red and blue Chevron sign, I thanked whoever was responsible for my good fortune. I pulled up to the pump and filled my tank. In the store, while paying for the gas, I overheard the locals talking about how they'd pulled old Mr. Conley out of a ditch, and several other stories, all having to do with the nasty snow. No one asked what I was doing out by myself with out-of-state plates and a two-wheel-drive truck.

Not long after I got back on the highway, the snow finally stopped. Little by little, the landscape showed less and less white. I could see pavement again and it wasn't covered with ice. That's about the time the winds with gale-force gusts picked up. They blew my little truck all over the highway. Thankfully, there still wasn't much traffic. Several times I blinked and found myself in the next lane over, like some giant hand had shoved me.

After what seemed like days, I reached I-95. Headed south, it should take me quickly to my next gig. The winds were still whipping me around, though, and now there was more traffic. My knuckles were white from hanging on to the steering wheel, especially on the many bridges where the gusts were stronger. I listened to the radio again and heard that many communities were without power because of the wind. I'd had enough. Gig or no gig, I was pulling over for the night. I searched for a motel, but most didn't look like they had lights. Some featured handwritten signs announcing they had no electricity. There was nothing else to do but keep heading south.

I needed gas again. Exiting the highway, I looked to my right to see a gas station with its roof being peeled off like a giant sardine can. I didn't even blink, just thought, okay, I can't get gas there, let's see what's on the other side of the freeway. I crossed over the highway and found a Shell station. Its stories-high sign swayed dangerously in the wind.

As I pulled up to the self-serve pump, an attendant came running up. "Our power keeps flickering on and off—I think it's gonna go off for good soon. The credit card machine won't work. Pump quick and pay cash." Like a member of a pit stop crew, I leaped out and pumped in record time, paid in cash and zipped back onto the road.

Wearier than I'd ever been in my life, I finally arrived at my next gig. The small seaside Florida town had signs of life—a kid's bicycle, a few cars, and houses of course, just no humans, like I'd stepped into some *Twilight Zone* episode. I walked around a bit, knocked on a few doors, and found no one. Just as I was about to give up, I rounded the corner of a building and I met a surprised woman. Looking like she was seeing someone come back from the dead, she raised her eyebrows and exclaimed, "Jamie?"

"Yes," I answered carefully.

"We thought you weren't coming. We canceled the show."

Later, during dinner with a few of the women who were to work on my show, I found out they'd had a tornado the night before. Many folks had left town and no one had power. I was invited to stay with a couple of the women, but with temperatures dipping into the thirties and no heat, I elected to stay with friends in Jacksonville, a half-hour's drive away. After dinner, I climbed back into the truck.

Fifteen minutes from Jacksonville, it started to snow.

CHAPTER TEN

Finding My People

It was Memorial Day weekend in 1995 and I was coming from Campfest, a great women's music festival in Pennsylvania. I'd seen lots of friends, slept in a comfortable cabin and received a standing ovation, so I was feeling pretty good as I drove west on my way to another festival. I was a bit apprehensive about this next one because it was the first time I'd been booked at a big folk festival.

I took my time with the driving, spending all day in the truck and stopping each of three nights on the road. A couple of hours from the festival my stomach growled just as I saw a sign for barbecue. When I walked into the rustic looking place, I was thinking that they should've called it House O' Meat. The walls were covered with mounted deer heads. The top of the beverage refrigerator sported a stuffed wildcat and a turkey. Above my head hung a chandelier made with antlers. Two good ol' boys in feed caps sat near me, chowing down on piles of beef smothered in sauce. I didn't love the gruesome décor, but damn, that smoky barbecue scent was so heavenly it was probably illegal everywhere except Texas. The smiling clerk behind the counter asked with a sweet drawl, "Honey, what'll you have?"

I got chicken that was so tender it fell off the bone, and a couple of yummy sides. If this was how Texas was going to be, I was all for it. I was feeling a little congested and worried that I was coming down with something, but I figured it wasn't anything a little mouth-watering barbecue couldn't cure.

By the time I pulled up to the festival gate, though, my throat had started a slow burn. I didn't feel any better when some man I'd never met engulfed me with a hug, enthusing, "Welcome home!" I'd never been to this festival, it wasn't even close to my home and who was this guy?

A woman behind a table there asked if I had a ticket. I replied, "No, I'm booked to play here."

"Where are you sleeping?" she asked.

I pointed to the camper shell on the back.

"It's five bucks a day for parking."

"What?" I asked, trying to smile, "I'm only making seventy-five to play here."

She blinked and slowly responded, "Well, I'm working for free."

Yeah, and I'll bet you have a job outside of this festival. Music is *my job.* I didn't say any of that because really, what would it do but make the start of my stay here worse? In the end, she agreed to give me a wristband that was good for a couple of days. Still not the whole time I'd be there. I figured I'd work that out later.

After finding a place to camp, I strolled around the desert campground cluttered with clumps of colorful tents, campers and tarps, looking for two particular sites. People don't just come to this event to hear the stage entertainment. Different groups set up campsites—some had come for years—and ran campfires every night. Folks wandered around, either playing their own music or listening to others. Some camps had a host of regulars and a reputation. If you wanted to hear well-written country and folk songs, you went to Camp Nashville. If you wanted goofy songs, try Camp Stupid. I was looking for Camp Cactus—a group of folks from my hometown of Tucson—and Camp Queer, because it always makes me feel better when I find My People. I couldn't find either. I saw some rainbow flags. No one was home, though. I checked the program, but the only lesbian performer I could see was Heather Bishop and she was playing after I'd planned to leave.

I did what a touring lesbian musician usually does in this circumstance—she finds the pay phones, calls her girlfriend and leaves a long whiny message on voice mail. A young hippie guy overheard me and after I hung up, asked if I wanted a hug. I grunted and said, "No."

"I didn't think so."

At least this one asked.

At that point, all I wanted was to feel better and find some lesbians. And sleep in a comfy cabin. And get a standing ovation. I was used to women's music festivals where there was an artist liaison to help me. All I had at this festival was a sore throat and strange men who kept wanting to hug me.

I longed to participate in the campfires, but my throat kept getting worse. After three days, I decided I either needed a doctor or the fire department. I asked someone at the front gate about getting help. He shrugged and after consulting with another volunteer, told me where he thought the doctor was camped. She wasn't there. A neighbor said she hadn't seen her recently. She described her car and suggested that I walk around and look for it. My energy was low, I was getting crankier by the minute, and I felt like crap. I shuffled my sorry ass back to the front gate and inquired about doctors in town. I was told to look in the phone book.

So, it was back to the pay phones. I think I heard a choir sing when someone answered at the first number and agreed to take me that day. I got directions, packed up the truck, and sped into town.

In the waiting room, I tried to ignore the magazines from Focus on the Family. The doctor turned out to be pretty nice—maybe he was used to disheveled musicians from the nearby festival. I probably had strep so he gave me a prescription. After stopping at a pharmacy I motored back to the festival. I downed the first dose of meds and slept for hours.

The next day, I found Camp Cactus and their neighbor, Camp Bungee—so named because they used a lot of them in an elaborate tarping scheme that defied most rules of physics. It was comforting to find some people from home. Still no lesbians, but at least I had someone to hang out with. The antibiotics were helping, too. As my health returned, my outlook improved.

I fell into a routine. Each day I'd sleep in, and then slowly wake up with coffee and a breakfast burrito from the little trailer where they sold food. It was also a place for folks to socialize, so there was often great conversation. Maybe someone would pull out a guitar. One day, there was a guy with an Etch-A-Sketch, doing these amazing drawings of the scenes around us. Another morning, a young woman laid out some beautiful hemp necklaces that she'd made and was selling.

After a couple of hours, I'd stroll back to my truck to read or nap. In the blistering heat of the afternoon, that's what a lot of us did. At night, there were performances on the stages. (I was scheduled for one a few days later.) After that, I'd mosey around to the campfires until the wee hours, listening and looking for opportunities to play. This was very much a songwriter's festival, with each original song more wonderful than the last. There were the famous folks, like Peter Yarrow (from Peter, Paul and Mary) walking around, as well as the people who were so good they should've been famous.

There were songs I didn't love, too. It was like the weather in Texas—wait five minutes and it'll change. I learned to avoid the fellow who sang the same song at every campfire and started to seek out my favorites.

For most of the campfires, you had to be invited to sing. It helped to know someone who was already playing. For others, as long as there was space, you were welcome to sit a spell and sing one of your songs when it came your turn. The more popular campfires had a huge ring of listeners.

One night, I went to Camp Nashville, where my friend Richard Berman was playing. He invited me into the circle. My voice shook a little when it came my turn. Looking around the ring of interested faces, I slowly gained confidence. I didn't leave until four a.m. The next night, I returned. We sang the sun up. When we started on the Crosby, Stills and Nash covers, I knew it was time to go.

Over the nine days I was there, I found a fun time at several of the campsites, including Camps Cactus and Bungee. One night we got started with a whole bunch of funny songs, so of course I contributed my "Menstrual Tango." A couple of the guys got all fired up about writing "Prostate Polka." They probably felt different after the beer wore off.

At Camp Stupid, I could always count on a solid circle of warped individuals who could truly appreciate songs like "When Cats Take Over the World":

When cats take over the world
All trouble will cease
You could jump on a bookcase
Knock over whatever you please
You could clean your butthole
In front of company
In public you could hurl
When cats take over the world

They were the only campsite with a drum set. Surprising, since drums weren't allowed at the festival—too loud, I guess. When I asked about the set, someone quickly responded, "What drums? These aren't drums."

All right, pass the beer.

The last evening I was there, I performed in a showcase on one of the stages featuring two other Tucson singer-songwriters, the wonderful Ron Pandy, and Stephan George, plus the best Tex-Mex Irish band on the planet, The Mollys. Afterward, we drank and carried on until four thirty a.m.

I never did find Camp Queer, if there was such a thing, but I'd certainly found My People.

CHAPTER ELEVEN

The Moon, God and Good Luck

My gig was at a tiny New England café in September 1996. I had a vicious cold. There but for the grace of Sudafed went I.

Yvette was in charge of running things. She told me it was her first time, but that was easy to tell, given the nervous way she glanced about the room like the audience was going to trash the place. We chatted as she set up tables. When I asked what kind of work she'd done before, she replied that she'd worked as an assistant for a Christian magician. Oh, I cracked, does that mean he pulled crosses out of a hat? She blandly replied, no, it's just that he worked to Christian music. She explained that she wore a tuxedo and that started our discussion of why male magicians usually wear a lot of clothing while their female assistants are expected to prance around in hankies masquerading as dresses.

The crowd was so small that I met each of them. I have family members I've met several times whose names still escape me, but on this night there were only seven names to recall. Before the evening was through, I also knew the names of their pets and where they lived. When one woman who was sitting by herself confided that she was being kicked out of her house in three weeks, and didn't know where she would go, I introduced her to the table of three next to her. One of them had told me earlier that she "takes in strays" and always has several roommates.

Just before I started playing, one of them said there was going to be an eclipse that night. I agreed to end the first set just before nine so we could all go out to gaze at the sky. I coughed my way through a ragged set. I hacked so much during "Midnight Alice" that I had to stop, then deadpanned that I always do that tune in two sections. They laughed. I may have sung like Lauren Bacall after a carton of cigarettes, but I could still make them laugh.

At the break, a few of the women went outside. They returned, saying there wasn't anything to see yet. While they were gone, I spoke with a couple of the others who offered thoughtful suggestions about how to get the word out about the next show. In my tired, half-drugged state, I didn't have the heart to tell them that at that moment I just hoped I could get through the next set without coughing up a hair ball. Promotion for the next booking—if I ever played there again—was not foremost in my brain.

I rasped through the second set. At the end I told them that if they wanted to hear me without a head full of snot, they should buy my CD and bless them, three of them did.

While I packed up my equipment and CDs, Yvette talked with me. She told me she liked how I sang in a girly-girl voice and then surprised them with a song like "Menstrual Tango." (Can I put "girly-girl" in my official bio?) She also liked the ballad "One Out of Three," a personal story about breast cancer. She switched the topic to abortion, which confused me at first, until she made the comment that women who had abortions were at a higher risk for cancer. I wanted to yell "Bullshit!" but answered with something more diplomatic, like "Maybe that was one study, but you need to look at all of them and you'll find that that isn't true." Expecting an argument from her, she simply answered, "Oh." At this point I excused myself and went out the door to see if the eclipse had started yet. Three quarters of the moon was covered with a filmy indigo mask. A thin crescent of bright yellow showed at the edge. Yvette stood with me as we silently admired the beauty.

I walked back into the venue and finished packing. Sometimes when a crowd is that small, the venue won't take out their percentage, but Yvette did. I made twenty dollars. As I was leaving, I found a penny by the door. The moon had changed to a luminescent orange. I tucked the penny into my pocket.

CHAPTER TWELVE

Straight Guys and Small Towns

It's 2001 and I'm sitting on a dock on a bay in Maryland. Unlike the song, I can't say "the" dock or "the" bay because I don't know which one it is. Or heck, it could be a river. At any rate, it's a large body of water, placid and a pretty blue-gray. The sun is setting to the right of me, giving the clouds a luminous lavender color, edged in pale yellow. They float in a watery blue sky, like a Maxfield Parrish painting. It's nice to be out of the truck after being cooped up all day, hunched over the steering wheel. I feel like I haven't inhaled deeply all day. I take in a big breath, let it out slowly, and smile.

Seagulls squawk behind me and traffic hums on the bridge to my left. The couple sitting behind me are talking quietly to each other. A kid's voice rises as he chases his friend around on the grass nearby.

Earlier, I walked all over the charming little town where I'm playing later. Most of the buildings are red brick with big front porches of wood. The windows are topped with arches, telling me that they're probably from the turn of the century, or maybe older. A plaque on one said it was built in the late eighteen hundreds.

I walked past the Methodist Church. A sign out front advertised a roast beef dinner. A wedding had just taken place at another church down the street. A young couple, the woman in a traditional lacy dress, posed on the steps next to her handsome groom, surrounded by the wedding party. As I passed them, I commented quietly to the woman walking ahead of me, "Should I tell them they're making a mistake?" She laughed.

Next door, a woman about the same age as the bride sat on a stoop and argued with someone inside the church, yelling that "I already cleaned the fucking thing." The curse hung in the air.

The sun is setting and it's time to head for the gig at a small restaurant with a listening room in the back. I'm opening for Sloan Wainwright. I'm excited because I don't know her work and because she's part of the famous Wainwright family. I figure she must be good. Also, my song, "I Wanna be a Straight Guy," is an answer to her brother Loudon's "I Wish I Was a Lesbian." I sent a CD to his booking agency—the only way I knew to reach him— but never heard anything. Maybe I could do it at this show and his sister could pass on the word. We've had a couple of easy, friendly conversations, so I'm hopeful.

Before the show, I sit at the bar in the front and eat dinner. The owner strolls over. With her short gray hair and brusque manner, my gaydar pings like crazy. It's not always accurate, but because we have a relaxed rapport, I'm probably right this time.

After she leaves, Bob takes her place. His hands float through the air as he speaks, he has a biting sense of humor and he wears a sweet-smelling aftershave. We talk for a long time about music, G. Gordon Liddy (neither of us like him), and getting older. I don't mention my sexuality, simply because it doesn't come up, and he doesn't mention a spouse, male or female. It doesn't occur to me until time for the show…was he flirting with me?

I start off my set with songs that don't reveal too much personal information. Bob laughs loudly at the jokes and claps enthusiastically after each song. When I play "I Wanna Be a Straight Guy," his wide grin disappears for a few seconds. I can hear the wheels turning as he slowly smiles again.

I wanna drive without a map
I wanna wear a jockstrap…just kidding
Kiss my girl for all to see, think everyone is stupid…but me
I wanna be a straight guy

Afterward, he shares, "I had no idea you were, uh, that way."

I enjoy Sloan's performance and she's very complimentary about my set. I give her the CD that has the straight guy song on it, hoping she'll give it to her brother. I never hear from him or from Bob. I don't care so much about Bob, but if you happen to know Loudon, ask him to call me.

CHAPTER THIRTEEN

Just Don't Say Uterus

It only took a few minutes after arriving for a gig in May 1998 for me to think, I'm in hell. Actually, I was in a Southern church basement, someone's idea of the way to heaven. The open mike preceding me was in full bloom, but in serious need of sun and water. I'd heard a comic with jokes that were greeted with silence, a piano player who screamed "Hey Jude," a toothless elderly guy who sang an off-key a cappella song about his mama, and a man who played an instrumental on a creaky banjo in so many fits and starts it was impossible to tap your foot.

I thought this could be a weird gig when they sent me a letter ahead of time telling me that they didn't allow profanity or obscenity. I don't usually use four letter words in my shows and the double entendres seemed safe, so I wasn't too worried.

I launched into my first set, feeling confident. Even if I missed a few chords or words, my guitar was in tune and I was hitting notes known to humankind. Some in the audience shifted uncomfortably in their seats, but many listened politely, tapping their feet in time to the upbeat numbers and laughing at the funny songs.

At the break, a few people left. I figured it was too late for them to be up. Since I was feeling pretty comfortable with the ones who stayed, I decided it was safe to do "Menstrual Tango" near the start of my second set. At the top of the song they chuckled a bit. Toward the middle they only smiled. At the end I didn't even see a grin, even when singing:

Do the menstrual tango, move your butt
Do the menstrual tango, eat chocolate
Do the menstrual tango, eat constantly
Let's all tango together, let's go out to eat

What I did see, out of the corner of my eye, was one of the coffeehouse volunteers. An older woman in a conservative print dress, she was wringing her hands as she stepped up to the side of the stage. As soon as I finished the song, she crooked her index finger, motioning me over. In a stage whisper, she said, "You have to stop with the sex thing or get off the stage."

I was truly puzzled. I hadn't even done my signature lesbian lust song "Dark Chocolate" nor had I cussed, not even under my breath when I missed a couple of chords.

I mumbled, "Huh?"

She repeated her statement as I remembered that I'd said "uterus" in the last song…and sung about menstruation. Okay, so maybe I pushed the boundaries a bit, but it wasn't any worse than those awful films they made you watch in the fourth grade.

It was clear she wanted me to be the good little lesbian and leave quietly. Instead, I made our conversation public. I turned to the small crowd and told them that I'd been asked to leave the stage. My reply was made to the entire room as well as her when I said, "But it seems like these folks are enjoying the show."

"I'm not enjoying the show," shouted a white-haired man from the back. He stood, hands on hips, and glared at me.

The woman kept squeezing her hands and looking frantically at him. No one in the room said a word, except a guy who blurted out that he'd gotten reprimanded earlier in the year for singing the Stones song "Let's Spend the Night Together."

All the while I'm thinking, did they listen to the CD I'd sent? "Menstrual Tango" was on there, as well as many of the songs I'd sung that night. Their booker wasn't at the gig—coward—and later she claimed that she'd only listened to "One Out of Three," my song about breast cancer. I guess she hadn't looked at my press kit, either.

I'd thought that by making conversation with the nervous woman public that someone in the audience would support me, but I was met with an uncomfortable silence. That made me angry at first, thinking they'd left me up there, to fall without a net.

There was no way I was going to be the obedient lesbian and meekly shuffle offstage. After a short public dialogue with the organizer, she blurted out that they'd shut off the lights if I stayed. Even if they turned off all the power, I could still sing, so that's what I announced I'd do. The angry man in the back yelled out, "It has to be the right kind of song."

"Oh, it's the right kind of song," I answered, a smile on my face as I willed my shaking hands to the right places on my guitar.

I invited the audience to sing with me on "A Family of Friends:"
Let us be your family
Let us take you in
Let us be your family
A family of friends

It was empowering to see everyone (except the sour-faced organizers) sing along with me. As the last chord faded I said, "See what love can do?"

My set ended there. As soon as I stepped off the stage, almost everyone in the audience came toward me. A boy of about twelve said it didn't matter to him that I was gay—he thought my songs were pretty. A woman, her words clipped in anger, said she intended to write a firm letter of protest to the organizers. Many of them bought CDs and signed my mailing list.

As I packed up my CDs, the woman who'd asked me to stop tapped me on the arm, repeating what she'd said earlier and adding, "You have such a pretty voice, it's just that you can't do those songs."

Yeah, like the next time I come I should do my medley of Pat Boone hits. She then handed me a fistful of change and one dollar bills, not even enough to cover my expenses.

An older guy standing nearby turned to me and wryly commented, "Welcome to the Bible Belt."

I had picked up my guitar and gig bag and headed toward the door when the same woman approached me one more time, extolling the virtues of my voice and chastising me about "those songs." At this point, I felt no need to appease her guilt, so I turned away from her and strode out the door.

Fortunately, at the intermission, I'd chatted with a table of lesbians and asked if they knew a place where I could stay. I was supposed to stay with one of the church members, a coffeehouse volunteer, but I was getting weird vibes from her. I figured that housing with lesbians I'd never met beat staying with a woman who might whack me over the head with a Bible in the middle of the night. Vera and Sharon provided a safe haven that night, along with some calming conversation where I learned more about life in their buckle of the Bible Belt.

I came to the conclusion that many in the audience were terrified, especially the gay folks who could lose their jobs, houses and kids by coming out. I, on the other hand, could just leave town.

So, if you're ever onstage in the South, be sure never to utter "uterus" into the mike. I'm pretty sure it's against the law.

CHAPTER FOURTEEN

Through Snot, Snow and Screaming Leaf Blowers

In April of 1999, I was having a lousy tour. The gigs weren't bad, but my body was worn out. Plagued with intestinal problems and a cold that dragged on and on, I doggedly forged through each gig, including a live radio show that was broadcast over half of Iowa. Thousands of complete strangers think I always sound like I just swallowed forty-grit sandpaper.

Des Moines was next on my tour. As I pulled into town after an endless five-hour drive, it started to snow. Snow! Where the hell was spring?

I performed in a favorite venue, a women's coffeehouse, at half my normal speed. Everyone was gracious and didn't mind that I quit a little early. I slept for most of the next two days. During one of the few times I was awake, I phoned my girlfriend. Really, though, what could she do? She kept telling me I would be home in a week. Yeah, and what about the days before then?

I arrived at my next gig, a university in Iowa City, feeling pretty sorry for myself. I sat on my hotel room bed drinking gallons of water, blowing my nose, and mindlessly watching TV because anything else seemed like too much effort. A breaking news story drew me in—students at Columbine High School had been shot. Then I watched a special on the bomb dropping in Hiroshima. I couldn't tear myself away, even as I plummeted deeper into despair.

My laptop had died the day before. My online friends might as well have been on Mars.

I did what anyone in that situation would do. I called my mommy. She listened patiently to my long list of woes. I also talked with my brother, Cris, who gave me a few ideas to jolt my dead computer back to the living. I felt a little better.

Next, I ran through a few of my songs, deciding against the ones with high notes, then realizing I couldn't sing many of the other ones, either. I tuned my guitar down a full step, lowering the key, and that helped.

At least I didn't have too far to go to my show—it was downstairs. I slowly dressed, then made my way to the performance room. The sound guy greeted me, saying he had bad news.

Great.

The university president was speaking in the room above us. The powers-that-be were concerned that my concert would interfere with that, so they'd moved my show from eight p.m. to nine p.m. Normally that wouldn't be too bad, but the guy who booked me didn't think to tell anyone else and this was a weekday. Most of my audience would have work or school the next morning, so doing a two-hour show would make it too late. And really? My acoustic guitar and vocal were going to be too loud? I was certainly no louder than the leaf blower that screamed just outside the window.

The sound tech suggested that I go to my room to rest. I was worried about the audience who didn't know about the time change, so I hung out and talked with them. They were a small, but mighty group, who didn't seem to mind my congestion and shortened show.

Afterward, I dragged my weary body back to my room. One of my best friends, Cheryl, called and gave me a great pep talk. The university had paid me and as I looked at the large fee, I thought, hey this isn't so bad. University checks don't bounce, my mom loved me, I had great friends and a wonderful audience willing to listen, even if I'm hacking up a hair ball every five minutes. On to the next gig, but please God, no snow.

CHAPTER FIFTEEN

Always a Cat in My Lap

I often stay in the homes of strangers, euphemistically known as community housing, 'cause that sounds more peace, love and Unitarian-like. Most folks are very courteous, often contacting me in advance to ask about my needs. If they have pets they get bonus points. I miss my critters when I'm away from home so I love sharing living space with animals, provided they are not of the barnyard variety.

In 2000, when women in Iowa told me that they had a lot of animals, I was unconcerned. The more the merrier, I thought. I was not, however, prepared for fifteen cats, two dogs and a rat. And that was just in the house. Outside in the barn and adjoining yard were three goats, a couple of rabbits, three horses and a host of chickens.

You'd think that the house would smell like a giant cat box, but that wasn't the case. The house had been carefully cleaned with the litter boxes confined to a little-used room in the basement. Every time I sat down, there was a purring feline in my lap, sometimes two or three. As we sat in their comfortable kitchen, I learned the stories of many of their pets, most of them rescues.

"See that black cat over there?" asked one of the women, pointing to a sleek kitty lying on the floor not far from me. "We found him in the middle of the road one night."

My hand flew to my heart as I gasped, "How badly was he hurt?"

"Oh, he wasn't…He was just lying in the middle of the road… He's an indoor cat now."

A few other cats were found hurt or abandoned and were nursed back to health by the two women. The two friendly pups got along well with the kitties. I think they might have been rescues too. The women had developed such a reputation that the local shelter called them when they got an animal they couldn't house. Hence, the rat. The rat normally resided in the guestroom, but they moved him to another space during my visit. I wouldn't have protested his presence, though. One of my brothers had had a pet rat when we were growing up and I remember him peacefully sitting on my brother's lap as he watched TV.

No, our last name isn't Munster.

One of the goats was a rescue from a nearby farm. Whenever they passed the place, the poor thing would be out in the summer heat, tied up with no water or shade. After complaining to the farmer, he simply gave it to them. Or maybe they just took him one night, I can't remember, but the latter makes for a better story.

They brought him home and found out shortly that the goat they already owned was female. Soon, baby made three. I visited the three in their cozy barn. The little one danced up to me on tiny hooves and lightly tapped my thigh with his head. I picked up the little critter and tried to cradle him—he wasn't much bigger than my cats—but was thrown backward when the little imp abruptly butted my face, knocking my glasses to one side and bruising my nose.

One of the best rescue stories concerned the chickens. The women had gone to a livestock auction to buy a horse and saw this farmer with a crate of scrawny chickens crammed into a wire cage. They'd been de-beaked, like commercial chickens often are, and they were losing feathers. Even though the women had no idea how to care for chickens, the animals looked so miserable they asked the guy how much he'd charge for them. He grumbled that they didn't lay and weren't worth much. If they gave him a few dollars, they could have them.

They brought them home to run free in the yard, fed them scraps and Chicken Chow until one of them got so big, I was sure it was a turkey. They laid eggs almost every day.

On the last day I was there, we rode a couple of the horses. In a meadow on a clear Iowa day, the dogs trotting happily behind us, I couldn't think of a better place for me to be. Most importantly, now I had a good argument for my girlfriend the next time I found a homeless cat while on tour: "But honey, he was laying in the middle of the road."

I wonder if they allow chickens within our city limits.

CHAPTER SIXTEEN

Closer to Amy

In spring of 2000, Amy Ray of the Indigo Girls was going to be at the Southern Women's Music Festival where I was playing and emceeing. I wasn't sure what one does to prepare for a gig like that, except listen to "Closer to Fine" over and over again and obsess about what to wear when I introduced her.

As it turned out, as long as I had on a pretty bra, I was good.

So, there I was at the festival. I'd already done my set the night before. Saturday night was the big night. There was someone on first, followed by the punk trio The Butchies and then, Amy Ray.

We were told not to bother Amy. Or maybe that was just a voice I heard in my head, because I knew I'd start gasping for air if I got too close. If I was passed out it'd be hard to do my job.

The stage manager strung a rope a few feet in front of the stage and around to the side, encompassing the little tent that served as a green room. "Amy has a stalker," she grimly informed us, "so we're trying to set some boundaries." At a rock concert they have six-foot-tall martial arts experts carrying guns. At a women's music festival, there's a rope and one woman politely telling everyone to step back.

Believe or not, they did. Women showed up two hours before the music started and waited patiently on the other side of the rope. They all had questions. "Will Amy be out early to sign autographs?" "Can I take her picture?" "Can we meet her later?"

Amy was sitting backstage with her model-pretty girlfriend, a bottle of water in hand, chatting with the three women from The Butchies. Not only were they friends, they were backing her up on her set. It might have been around the time that Amy came out with her first solo effort but don't quote me. I'm not writing as a music journalist who's done a lot of research, just a menopausal woman who does well to remember where she put her car keys.

I don't remember who was on first that night. I'm sure they were very good. I was too busy not looking toward the little tent next to the stage WHERE AMY RAY WAS SITTING THAT VERY MINUTE.

As the notes from the first act faded into the night, I took my place at the emcee mike. All around me, equipment was being shuffled around. I babbled on about festival rules like where to put your recycling and reminding women to drink enough water. I could've been naked and doing a pole dance and no one would have noticed me, because THERE WAS AMY RAY SETTING UP HER GUITAR...TUNING HER MANDOLIN... ADJUSTING HER MIKE.

It was actually kind of nice to be invisible. I thought about making a totally bogus announcement to see the reaction..."A giant spaceship has landed in the field south of us and aliens are handing out free vibrators to everyone"...But I knew someone would be listening and we'd have to have a political meeting the next day with a lot of processing about Martians and sex toys. I elected to stay in my somewhat serious position as queen emcee.

The stage lights dimmed, my spotlight brightened and the stage manager tapped me on the shoulder. "We're ready," she intoned.

I straightened my shoulders and looked down at the clipboard where I'd jotted a few notes. I looked to my left and saw Amy standing in front of her mike, her mandolin on a strap and held in front of her. I took a deep breath and listed a few of her accomplishments. As if I needed to do that. Her fans, arms up and straining against the rope, were already breaking the sound barrier.

I went on, "This performer is so hot I have to take off my shirt to introduce her." And there, in front of several hundred stunned audience members, I lifted my shirt over my head...to reveal a plain black bra. The ASL interpreter, Caryl, removed her shirt too. The crowd went nuts. I hoped Amy wasn't jumping off the back of the stage. On the contrary, she had her head back in a hearty laugh.

I wiped my brow and screamed, "Give it up for Amy Ray!" The crowd noise increased to the level of a jet plane engine as I gracefully made my exit.

She ripped through a great set. Somewhere in there The Butchies did some songs. (Forgive me if I don't remember the details. Have I mentioned the thing about the car keys?)

After the music, I hung around thinking I'd stroll up to Amy, look her right in the eye and say, "Good set!" Instead I busied myself with I don't know what as the stage crew carted off amps and turned off the stage lights. Amy graciously met her fans to sign CDs and T-shirts, and then I heard her ask the stage manager if it was okay if she drove up to the stage to load her stuff.

She asked? Don't Big Stars just have their people take care of things? Or otherwise do whatever they damn well please? No. Amy had driven her own car and loaded up her own equipment. She didn't assume anyone would wait on her. Now that, my friends, is a musician who deserves respect.

Since then, I've seen her milling around at other festivals and she always seems so nice. I don't want to bother her though, so I've never said anything to her. Maybe one of these days I'll just casually remove my shirt again.

Where did I put that black bra?

CHAPTER SEVENTEEN

Aloha State of Mind

When I told my friends I had *only* five days in Hawaii in March 2003, they felt really sorry for me. Their opinions didn't change much when I added that in that time I was visiting two islands, doing two full concerts and giving a radio interview. I felt like I was working a lot, but as one of them reminded me, it's Hawaii…quit dabbing your forehead and put away the lace hanky.

Coming from the East Coast, it made sense to add this island adventure to a West Coast tour. However, I had the audacity to be away from home more than a month, so they penalized me accordingly and charged me an additional two hundred dollars on top of the normal airfare. I purchased a box of hankies for the trip.

I arrived at the beautiful Honolulu airport filled with relaxed smiling people in Hawaiian shirts. I felt a tad overdressed in my heavy jeans and long-sleeved shirt. A smiling woman greeted me warmly with "Aloha," gave me a quick hug and drove me to my housing. My gracious host had a wonderful mountainside home. Right outside my window was a thick bougainvillea bursting with red blooms. A small pool was just beyond and in the distance a bright blue bay with the jagged black Diamond Head rising up on one side.

I could've spent my whole visit in satisfying repose next to that pool, reading a deliciously good book. However, when my host offered to take me on a quick tour around the island I didn't think about it too hard before I said, "Hell, yeah." She took me to her favorite beaches of brilliant white sand and turquoise water, and then we went hiking in a cool rain forest laced with delicate vines. The trail ended at Manor Falls. Several stories high, the white water rushed into a pool. I stood and watched it for a long time. I'll bet my friends were feeling extra sorry for me then.

The concert that night in Honolulu was a blast. I started with my song "Drive All Night," then briefly stopped in the middle. "I guess you can't drive all night here," I teased.

Someone in the back yelled out, "Yeah but we can drive around and around."

Somehow that didn't sound as romantic—"Baby, let's drive around and around."

After moving through a selection of ballads and up-tempo songs, I finished the show to a standing ovation.

I told my concert producer that I wanted real Hawaiian food and asked if I could go to a place that wasn't featured in tourist brochures. She and a couple of friends took me to a diner with battered chairs, wobbly-legged tables and harried, but efficient waitresses dressed in T-shirts and jeans. After the different foods were explained to me, we ordered a sampler of dishes. I enjoyed most of it except poi, a purplish pudding-like dish. One of my companions likened it to library paste, and since I was a paste-eating child, I thought I'd love it. Maturity has changed my taste. Or maybe it was only good if I was sitting in a tiny little chair.

My time on Oahu only lasted a couple of days before I had to fly to Maui for a college appearance. Where were those hankies? Again I was met at the airport by a friendly woman and whisked away to housing.

Just before I got up onstage for the show, I noticed a smiling older woman wearing a large, colorful rayon scarf, alive with pink and purple flowers in batik, over her shirt. I told her it was gorgeous. She smiled, took it off and said, "I designed it. Here, you wear it." It looked great with my otherwise plain outfit of a brown skirt and cream-colored top. I was overdressed again, though, taking off my dark stockings and boots halfway through the concert, but still wearing the scarf. Afterward, I removed it and handed it to her.

She waved me off. "You keep it." I gave her a CD in return, hardly payment for the beautiful wrap.

My hosts were two wonderful women and because they had a small studio apartment, we all stayed in a borrowed, roomier apartment. Like many people who live on the island, they were escapees from the mainland. One was an artist who did magnificent creations with coconuts, making them into whimsical cartoon-like fish. My favorite was a "cow-fish" complete with black and white spots, pink udders and glasses perched on its nose below comically bulging eyes. Their apartment was hung with dozens of them, like colorful schools of fish swimming through the air.

The day after my show we stopped at a small market and bought a pineapple, some star fruit and an apple banana (a special kind you can only get there). We drove out to a beach sparkling with black sand and watched whales off in the distance, jumping and diving. Then, we traveled to another beach, this one jagged with black volcanic rock, the ocean splashing up through blowholes. We sat on the warm sand several feet from the water, ocean breezes blowing my hair back, and sweet pineapple juice running down my chin as I bit into the luscious fruit. I couldn't think of anywhere else I'd rather be.

A month before leaving for the islands, I had contacted Ginni Clemmens. I knew her music from the folk and women's music circuit and even though I'd only met her once, my friend Toni suggested I talk with her about Maui, since she lived there. Ginni said she'd love to show me around her island. Sadly, just days before I left on my trip, she was killed in an auto accident.

Her memorial service was the same day we had planned to go sightseeing. Her friends and I gathered on her favorite beach, where I was honored to read a letter from her friend Laurie Fuchs, founder of the women's music company Ladyslipper. It was such a moving ceremony, with readings, dance and music from her friends, including traditional Hawaiian slack key guitar and singalongs. Ginni loved for people to sing at her concerts, so of course we sang at her service. As the peaceful sun sank on a blue-green ocean, we put our leis into a kayak. Friends towed the vessel into the waves, and tossed the colorful blossoms as we said our goodbye to Ginni.

Music lasted late into the night as we sat around campfires, remembering the songs she loved. One of the guests was Spanky, from the sixties group Spanky and Our Gang, and who went on to replace Cass Elliot in the Mamas and the Papas. She toured with them for twelve years. When the guitarist started "Monday, Monday," she beamed, "I know this one!" and delighted us all with her part as we sang the rest. I could swear I heard Ginni's harmony.

Too soon, I was sitting on a plane headed for northern California. I arrived in San Francisco to a misty cold evening, but I had beautiful memories, a gorgeous new scarf to keep me warm and a sudden craving for paste.

CHAPTER EIGHTEEN

The Miracle of Duct Tape

In the summer of 2002, I waited at my housing for a ride to my sound check at an outdoor festival in New England. When no one showed up I started making phone calls. After reaching only voice mail on two different numbers I finally got a real person. "No one told you the event was canceled?" wailed a voice on the other end.

No, I told her, hoping they wouldn't neglect to pay me for my airfare and hotel.

"We might have you play at the bar. I'll get back to you."

Since most of my gigs from hell have been in bars (too noisy and too many drunks), I wasn't eager to switch venues. Still, I was there and figured I might as well do something.

After some negotiating it was agreed that I'd perform at the local lesbian club. I arrived to find a chummy neighborhood place with a tiny dance floor, a pool table and a friendly bar owner who promised to do everything she could for me. I asked about the sound system and she pointed to two women stringing a wire from the DJ booth. She explained that the stage was on the other side of the room so they were taping the mike wire to the ceiling to bring it over to me. I cringed, thinking about the tinny sound quality I'd gotten from every dance DJ's mike I'd ever had the misfortune of using. They're good for talking but crap for anything else.

A guitar amp the size of a briefcase was carted in from somewhere. I coaxed sound from it. At least my guitar was loud enough to be heard over the din of people talking. The mike stand was straight up and down—not good for a musician with a bulky acoustic guitar. The same women who'd strung up the wire duct-taped a piece of wood to the top of the stand, angled it toward me and taped the microphone to it. It worked fine as long as I didn't touch it.

We turned on the mike and I asked the audience if they could hear me. When they answered affirmatively, I thought, Good enough. I played my set. Sometimes the audience talked loudly, but for a few songs they quieted and I figured, they invited me into their space and set up something as best they could, so I relaxed and enjoyed myself. Afterward, I joined one of the tables and had a few drinks. The festival organizers came through with the money for my airfare and hotel, so even though I didn't make much money, I didn't lose anything and heck, I had fun.

With a few smart women and a roll of duct tape all things are possible.

CHAPTER NINETEEN

One of the Family

It was October 26, 2002, just three days before my birthday. I was about to walk onstage at the ArtsCenter in Carrboro, NC, to introduce Holly Near and Cris Williamson to a full theater. Appearing with them were three more of my favorites, Teresa Trull, June Millington and John Bucchino. The audience of three hundred were practically levitating because they were so excited. Me too.

I welcomed everyone, brought on Holly and Cris, and then made my way into the audience to take my seat and enjoy the show. It was like the old days as I sat wide-eyed in the audience, surrounded by women, joyfully singing with the songs we knew. Only now, I'm about to turn forty-five and I know Holly and Cris.

They sang a great combination of old and new songs, with familiar themes of love and peace, separately and together. They included a medley of "Sweet Woman," "Something About the Women" and more. I was in heaven.

Then, a most marvelous and unexpected thing happened. Holly invited me onstage. I was in the front row, but there were no steps leading up to the stage. Fortunately, I'd performed in that venue before so I knew the way backstage…if only I could find the door. I felt my way along the wall in the darkened theater as Holly and Cris joked about losing me. I yelled out that I was coming, eliciting laughter from the crowd.

Finally, I found the right door, scurried down a hallway, turned right and there I was, surrounded by all these great performers I've admired, in front of several hundred about to sing…something. Not only was it a surprise that Holly was inviting me up, but I had no idea what we were about to perform. Thankfully, as soon as they started, I knew it was Ferron's "Testimony." I relaxed. We heard the audience's voices rise up with us. In the middle, we stopped singing onstage, just to hear those beautiful voices out there. We joined them to finish the song. The applause was sweet and warm.

I turned to leave. Holly grabbed me gently around the waist and asked me to join them for the next song. Gladly! Unfortunately, it was one of Cris's that I didn't know well. I watched and listened to the others, then offered my voice partway through the song.

Afterward, the audience leapt to its feet in applause that could've lifted the rafters. Teresa, June, John and I tried to step back to let Cris and Holly take the applause, but they motioned us forward. We all stood there holding hands, taking in that wonderful energy—June on my left, her hand strong and a little rough, and Cris on my right, a smaller and softer hand.

Cris and Holly were called back for another song as Teresa, June, Stella (the concert producer) and I stood backstage. They performed "Singing for Our Lives." June looked puzzled and asked Stella about the song. When Stella explained that it was Holly's song, June laughed and joked that she still hadn't made the transition from rock to women's music.

My following isn't as big as Holly's and Cris's. They were there in the early seventies at the start of women's music, and I was an upstart who didn't appear until fifteen years later, so there have been many times when I felt like the poor stepchild of women's music. That night, though, I was definitely part of the family.

CHAPTER TWENTY

Leave the Light On For Me

In March of 2003 the Dixie Chicks were vilified by some for their statement about being ashamed of the president. I wasn't wild about him either, but that's about all we shared. They stayed at Hiltons and I stayed in strangers' homes. It usually turned out well, but sometimes it was an adventure, like the housing in this small coastal town. The concert producer said she'd found me the perfect place to stay. After touring for many years, I knew that "perfect" could range from "Hey it's got a bed!" to "You'll have your own wing in a mansion!" After following confusing directions that included going the wrong way on a one-way street, I found the large old house. As I parked out front, a young woman walked up to lead me into the house.

She looked strong but didn't offer to help me up the stairs with my larger-than-Rhode-Island suitcase, a bulky backpack, my purse and a guitar. When I saw that the last flight of stairs was really a ladder, I must have groaned audibly because she offered to take my suitcase. With her a few steps above me pulling, and me pushing below, we managed to get it up to the room. Rather than struggle with my backpack and guitar, I dumped them at the foot of the "stairs."

I collapsed my five-foot-eight frame into the tiny attic room, then moved into the very center because it was the only place where I could stand upright. I tried not to hit my head on the lone bulb that swung from the low ceiling as I stuffed my suitcase into a corner next to a mattress covered with only a stained comforter cover and a tired blanket. Candy wrappers and dust bunnies blew across a little slice of grimy carpeting like tumbleweeds in a bad Western.

My host casually explained to me that there was no heat up here, but I should be pretty warm anyway (despite the fact that I was in a coastal town in March). She explained that a roommate would be putting sheets on the "bed" later. I nodded my agreement, and then carefully followed her back down the ladder.

After she'd introduced me to several roommates, I realized I was in a classic college rooming house. They all seemed like nice folks, but there were a bunch of them. Did Larry live here or was he the boyfriend of Anne? Did all those people at the kitchen table reside here or were they just Jude's study group?

I was glad my room was in the upper reaches of the dwelling, so no one was tempted to wander in my room to check out my stuff. I don't think students are inherently thieves, but if I didn't know who's supposed to be there, I'd have no way of knowing if a stranger I think is Jude's cousin is really some crackhead off the street who's there to rip off the TV. Maybe the residents weren't worried, given the amount of dust lurking everywhere. A thief wouldn't be able to find the TV without a good metal detector. If he was hungry, however, he would be able to find food in the kitchen. All he had to do was follow the ant trail.

The bathroom on the second floor had corners packed with brown goo—the kind you get when the floor is never cleaned well. The tub edges were overflowing with enough grimy bottles of shampoo and shaving cream to stock a Super Target. On the stained sink were more jars and a hairbrush sprouting a cluster of long blond hair.

I had an hour or so before the gig. After searching through the dirty kitchen and finding only takeout cartons sporting someone's name, some condiments, and rows of uncooked pasta, I elected to eat some dehydrated soup and an orange I had out in my car. While eating on the front porch, one of the roommates encouraged me to help myself to "whatever." I figured that was code for "find a restaurant."

After telling my host I'd put her on the guest list—free should sound pretty good to a student—I headed out to the gig. I've had better shows. I failed to connect with the small crowd and looked forward to a restful night of sleep. The house was completely dark when I arrived. Even Motel Six leaves a light on. After grappling with the heavy front door, I blindly patted the walls nearby for a light switch. I didn't find one, but after my eyes adjusted I could see that a light from the second floor illuminated the stairway enough for a ghostly outline of each step. Carrying my guitar and heavy purse, I carefully negotiated the stairs. Coming to the second-floor landing, I saw that the light guiding my way came from under my host's door. I could hear her on the phone.

My room looked the same, with no sheets on the mattress, only the comforter cover and a blanket studded with a few hairs. Using the cover as a barrier between the mattress and me I pulled the blanket up and tried not to put it too close to my nose. A little chilly, I wondered if I could find a match to light the dust bunnies, but gave in to a restless sleep instead.

I got up early and not surprisingly was the only one awake. For a couple of minutes, I stood at the top of the ladder planning how I was going to get the massive suitcase down to the landing. I opted for zipping it up tight, lowering it partway, then dropping it when I couldn't hold it any longer. I carefully inched down with the rest of my stuff, dropping the key off on the carpet outside my host's door. Once on the ground floor, I fled like the Christians from Rome.

That night, while relaxing in a goo-less motel room, I caught up on my emails which included a note from my recent host. She apologized for the lack of clean sheets, saying her roommate forgot to do it. Clearly she'd been too busy chatting on the phone to attend to it. She then asked about the key, since it was her only one. I was so tempted to ignore her plea, but decided God would get me and make me sleep on a bed of nails before my next gig, so I told her where I left it. I wonder if I would've gotten the apology had she not needed a way to open her front door. But hey, who was I to complain? The place had a bed.

CHAPTER TWENTY-ONE

Don't Stand Too Close to the Bird

If I'd been listening to country radio in October 2003, I would've heard Alan Jackson and Jimmy Buffet sing "It's Five o'clock Somewhere," but my listening tastes on the road ran more to tapes of Bonnie Raitt and Ani DiFranco. It happened to be after five p.m. in this small Nashville café, though, and it was crowded with middle-aged couples, waiting for the concert featuring four female songwriters, including myself. I felt a little out of place in this music industry haven, the lesbian hippie in a sea of straight folks, but honored to play in a legendary venue that has featured so much great music over the years. We sat in the middle of the room, facing each other in a circle, a tangle of mike cords and mikes in front of us, guitars squeezed in close to our hearts, careful not to bang into the audience mashed in around us. The other performers were standard country writers, each hoping their songs would get noticed by the music industry elite.

A packed room is always better to play for, and this audience was no exception. As we went around the circle, each taking a turn singing our songs, they quieted and listened. My songs were just as solid as the others, so I felt myself relax after a while, getting into the rhythm of being there and not worrying so much about being the big weirdo hippie babe. When Joyce, the songwriter to my left, started one of her songs that was made famous by a big star, the crowd clapped as they recognized the opening bars. At the chorus, my fellow songwriters joined in. Putting on a confident face, I mouthed the words until I could follow along, even putting on a harmony like, hey sure, I know this song, doesn't everyone?

Halfway through the evening, the leader of the circle announced that one of the songwriters had a famous husband and wouldn't we all like to hear him? The crowd cheered its approval while I clapped, clueless about who he was, but with a sure smile that would have won me an Academy Award. As he took a seat in our circle, our leader laughed and commented that he was the only guy performing and he'd probably show us all up. Yeah, like four women songwriters couldn't possibly compete with his manly songs. He did his hit. It was a great song that everyone seemed to know except me. Then he accompanied his wife on another tune as she explained that she just didn't consider herself a guitar player. Funny, we'd seen her play credibly through several songs. Then it moved around the circle to the songwriter on my right, who called up her own guy to play a song with her, also making a negative comment about her guitar skills. Suddenly, we all become lesser musicians because some big handsome man will play for us?

The circle went around a couple of more times. I took a chance with my tongue-in-cheek "I Wanna Be a Straight Guy." Bolstered by the audience's easy laughter at the jokes I'd cracked all through the evening, I figured they might like it, even though by singing the song I'd come out. The women laughed loudest, one of them behind me saying how could any woman who's married not laugh at that song? Maybe she missed the line, "I wanna kiss my girl for all to see."

After two hours, the leader announced that I would have the last song. I introduced my tune by saying it was a sing-along that some of them wouldn't like, and I hoped they hadn't brought their guns. They were still chuckling when I began "Woe to the World," my anthem of how our esteemed President Bush had screwed up, all to the tune of "Joy to the World," the Three Dog Night tune penned by Hoyt Axton:

George W. was a frat boy
Did his share of coke
Now he's the U.S. President
Even though he didn't get the vote
Singin' Woe to the World…

I could see pockets of people with broad grins, singing—my friend Kurt Fortmeyer and his wife over in the corner to my left, another straight couple in front of me (who'd also laughed loudest at the straight guy song), two lesbians to my right almost in the back and two more dykes to my far right. The rest of the crowd looked like they needed a good laxative, their mouths set in a hard, thin line. I left out the verse about the war, simply because I forgot it, but looking back, it was probably better just in case there really were firearms stashed in denim coat pockets and vinyl handbags.

Just as the last note died down, a chorus of boos started from behind me. It didn't start with the people in front of me that I could see. Cowards. They were soon joined by others. I laughed loudly, knowing I'd gotten a rise out of them. The circle leader leaned over and with a sly smile quietly asked why I hadn't opened with that song. The straight couple who'd sat in front of me came up and kidded that they'd be my bodyguards to escort me out of the room. A few minutes later, I met several people in front of the café, including my buddy Kurt, who said I certainly had balls to do that song in a place like that. No, I replied, big ovaries.

My "bodyguards" bought a couple of CDs, and we chatted for a short while. Walking over to my truck, I noticed two lesbians from the crowd. They said it was great to hear me and asked about buying CDs. I pulled a couple out of my truck, took their money, and thanked them. I finished packing my truck and pointed it toward a friend's house for the night.

The show after mine featured Emily Saliers of the Indigo Girls, but it was sold out. The tickets were twenty-five dollars anyway, and money was tight on this tour. I hoped the café would offer me a free ticket since they didn't pay me for the gig I'd just done. No dice. I also asked if I could stand in the back for a discounted ticket and again, I was told no. I'll give them the benefit of the doubt and say it was probably because of fire regulations.

As a full-time musician, I don't usually do gigs for free, but it was such an honor to play there that I took the engagement, as did a lot of performers. They didn't even offer a sandwich and after seeing all that steaming food and frosty beer go to the tables, I knew they were making money from these shows. Good thing I sold a few CDs to pay for my gas. My mortgage would have to be paid out of income from some other concert.

A month later, the experience almost forgotten, I checked my mailbox at home. In it was a card from one of my lesbian audience members. When I opened it, a check for a hundred dollars fell out. The card read, "I loved your performance. It was worth this and much more."

I decided to make up a T-shirt with this saying and wear it proudly, "I Got Booed at the Bluebird and Still Made a Hundred Bucks."

CHAPTER TWENTY-TWO

Sex, Drugs and Rock 'n' Roll

You turned right to this chapter, didn't you? I'll be systematic here:

1. You think I'm going to tell you about that?
2. I don't even like to take ibuprofen.
3. I'm a folksinger.

Now go back and read the other chapters.

P.S. Well, there was that time in Southern Florida...never mind.

CHAPTER TWENTY-THREE

Black Cats and "My Wild Irish Rose"

In April of 2004, I played in a beautifully restored building in an industrial section of a small Iowa town. My guess is that it used to be a factory or retail establishment in the early 1900s. The huge oak-framed windows and high pressed-tin ceilings were beautiful. At one time in its life it was probably a dance hall, as evidenced by the large wooden bar in one of the big side rooms. Several other rooms lined the main area, some serving as art gallery space and some as offices.

The stage sat at one end of the main room and beneath it, down a flight of stairs, was my housing for the night. The charming three-room apartment featured a living room, bedroom and small kitchenette. The bathroom was down a hall and shared with audience members during the show, so it was a bit unusual for an apartment, with its two toilets in stalls and a showerhead sticking out of the wall over a plain cement floor with a drain. I had my own telephone, TV with cable, queen-sized bed, refrigerator and microwave. It was neat and there were clean sheets on the comfortable bed.

After the show an audience member, with raised eyebrows and a joking tone to her voice, told me about the ghosts that wandered the large building at night. Shadowy corners began to take on a sinister look. I laughed, telling her to stop it.

I'd opened for my friend and singer-songwriter Erica Wheeler. She stayed after the show. We sat in the little kitchenette, eating popcorn and laughing while we told tour stories. I forgot about the ghosts until I escorted her to the front door. As I walked through the performance area back to my living quarters, the creaks of the old building seemed even louder now that I was alone.

Back in the apartment, I closed the myriad doors that opened into the rest of the building. None of them locked, but with the space closed off, it felt a little smaller and safer.

In the living room was an old record player with a crank in its side. A dusty seventy-eight of "My Wild Irish Rose" sat next to it. While I was curious, there was no way I was going to crank the thing up. I prefer my ghosts to sleep rather than dance.

Pleased with having a phone line to myself, I cranked up my laptop. (Back then dial-up was the only option.) Playing on the Internet and talking to a few friends calmed me and made me tired enough that I figured I wouldn't care about my surroundings. If I could nap curled up in the front seat of a Toyota pickup like I often did at rest areas, then I could sleep anywhere.

Just as I was finishing my last email, a blurred movement caught the corner of my eye and then I heard an odd scurrying sound. Startled, I glanced over to the floor on my right and saw one of the resident kitties, her black furry head buried in the pocket of my backpack, trying to pull out an extra phone cord I had stored there. How had she gotten in here with all the doors closed? I checked all the doors again. They were still shut. But I found a mysterious doorway in the kitchen area that was only covered with a blanket. Behind it was a wooden stairway leading to an upper level. She must have snuck in through there. I found a piece of string she could play with, so she batted that around for a while, and then slipped out as quietly as she came in.

I washed up, changed into pajamas and crawled into bed. The two large bedroom windows let in the pale yellow of a streetlight between the slats of the blinds, giving the room an eerie, striped look. The hoot of a train whistle sounded from a few blocks away and the rumble of trucks from the highway filtered in. I closed my eyes and tried not to think about ghostly dancers.

Just as I was drifting off, I heard click…click…scratch…click. My eyes flew open as my heart raced. I thought of all the dumb things characters in horror movies do while the audience yells at the screen, "Don't do it!"

I did it. I put on my glasses and crept out of bed, quietly moving over to the door where I'd heard the noise. Hoping the doorknob wouldn't move of its own accord, I placed my hand on it and turned it slowly. Just outside, in the dim light I'd left on in the hallway, I saw a small shape. Hoping it wasn't a rodent, I finished opening the door to find a very indignant cat. She strutted into the room to claim her space. Okay, I told her, the door is usually open. I left it that way, petted her a few times, and then lay back down. A few more strange scratching sounds jarred me, but I convinced myself that it was the cats prowling around and not some ghostly party. I finally drifted into a restless sleep.

Morning light came in early. My watch said seven a.m., much too early for someone who'd gotten to sleep after one. I put on an eye mask to block the brightness, inserted earplugs, and then rolled over to get some more shuteye. It was useless, though, my brain already contemplating the long drive for that day, so a little before eight I rolled out of bed. Skipping the cold, uninviting shower, I quickly brushed my teeth and climbed into my clothes. Just after putting on my shoes I heard a door creak open. At least in the daylight I'd be able to see an intruder.

"Hello?" I called out and was greeted with a man's voice answering.

"Hello? I'm the plumber. I need to look at the sink in the bathroom." Seconds earlier I'd been standing there in my underwear.

After a quick breakfast, I sat down to write this story. Part of the time a friendly, longhaired kitty lay in my lap. What was it like for her to live in this cavernous place, a rotating list of guests to pet her and ghostly partiers to keep her company?

Next time I stay here, I'm bringing sage and a witch.

CHAPTER TWENTY-FOUR

I Love My Car…Go Car

Part of a collective that put on a folk coffeehouse, it was Bea's turn to house the musician. I arrived at her duplex in a small Oregon town a couple of hours before the show. With a wide grin on her face she waved me into her home like it was a grand hotel. "Welcome!" she shouted as her disheveled dishwater blond and gray hair flew around her head.

Her small living room was so crammed with cast-off furniture that I could barely maneuver my small suitcase and guitar through it. All of the pieces had been free, she proudly told me, isn't that great? One of the couches, a bright red plaid, was leaning crazily to one side; another, a washed-out floral print, had been pretty well shredded by a cat. A third couch huddled in the corner, a tired afghan thrown carelessly over it. I've stayed with a lot of folks who were poor, and it's not that I think everything should be pristinely new, but three couches? If that wasn't enough, the room also sported several tables, all of them heaped with mountains of papers, books and dusty knickknacks.

The guest room was more of the same. It had its own couch, coffee table and thankfully, a bed, all in a space really only big enough for a small bed and dresser. There wasn't enough floor space for my suitcase, so I set it on the table. An odor of cat pee mixed with mildew hung in the room.

When I saw that the kitchen counters were covered in crusty dishes, boxes of food and discarded mail, I suggested that we go out for dinner. We decided to grab takeout on the way to the gig. Her old station wagon rattled loudly as we reached top speed on the highway. Her mantra of "This is my car...my car...I love my car...Go car..." seemed to soothe her—maybe it even kept the car going. I looked around. My guitar was sitting on bags of recycling that were splitting open at the seams, barfing out empty cans and stacks of yellowed newspapers. The dashboard had a gaping hole stuffed with rags where the radio used to be. The top of it was layered with dead weeds. I don't mean dried flowers—piles of brittle dusty plants several inches high. The glove compartment and every other available surface were covered in peeling stickers like some grade school kid's notebook.

We stopped at the restaurant. I stepped out, and just as I put my hand on the door lock, she yelled, "No! The key doesn't work!"

"What about my guitar?"

She waved her hand and said, "Oh it'll be safe."

Perhaps she was right. The dented car with the weeds on the dash certainly didn't look like a vehicle that would harbor a two-thousand-dollar guitar. Still, I kept a wary eye on the car while we were inside getting our sandwiches.

The gig went pretty well. No one asked about my housing. Maybe they'd never been there.

After another harrowing trip back to her place I managed a fitful sleep. I got up early the next morning before she was awake. Since the mold-covered bathroom looked like it hadn't been cleaned in years, I skipped a shower and hit the road.

I played that coffeehouse again a few years later. That time I asked pointed questions about housing and ended up staying with a very nice couple who had a comfy and, most importantly, clean apartment. And only one couch.

CHAPTER TWENTY-FIVE

Just the Opening Act

In 2003, a month before an East Coast tour, I was still without a gig for one Sunday. After searching the web for opening act possibilities, I found that Holly Near was performing about an hour's drive away from my Saturday gig. I had her email address so I wrote and asked about perhaps sharing the bill with her. After checking with a couple of people, she said yes, I could do a walk on. Usually that means doing a couple of songs in the middle of someone else's show. It sounded a lot better to me than watching TV in my motel room, so I thanked her and said I'd be there.

The gig was at a small library in rural New Jersey. Nestled in a wooded area, it looked too small to have a separate theater like some libraries do. When I walked up to the front doors, I saw that they'd pushed aside tables and bookcases to clear an area in the middle of the room now filled with rows of chairs. A stage at one end featured a grand piano and some sound equipment. On the checkout desk was the soundboard.

The cheerful woman who met me said that Holly was running late. Would I like to do a sound check? "Sure," I answered. It was great to be treated so nicely. I've done similar types of gigs before where I wasn't allowed to sound check or use the dressing room because the Big Star needed all that. Ed, the sound guy, was very easy to work with, so the sound check went quickly. Not long after that, I saw Holly and John Bucchino, her pianist, come in. I already knew them from doing various events together. After briefly hugging each of them I left them alone to do their sound check.

I sat in the back of the room talking with the friendly volunteers. Even though I was a last-minute addition to the show and not their choice, no one seemed the slightest bit put out. After her sound check, Holly asked if it was okay that I open the show with three songs instead of singing in the middle of the show. That way, she said, I can sell more CDs, since there'd be a break not long after that. She laughed and called herself a capitalist. Then she and the volunteers invited me to the dressing room to eat lunch. Now, I've opened for people where not only was I not allowed in the dressing room, but the food was strictly for the Big Star. This saved me from pulling a can of tuna and a box of crackers out of my truck.

While we ate a light meal of salad and stir-fry, we all chatted. Both John and Holly are warm, gracious people, and while talking with them I felt like their peer. I am in most ways, but I don't have the following they do. I didn't do my last event with Gloria Steinem and I've never worked with Pete Seeger or Judy Collins.

The three gigs I'd done before this show were comedy shows with two other musicians. While I enjoyed the performances, they drew a somewhat conservative and probably straight crowd. As I watched Holly's audience come in, I saw smiling lesbian couples, straight hippie folks and the kind of audience you'd expect at a peace rally. Ah, My People.

Came the big moment when I was introduced. The 160 people there—many more than I could draw myself—warmly greeted me even though most didn't know there was an opening act until that moment. I sang the first song, and then noticed a buzz. It stopped when I fiddled with the cord leading from my guitar. I joked that I shouldn't move when I sang, then did the next song. Again, there was a small buzz. I asked them if they heard it. Yes was the answer. Figuring it was my guitar and not the sound guy's fault, I simply unplugged the guitar, stepped to the edge of the stage and sang the last song without amplification. It was great to sing without the barrier of mike stands and monitor speakers. The audience sang "A

Family of Friends" with me. I could really hear them without the microphones, and since it was the afternoon, I could see them, too. It made for quite a connection.

The best was yet to come. Holly did a great set right after mine, then we took a short break where people generously bought CDs. Just before the second set, Holly asked if I knew a couple of the songs she was going to do. I knew one of them—a song by Ferron—but told her it'd been a long while since I'd heard the other. The truth is that I couldn't remember ever hearing it. I'm a Holly Near fan, but I suspect this song was on one of the albums I didn't own.

As she stepped onstage, I settled into my seat. I assumed the songs she'd ask me to sing were toward the end of the show, so I popped a piece of candy in my mouth and got ready to listen to some more great music. After only one song, Holly invited me to the stage. I still had the hard candy in my mouth. At the time, I was having some tooth pain and couldn't chew hard things very well, so there I was, in front of all those people, trying to chomp down on the sweet without wincing or swallowing it whole. She started singing and I looked as confident as I could, about to sing a song I'd never heard while surreptitiously chewing and swallowing. She got to the chorus and I mouthed the words. I could see the sound guy in the back, shaking his head and turning knobs. I hoped he wouldn't crank it up so loud that the crowd could hear me breathing in panic. The next time the chorus came around, I had an idea of what the melody sounded like—and fortunately, Holly likes to have the words in a book close by—so I could sing. The next time, I confidently added a harmony. Holly looked over at me and smiled. Yep, I sing with Holly Near all the damn time. The Ferron song was next. I knew this one, so the melody was easy. I tried a harmony but couldn't find my notes. I'm hoping the audience was singing loudly enough that they didn't notice. She invited me up one more time for the final song, "We Are a Gentle Loving People."

Holly and John's show was inspiring and beautiful. The audience looked happy and I felt like Wonder Woman. I was one lucky musician.

CHAPTER TWENTY-SIX

You Can Play for Us

It was the day before a Midwestern gig in 2000 and I still didn't have directions to the bookstore where I was performing. In the days before cell phones and the Internet, it was often hard to reach people. I knew how to find the city, though, so the next day, I set off in that direction. At a gas station along the way, I found a pay phone and finally caught the store owner.

I arrived at the small storefront an hour before I was to play. There were no fliers advertising my show and although they had a small selection of LGBT music, they didn't carry mine. All of it was on sale.

The store stereo was playing a pop song with some woman warbling about what she'll do for her man. (Maybe if the store played the music they sold, they wouldn't have to put it on sale.) The ceiling above my head had a huge hole, revealing dusty ductwork. A large, garishly colored banner hung from the wall opposite a case with a sprinkling of books. I sat on a sagging sofa that didn't match anything as the owner spent fifteen minutes on the phone with her girlfriend.

I was just a tiny bit cranky.

At seven p.m., when the concert was supposed to happen, there were four people there, including the owner. As we waited, I gave her suggestions for promotion. For me, it was closing that proverbial barn door too late, but at least they wouldn't make the same mistakes with another musician. After a few minutes it was clear no one else was going to show up. I told the owner I'd cancel.

Using a sympathetic voice she implored, "You can still play for us."

"Thanks," I said, smiling, "but it's better for me to go." I'd done a seven-hour drive that day and I was fried. If there'd been even ten people, I would've found the energy and had fun with a show. But for the twenty dollars I'd earn with them, it didn't seem worth it. A clean motel room, a hot bath and sixty glorious channels of cable TV awaited me.

The owner asked if I'd been at a recent women's festival not far from there. When I replied that I did it that year, she replied, "Oh. I don't remember hearing you."

I made a gracious exit. At my motel room that night, I indulged in some good chocolate. I phoned supportive musician friends and just before sleeping, called my girlfriend, who told me I'd been chosen as a finalist in a prestigious contest. Their concert where they chose the winners was in a few months. I crossed my fingers and hoped I'd be playing for more than four people. I didn't even care if the couch matched.

CHAPTER TWENTY-SEVEN

Pork Predicament

In 1995, just before heading out on tour to the East Coast, I talked with one of my housing hosts. She asked me the standard question about pets and like I always do, I said I loved sharing space with them. When she replied that she had a pig, I said, "Oh a potbellied pig?"

Yes was the answer and so no, I didn't have a problem with that. They're very intelligent and can be great pets.

My cheerful host opened the door to my knock. At her side, and attempting to push through the closed screen door, was an enormous barnyard animal. He stuck his snout up at me, then grunted, turned his back and waddled away. I'm guessing he weighed over a hundred pounds, with his fat belly nearly dragging on the ground. A few bare patches of pink skin showed through tufts of black wiry hair that stuck out at odd angles. Giant slivers of dead skin hung off his body where he'd had recent sunburn. (Pork rinds? Ew. Sorry.)

Most of his time was spent sleeping in the small bed in the guest room, although he seemed to enjoy strolling around, wiping his nose on the furniture or begging for food and grunting in disgust if he didn't get any.

We ordered a pizza, and as the delivery guy waited, the pig rushed across the room, squealing his displeasure at the stranger, and almost knocked the poor kid on his butt.

Maybe a pie with Canadian bacon was a bad idea.

His owner fed him by sprinkling pig chow on the carpet in the living room. Pigs are very clean, and he always found every morsel but still, it was odd to see his huge pink and black body nosing around a living room, scarfing up those little cereal-like chunks (along with the lint and stray dust). I was told he couldn't be fed in the kitchen because his hooves slid around too much. In fact, when he was let outside, the owner put down carpet pieces through the kitchen and to the door so the poor dear wouldn't fall.

When I first arrived, I was with someone so our host generously gave us her room because it was the only room with a double bed. She warned us to always make sure the door latch clicked so the pig wouldn't bust in. He had a habit of nosing everything within snout's reach.

Toward the end of my stay, my traveling companion left. As I drove back from dropping her off at the airport, I realized that I'd be moving into the guest room with the single bed, the same one where the pig settled in every day. The door to this room had no latch.

Arriving at the house, I didn't immediately see the pig, but noticed that the door to the room with the double bed was slightly ajar. In my haste to get to the airport on time I'd neglected to shut the door tight. I rushed into the room. My underwear and socks were scattered about the room. A box of tampons had been torn apart, but a half dozen sat in a neat pile, the ends chewed to a slobbery mess. The pig was on his back, a container of almond scented soap between his hooves, happily sucking it down. He looked at me with a serene expression before I screamed, "You fucking pig!" and rushed at him with a raised fist. I wouldn't actually hit him. Not only am I against hurting pets, but he would've trounced me in any battle. He squealed and scampered into the other room while I scooped up my belongings, muttering that I had to get my ass out of that house.

Thankfully, I knew someone else in town. I called her and pleaded my sad case.

"Of course you can come here," my rescuer assured me, "but I won't be home today. I'll leave you a key. You know where the guest room is."

When my current host came by, I made excuses about not wanting to overstay my welcome and said I'd arranged to stay with a friend across town.

I arrived at my friend's house, found the key under the mat and let myself in. There on the freshly made guest room bed was a toy pig. At least with that one, I knew my tampons were safe.

CHAPTER TWENTY-EIGHT

No Room at the Inn

It was a pleasant middle-class neighborhood on the West Coast with neat split-level ranch homes and trim green lawns. My housing was the only place on the block with thigh-high yellow weeds and a long-dead tree, fallen across the yard. I stepped around cardboard boxes piled as high as the roof of the front porch and rang the bell. Marcy, my slightly harried host, answered the door. As she waved me in to the foyer, also crowded with cartons, I commented, "So you just moved in?"

"Oh no," she answered breezily, "I've lived here quite a while."

As my eyes adjusted to the semi darkness of her living room, I saw that it too was piled high with containers. I could just make out a sofa and coffee table. That furniture, as well as the top of every box, was piled with junk mail, magazines and other items. A narrow path wound its way to the side where I assumed there was a kitchen. Another trail branched off in the opposite direction, down a dimly lit hallway. Marcy led me this way, my luggage bumping against still more containers lining our way. We passed a room belching out its contents of paper and junk, several file cabinets peeking out from the mess, and turned right into what would be my room for the night. Half filled with cardboard cartons and an old chair missing a leg, the room, she proudly told me, had been cleaned out just for me. In one corner slouched a tiny single bed, listing slightly to one side. I wedged my suitcase and guitar next to it.

Then she led me into the bathroom. Reaching into the shower to point at a plastic container of water sporting a thin layer of scum, she informed me of a leak she was catching to water the plants. What plants? The only plant life I noticed was the gummy green mold on the shower tile. Coupled with the thick dust and powder coating almost every other surface in the room, plus the brown slime ringing the sink, there was a whole ecosystem in there, I figured. I could avoid using the shower and sink, but aside from peeing in the backyard, I had no choice with the commode. Later on, I settled for closing my eyes as I lowered myself down. Better not to see some things.

Next, it was time for dinner in the kitchen. There, amidst what seemed like hundreds of pieces of Coke memorabilia crowding the walls and every flat surface, she fed me pasta.

The gig that night was uneventful, except that they served me dinner in the green room beforehand. They didn't know I'd get two meals that night, so I felt obligated to eat the second one. Marcy poked her head in, laughed, and yelled "Pig!"

I hope she was happy that I didn't wipe my nose on the furniture.

CHAPTER TWENTY-NINE

DIY Festival

It was the nineties and I'd been touring for a few years so I should've known something was up when it took several phone calls, the last one just a few days before my arrival, to figure out how I was getting from the airport to this particular outdoor festival in the Southwest. At first, the organizer told me I'd have to find my own transportation. While I knew a few of the other musicians, I knew no local folks who could help me out. With the small fee she was offering, I didn't have the dough to rent a vehicle or take a cab, even if I could get one to take me to the middle of nowhere. Finally, the organizer reluctantly agreed to send someone.

There was also a housing problem. Most of the locals were camping, but it would be difficult for me to bring a tent and sleeping bag plus guitar, recordings and other gear on the plane. In the end, the organizer consented to renting a condo about a mile from the festival for several of us musicians. She insisted that we pay for half of it.

At the airport my ride screeched up to the curb, stuck out her hand and introduced herself as Lead Foot Mary. She proved her name as we careened from intersection to intersection, empty Bud cans rattling from behind the seat.

She dropped me off at my accommodations, a pleasant three-bedroom condo. Some of the other musicians were already there, four of them plus equipment, squeezed into a rented sedan. I dropped off my suitcase then smashed myself into the car for a ride to the event. Everyone was friendly and when a festie-goer named Doris found that several of us were stranded without a car for the three-day festival, she loaned us her seventies-era Buick.

That afternoon several of us showed up for our sound check. We found one overworked sound tech and no support staff. In the broiling sun, we made sure the mikes worked then came back that night for the show. Since there wasn't any stage crew, each act set up its own mikes, amps and drums. I was asked to emcee so I figured it was just a step further to stage-manage. That meant it was up to me to keep the show running, to make sure that the next act was ready as the one before finished up. This could have been a disaster with too many divas, but this bunch worked like champs.

The audience made far more noise than the small numbers I could see. It was like playing with an applause track. The next day, as more and more bought nearly every recording we'd brought, they told us that they were listening in their tents. Hey, if you're cozy in your tent with your girlfriend and a case of Bud, why leave?

Too bad one woman in particular didn't stay in her tent. All through the first half of my set, she stood at the edge of the high stage, looking up at me longingly with bloodshot eyes and slurring, "Hey! Hey! Wanna go out with me? Hey!"

I tried all my tricks. I looked directly at her, exclaiming, "It's MY show." I gently talked with her off mike and asked her to leave. I offered the audience a prize if they'd cart her off, but there she stood, doe-eyed and clutching the edge of the stage while shouting in the middle of a ballad, "That's pretty!" My buddy and fellow musician, Sue Fink, rescued my sorry butt by putting her arm around the pest and gently guiding her away. If I ever have kids, I'm naming them all after Sue.

There was a tent behind the stage that we musicians were supposed to use to store our instruments. Off to the side were tables for our merchandise. We were assured that there'd be a security crew who'd look after our stuff all night. That would have worked great had the crew not gotten drunk and left halfway through the show.

The next evening was more of the same except at one point, all the lights went off. Our sound tech couldn't leave her board so it was up to the performers to determine the problem. One of them was on her knees, following cables while I stood onstage and asked if anyone could help us. Finally, I heard a voice exclaim, "Someone tripped over the extension cord...again." The lights miraculously clicked back on.

The last night at the festival our condo group got a bit loopy. We sat up late, shaking our heads over all that had happened. One of us drained an almost empty bottle of vodka and tossed it in the trash. Everyone else had soda and something to eat, including a couple of sandwiches that were wrapped in foil from which one of the musicians busied herself making little foil animals as we talked into the night. We laughed ourselves silly telling road stories then wandered off to bed.

I sleepily arose the next morning, packed and then looked for a ride to the festival to collect my check. Unfortunately, the band with the rental car had already left and I hadn't seen Doris's Buick since the day before. The organizer sent someone to see if we'd checked out yet and she gave me a lift to the event. I'd hardly stepped out of the car before the producer started screaming that I was costing her another day of rental because we left late. That was the first I'd heard about a checkout time.

I asked several at the festival for a ride, finally finding someone who could take me if we left *right now*. I threw my possessions into the back of the stranger's truck and we were off in a cloud of dust. Thanks to my ride's skillful avoidance of our nation's finest, we made it to the airport in record time.

I found out later that when cleaning our accommodations, they found the empty liquor bottle and bits of foil in the garbage, had proclaimed us drug addicts and banned us from playing at the festival ever again.

I never did pay for the condo.

CHAPTER THIRTY

It Sounds Like a Train

It was one of my early tours to the Midwest, probably 1990, a desert dweller alone in an unfamiliar landscape. I was staying with a friend in St. Louis for a few days in a big house built in the early 1900s.

One afternoon I was alone in the home watching TV when programming was interrupted by a report from a calm reporter saying a tornado had been spotted in the area. About then, the wind that'd been blowing all day ceased as a siren went off. Visions of Dorothy and Toto filled my head as I wondered what to do.

Somewhere in the musty depths of my brain I remembered that in the event of such things one should go to the basement. (Living in the desert most of my life I never had to deal with tornadoes or any other natural disasters unless you count our string of Republican governors. We didn't have basements, either. If so, I might have spent most of the eighties in one.) I gingerly made my way down the uneven stairs into the dank basement and settled myself on an ice chest. The siren continued to wail as I nervously waited. My host, a recent transplant from Arizona, came home and joined me. We both talked about the big wind outside as we split a bottle of wine. No wicked witch appeared outside the window, but we vowed to stay there until that eerie siren stopped.

We heard the front door slam and footsteps echo through the large house. We recognized my host's girlfriend calling out, "Jamie! Kathy!" She couldn't hear us answer and we weren't about to leave the safety of the basement. For several minutes her footsteps clicked and faded throughout the house. At last we heard her clomp across the kitchen floor and to the top of the basement stairs. She poked her head around the corner, looked at us huddled around the bottle of wine and exclaimed, "What are you doing down here?"

"The siren!" we sputtered.

The longtime Midwesterner had a good laugh. "You don't need to do that," she said between giggles. "You can tell when a tornado is about to hit. It sounds like a train."

All the same, we elected to stay beneath ground level. We heard her bustle about the kitchen, making coffee as we finished the wine. A friend joined her as she sat on the back porch with her hot drink, looking over the greenish-gray sky for any signs of a funnel cloud, emitting an occasional guffaw as they remembered the crazed desert rats in the basement.

Not ten yards from the old dwelling were train tracks. Every time I heard that rumble, I jumped out of my skin. It wasn't until I heard the whistle that I knew we were okay.

The siren finally quit, and the sky lightened to something less scary than a disaster flick. Although patches of threatening clouds still littered the sky, the heroes were safe.

The rest of the day, every two or three hours, that damn train would chug through and every time, my heart raced with fear. That night, alone in the third-story guest room as lightning flashed on the walls, I couldn't sleep. I stepped downstairs and knocked on the door of my friend's bedroom. She was wide awake, too. I figured I was safer on a lower floor and asked if I could sleep with her. She said yes. Good thing her girlfriend didn't live with her.

The next day, I was scheduled to drive to Kansas for my next gig. The sky being an ugly gray, I wasn't surprised that more tornadoes were forecast. With visions of a wicked wind whirling my small truck off the interstate during the four-hour drive, I was sure that my concert would be canceled, so I phoned my producer to confirm. I could tell she was smiling as she said, "Of course we're going ahead. Tornadoes don't strike in cities because it's too warm there. Besides, we'll be outside watching for it." I'd bet they'd be drinking coffee, also. I arrived there safely and had a great show. My housing sported no nearby train tracks, ruby slippers or little dogs. I slept by myself. If I heard a train, I knew exactly what to do, as soon as I found the basement stairs…and the wine.

CHAPTER THIRTY-ONE

Finding Emily

It was Mother's Day in 2001 when my buddy Kara Barnard and I headed home after finishing our Midwest tour the night before. Plans were to drop her off in St. Louis to get her truck so she could drive to her house in Indiana. I'd continue on by myself to North Carolina, where I now lived. Stopping at a rest area just west of St. Louis, I saw a young woman dressed in khakis and a white T-shirt, oversized glasses perched on her nose, sitting on the ground petting a relaxed tortoiseshell cat. Nearby were dishes filled with food and water. Crouching down next to the woman, I brushed my hand over the cat's soft fur and asked if it was her kitty.

"No," she shyly replied. "Someone dropped her here yesterday, so I brought her something to eat."

We talked for a while. The young lady spoke simply and with a small stutter. She mentioned that she was part of a crew who regularly cleaned the rest area. I asked if she could take the cat home, and she said she couldn't because she lived in a group home that didn't accept pets.

"Someday," she assured me, "I'll be able to take her home."

We discussed what it might be like for a kitty to live outside in a busy public space for that long. I gave Kara a pleading look. So many strays seem to find Kara that I figured this one was the latest.

"No," she commented with a grin, "I think this one's yours."

I hefted myself off the ground and headed for the pay phone.

My girlfriend and I only had two cats at the time. I explained about the abandoned kitty. She was skeptical, but finally relented. "By the way," I added, "the cat is…pregnant." Her skinny frame barely supported the weight of the huge bulge around her middle. She looked like a football with legs.

I walked back to the truck, the young woman behind me, cradling the cat. Kara got in the driver's seat and I in the passenger side. Through the open window, the young woman handed me the kitty, her eyes sad but hopeful and said, "Happy Mother's Day."

We stopped at a store and bought a cat carrier and other supplies. A few miles later, I dropped Kara off at her truck, and then continued on the two-day drive home, my caged companion on the seat beside me. My mantra with every mile was "Please don't have your kittens yet…Please don't have your kittens yet…" Fortunately, she listened to me and had six healthy babies a week after I got her home.

I named her Emily, short for Emilita-citabita-boo. She prefers the short version, mostly because the long form has its own ridiculous song. She doesn't like music, especially mine, but she's a cat, so I try not to take offense. All the same, I named a song after her mostly because she was crying the whole time I was writing it. Maybe she was penning lyrics. She missed the deadline—cats are so bad with deadlines—so I recorded the song as an instrumental.

We found homes for four of the babies, keeping one for ourselves and one for Kara, who'd promised to take a kitten back when we found Emily. Her kitten, Maggie, appears on the cover of my album *Listen*. She'd jumped into the photo shoot while dashing madly about the house chasing her sister. I'm glad I listened to my conscience and brought Emily home.

I still have Emily and two of her babies, Zoe and Vito. (Vito came back to me after his owner moved overseas.) I think Emily likes my music a little more, or maybe in her older years she just can't hear it as well. She still stinks at deadlines unless it has something to do with dinner.

CHAPTER THIRTY-TWO

Things That Go Thunk in the Night

It was the early 2000s and by then, I'd played at a couple hundred folk coffeehouses.

This one is more brightly lit than some, but the other trappings are the same—a harried group of over-forty hippies, women in big earrings and full skirts, and bearded men who want to talk about Pete Seeger. The warm scent of coffee and freshly baked brownies greets me as I arrive on time for my sound check. The sound guy is sorting through mike stands, a confused look on his face. As he consults with another volunteer, I settle into a front row seat and look around.

The room could be any school basement constructed in the sixties, with a low stage at one end, dull white walls covered in posters and bulletin boards, and overhead a ceiling covered in yellowed acoustical tiles, some that hang on for dear life. Behind the stage, a curtain holds a sign proclaiming the coffeehouse name. It sports a few ragged tears and threads that dangle from the edges and scream "low budget," but then, so did everything about this room. It's not like I play Carnegie Hall, so I don't expect plush theater seats and an orchestra pit. But it helps if there's a little cozy ambience—candles and tablecloths, maybe—but there was none of that in this dingy room filled with folding chairs.

One of the volunteers is scribbling the list of performers on a white board that would be placed outside the venue. She is carefully writing "J-a-i-m-e" when I point out that my name is spelled "J-a-m-i-e." She tells me that's what the publicity said and asks if that isn't the most common spelling. She dutifully erases it. I walk away muttering quietly that I know how to spell my own name.

The sound guy wears a shirt that says "My Job Is Not My Life." It's clear that running sound is not his as he untangles cords, his brows knitted in concentration. He asks me twice what my sound needs are. It's not like the one mike and guitar input I need is complex.

I dutifully wait…and wait. I clean out my purse, answer a phone call, file my nails. Finally, he asks if I'm ready to sound check.

I pull out my guitar and plug it in. I adjust the vocal mike to my height and start singing. After a few notes I stop and tell him that I can't hear a thing. The monitor speaker—the one pointing toward me—is dead.

Raising his eyebrows, he asks, "Are you sure?" He ambles over, puts his ear to the speaker and says, "Hey it's not working." He strolls back to the board, makes an adjustment and asks, "How's this?"

"Still no sound," I reply. He wanders back up, unplugs the speaker, plugs it back in, then walks back to the sound board. He mumbles to himself, touching various knobs and wiggles connections. He flips a switch and suddenly, my voice fills the venue. I thank him and gratefully step offstage so that the rest of the performers can check too.

There are two other acts. The coffeehouse folks tell us that the performers decide the order. I call forth my inner diva and tell the other musicians that as a solo, it's hard for me to follow a band. After their wall of sound pumps through the speakers, no one is going to hear my little solo guitar (especially if the sound guy forgets to flip that one lever). I ask the other singer if she's a solo too, and she replies that she's got "one, two and three." Three people? A recording pedal that duplicates her voice? Other personalities? Then she adamantly states that she wants to be second on the bill. I convince the band that they should be last. That means I'm on first. Good.

We have some time, so a friend and I slip out to find a quick dinner.

We arrive back a few minutes before the start time. As I stuff a burrito into my mouth, one of the organizers says that she hoped I was finished because she's about to announce me. I mumble through the beans that I just need enough time to tune. I wrap up the rest of my dinner and dash up to the stage. I slap the tuner on my guitar just as she announces my name. A calm look on my face, I plug in my guitar and step up to the mike.

I could barely hear my voice and guitar. I ask the audience if they could hear me and they nod yes. That means the monitor speaker is not working again. The sound guy shrugs. I leave well enough alone.

Three of my friends are in the front row, pleasant looks on their faces. Across the aisle are two people in their seventies wearing matching brown plaid shirts and sour looks.

Slumped in a seat two rows back is a disheveled young man who I'd seen wandering about the room earlier, making repeated visits to the table holding the cookies. He didn't talk to anyone. In fact, he didn't seem to engage with anything but those cookies. During a quiet ballad, he pulls out a newspaper and rattles it so loudly that someone in the row ahead shushes him. During most of my set he stares at the ceiling. Maybe he's thinking about those cookies. If they're homemade chocolate chip, I don't blame him.

Further back sits another friend. Next to her is a guy who is stone-faced through my entire set.

Scattered about the room are a lot of gray hair and beards, some nodding in time with the music, and some who wish I were Joan Baez.

My song "Your Mama Scares Me" elicits a few nervous chuckles. My funny between-song comments are greeted with uncomfortable silence. I get some applause when I mention supporting independent music, but mostly, I play to what could have been rows of wooden heads. Thank God my friends look engaged.

I finish a couple of minutes early, and then take my place at the CD table. I get some very nice compliments and sell a few CDs, including one to the stone-faced gentleman who informs me that he's a comic, too.

Soon the lights dim and the next performer is on. Dressed in a short, straight skirt, her skinny legs stuck into ankle-high boots with sagging red socks, she launches into her first song, her legs spread and her rear stuck out in a rock star pose, completely incongruent with the folk song she warbles. She has only one accompanist, a guitar player who plays about a half a beat off and sometimes in a different key. She ends with a screeching high note, and then strides over to the piano, yammering on about something that has nothing to do with her songs. She does another song with the guitar player. The guitar or the piano needs tuning. After that, she picks up her guitar, and they start another tune.

One of the guitars distorts badly—perfect for a metal band, not so good for a folksinger. The sound guy darts up every minute or so to fumble with the cords. At one point, I call him over and tell him that maybe the electronics in the guitar aren't working and suggest that he mike it. He scurries over and puts a mike on the wrong guitar. Even my friend who isn't a musician is shaking her head. She taps him as he rushes by and says, "No, the *other* guitar." He nods, sweat dripping off his brow, and moves the mike to the other guitar. (Meanwhile, the musicians are laboring through a number, the guitars still out of sync.) The mike falls into a music stand with a big clunk. He pulls it back and it falls again with a huge crash. He works like he's under an invisibility cloak. Dude, we can see you.

I'm sure I'm in the middle of a *Saturday Night Live* sketch. I'm tempted to yell out, "More cowbell!"

After playing for an hour—we aren't supposed to go over forty minutes—she does her last song and for that, she decides to stand in front of the stage. The harried sound tech carefully picks up each mike stand. One falls, then is righted. A long intro ensues and then we are commanded to sing because "three-quarters of you know this song." She sings an original I have never heard while I move my lips, eager to look like a good sport.

After a second break the band takes the stage. Every song has the same laconic tempo and features three-part harmony that wavers in and out of pitch. Almost every song is introduced like it's a grade school concert. "And now, we will do a song by Jane Smith…it's about the environment…now we will do a song by Bill Greene…it's about war."

One of their singers, a cherub-faced woman in a lace skirt, wears a tiny red velvet jacket that would've looked stunning on someone else, but on her it looks like she'd mistakenly put it in the dryer. She teeters on impossibly high-heeled boots, looking very out of place in this laid-back group of worn jeans and hippie skirts. When she isn't singing, her wide eyes scan the room, as if she's looking for something far more interesting to do.

We again are instructed to sing. One of the words "hobo," is changed to "homo" by one of my buddies. He's going to hell for that.

Finally, the show is over. I collect my pay and walk over to my group of friends. "I need a drink," I firmly inform them. As we traipse out of the room and on to the street, I notice that their sign says "Jaime."

CHAPTER THIRTY-THREE

Emcee Boot Camp

Thrilled about my booking at a big women's music festival in 1991, I suggested to the producer that I emcee also. I didn't have much experience but I knew how to talk and it would give me more stage time. She liked the idea and told me yes.

On one of the first nights I introduced the second act. Partway through their performance, a clap of thunder sent a shower of rain. The duo stopped playing as I stepped up to the mike to tell the audience that we were moving into a large building nearby. I ran over to the building through buckets of rain as the stage crew gamely packed up equipment and carried it to the nearby barn.

In the new space women were milling around, not sure what to do. Some started setting up chairs, and gradually order was restored. As the crew busily set up an alternate sound system (the previous one was too wet), I decided the crowd needed some entertainment. After the sound crew had enough gear set up to put on a tape of dance music, I shook my booty across the wide expanse of stage, maneuvering around busy sound people. I felt stupid in this spontaneous act, but it was the only thing I could think to do without a working mike. That was good for a few minutes as the crowd clapped along and laughed—at me or with me, I'm not sure.

When the crew got one mike up and running, I stood before it, babbling about whatever crossed my mind. That might have been one of the times when I had an impromptu contest to see who had the most tattoos or who could guess the color of my bra. (Aqua. I still have it.)

After what seemed like hours, the stage crew got everything up and running. We continued the show. It actually took an amazingly short time, given all they had to do, but when you're onstage in front of a few hundred women thinking up ways to kill time, the minutes balloon into what feels like months.

Later that night, while I was introducing a performer, a commotion started toward the back of the hall. I saw a group of women rush over to a spot. I heard excited voices and the scraping of chairs, but couldn't make out what was going on. Several yelled "Lights!" When the houselights were brought up, I could see that some of the several hundred audience members had started to panic and were headed toward the two small doors at the rear of the venue.

Here's where having a microphone comes in handy. I used my best grade school teacher's voice, asked everyone to sit down and for one person to yell out what was happening. A woman was having a seizure, I was informed, and now that people were sitting down, I could see her thrashing on the floor where folks had moved the chairs away.

In a calm voice, I asked for the doctors, nurses and paramedics in the crowd to raise their hands, and then sent a few of them over to the woman, telling everyone else to sit down. After the woman settled, they carried her outdoors, then transported her to a medical facility. I thanked the audience, introduced the next act, and then walked backstage to have a crying jag.

I found out later that the woman taken to the hospital was someone I knew. She hadn't had a seizure for years, and joked that seeing half-naked women probably set her off. (It was a clothing-optional festival, as many outdoor women's festivals are. Hey, when it's only women, who cares what you're wearing or not?)

Already I'd dealt with a thunderstorm, a restless crowd that needed entertainment despite the lack of a sound system and a medical emergency. Somewhere in there, I did a musical set, but I hardly remember it.

It wasn't over.

The next night, as I was making a few announcements, a small group of women started yelling from the back of the room. I had no idea what they were saying, so I continued on. As they marched up the center aisle, I began to understand them. They were upset about what they perceived was the exclusion of some women from the festival. One of them yelled at me to tell the audience their demands, but the festival had a strict policy about political statements from the stage, so I kept on with my benign announcements, hoping they'd go away.

They didn't. Their faces contorted in anger, they continued to the front of the hall until one of them reached up to grab my mike, and when that didn't work, came up onstage. At this point I didn't want to fight, so I moved aside for her to make her statement through the PA. She took a few minutes, and then stepped down. Some in the audience were restless, calling out to agree or disagree, but I ignored it all. I simply introduced the next act and got the hell offstage.

After my experience at emcee boot camp, I knew I could tackle any event. I went on to host many pride events, coffeehouses and festivals. So far, there have been no more seizures, unless you count my dancing.

CHAPTER THIRTY-FOUR

Almost the Middle of Nowhere

In December, close to Christmas, I was driving in southern New Mexico, just outside of the small town of Silver City. I knew I was in the middle of nowhere because not too far from there, at a desolate crossroads, was a lone building with a peeling sign that proclaimed it the "Middle of Nowhere Bar."

I was taking in the beauty of this desert drive—an enormous vivid blue sky over rolling hills dotted with pale green sage and creosote—when I heard a thump, thump, thump from the right rear of my truck. Sighing, I pulled over and checked the offending tire. Depressingly flat.

I'm a capable woman, I thought to myself, and yanked the front seat forward to remove the lug wrench and jack. Dredging up a long-ago memory from some high school driver's ed class, I confidently fitted the wrench on a nut. It slid off, the momentum pushing me to my knees. Humming "I Am Woman" while delicately but firmly brushing off my dirty knees, I lifted the heavy wrench again and aimed for a nut. The wrench spun around without grabbing the nut. I examined the wrench, then the nut, like they were going to suddenly change size. It was a lousy time to find out that Toyota had given me the wrong size tool.

No problem. I took out my cell phone and punched in the number for Triple A. It beeped at me, flashed a battery sign, and then fell silent. Looking around at the tiny highway with few cars, I wondered what to do as a dented pickup pulled up behind me. All my senses went on alert. I travel alone and make a point not to talk to strangers, much less depend on them for anything. A skinny guy about my age and a boy about ten ambled up and asked if I needed help.

"Oh no, I was just calling for assistance with the tire." With that, I furiously poked at my phone like it was going to suddenly spring to life.

Sensing the futility of my efforts, in a soft voice the man asked if he could change my tire for me.

"Thanks, but, no. Do you have a wrench I could borrow though?"

He went back to his truck and returned with one that settled easily on the nuts. He loosened them as I played damsel in distress like so many stranded female motorists I'd seen over the years. The feminist part of me wanted to jump in and take the wrench from him, but the princess part of me thought, Hey, he's saving me from getting dirty. I'll change the tire myself next time.

He removed the spare from its nest under the chassis, and then jacked up the truck. I talked with him and his boy. "I've got two dads," the kid says. My ears perk up. "My birth dad lives with my other mom and this is my stepdad."

Oh.

They asked me where I was going and I said to visit friends. I lied—I was really headed to a house concert, but didn't think a small-town straight guy and his son would feel comfortable at a party hosted by the local LGBT group.

He changed the tire quickly. Worried that I wouldn't find an open tire store late on a Saturday afternoon, I asked the guy if he knew of one that might be open.

"Sure, there's one right on this highway, about a fifteen-minute drive toward town."

He didn't want any money. I thanked him just before they got in their truck to motor away. He was right, the store was close and they'd be open another hour. I was grateful, since I had a long drive to Albuquerque the next day for another gig, and I knew I wasn't going to find anything open on a Sunday in Silver City.

I explained to the tire store employee about needing a new tire because the old one was punctured beyond repair. We looked at new ones until he remembered that he had a used tire in really good shape that'd be a lot cheaper. I told him to put that one on my truck and headed into the office to wait. After a half hour, he called me to the front desk to tell me it was done. He'd noticed my North Carolina license plates and asked if I was from out of town. I told him I was there just for the night. He slid my keys across the counter, eyes crinkled in a smile, and said, "No charge. Merry Christmas."

CHAPTER THIRTY-FIVE

A TV Star in Pensacola

It was the first gig of 2006 and I hadn't done a concert for three months. Most of my recent guitar playing consisted of plucking out "Skip to My Lou" with ten-year-olds. Walking into the spacious venue in Pensacola, Florida and seeing the TV cameras, I felt a flutter in my chest. TV? I knew the show was being broadcast live on public radio, but pictures too? My hands flew up to my hair, frizzy in the beach climate, and I looked down at my plain, baggy blue jeans. At least I'd worn a pretty flowered top, but did I have the right makeup? Decent shoes? Would I remember my songs or look like a big dork as my fingers flailed around for a C chord?

Feigning confidence, I headed backstage, my guitar on my back and pulling a small suitcase of gear and CDs. I met with the friendly stage manager, Enid, and two twenty-something kids, one with an adorable apple-cheeked baby on her hip. (When you're my age, you can call anyone under thirty "kid.") The guy had one of those mod, blender hairdos. The woman, Jen, had tri-colored hair that stuck up like a surprise. These were the kind of coifs that would look ridiculous on a woman my age, but were adorable on them.

As I was introduced I realized that they were the duo Martha's Trouble, one of the other acts on the bill. The stage manager said cheerfully that they wanted all the performers to do a number at the end of the show. The three of us smiled politely, because you don't want to be the temperamental diva who doesn't get booked again. Inwardly, I'm frantically running through the Rolodex of songs I know and wondering if Martha's Trouble knew the same ones. It's hard when you're all songwriters and mostly you do songs you've written; even harder if you've never heard each other's music.

I continued backstage and met Colombo...no...Malcolmb Holcombe. In rumpled clothes, wearing a ball cap, a strong scent of cigarette smoke hovering around him, he stuck out his hand and in a honeyed but gruff Southern voice, introduced himself. He moseyed about looking for coffee, after asking me if I wanted some. "No, I'm good," I replied.

I tried not to think about the two hundred chairs and TV cameras out there as I put on my makeup. I didn't have any foundation—a must for TV—nor did they have makeup people, so I covered my face in the cover-up I usually only use under my eyes. It gave me kind of a yellowish tint, but I hoped that under the lights I would look natural. I applied my eye makeup a little heavy and tried to remember an article by Janis Ian that I'd read a few years back about how to apply makeup for TV. All I could remember was that red shows up darker than it is. All I had was red lipstick.

I wetted down my hair in the bathroom and willed it to lay flat for the next couple of hours.

Meanwhile, Ed Gerhard was playing some lovely lap steel for his sound check. Ethereal, it floated over the almost-empty venue. I'd long admired his guitar work. I knew he'd recently won a Grammy (for a cut of "Moon River" on a compilation) and wondered if he'd be the kind of star who always looked like there was something more important for him to do when you talked with him. My fears were soon dispelled though, when later on he offered his meaty hand and warmly introduced himself.

I sound-checked after him, kidding with some early folks in the front row and telling them they'd better behave themselves while I was onstage. The experienced sound crew took about two minutes to get my sound right. I joked with the guy behind the board that

I wanted him to tour with me, and how much did he cost? The rest of the staff exploded in laughter at that one. That's not what I meant, I protested, smiling.

During the next hour, between bites of tuna salad and crackers, I queried the other performers about that last song we were supposed to do. I suggested a zipper song, one where a new line can be inserted with each verse. That was greeted with blank stares from Martha's Trouble. Jen, the woman of the duo, suggested "Material Girl" by Madonna. "You know all the words?" I asked. "Yep," she answered. "I dunno," I replied, "I just can't see Malcomb singing that one. How about 'This Little Light of Mine?'" I hopefully suggested. No one jumped on that.

Malcomb's wife was making suggestions like "Blowin' in the Wind" and other folk songs, but no one knew all the words. I mumbled that the only cover I knew all the way through was "Angel from Montgomery," the John Prine tune also covered by Bonnie Raitt. Malcomb brightened and said, "Yeah! I know that one." The duo didn't but I suspected Ed did, since it's practically a standard, at least for performers my age and older. Besides, when you've got guitar chops like his, you just need to know the key and you can jump in. I started singing the song. Jen remembered that she knew the chorus and started on a nice harmony. Malcomb could sing one of the verses. Ed wandered in about then and commented that if we did it in C instead of D that he could play slide. Perfect. Right about the second verse, the stage manager came in and said, "Two minutes, Jamie." I dashed off, not completely tuned up, for my set. I was on first and this was live radio. It's like catching a train. If you're late, it leaves without you.

The place was standing room only, with six rows in front of me and ten or so on each side. They looked relaxed and ready for a good show. The sound board and technicians were behind them, cameras on stands were scattered throughout, bright lights on either side, and a row of mikes and monitors stood just in front of me. Just before we went live, the emcee told me there was even a camera in back of me, so I stuck out my butt and slapped it, getting a laugh from the audience.

After a last-minute tuning, we were on the air and the emcee was welcoming everyone in a relaxed voice, using a few funny lines like Garrison Keillor, but without the deep breaths of air. He introduced me as a music instructor at Duke and as being from Asheville. Actually, I was from Durham and I hadn't taught those non-credit courses at Duke for a few years, but hey, I'll take that intro.

I started right into "Drive All Night," a song I'm usually very comfortable with. I knew I had to open with a tune like that since my hands were shaking so much. Yeah, I've played for bigger crowds before, but I couldn't forget those damn cameras and yikes, this was being broadcast right that very second to who knows how many people out there.

Okay, I made it through that one, never playing a chord unknown to humankind. I stumbled with retuning and talked about the last song. It's stuff I've said many times before, but it came out like someone had slapped me upside the head and I'd momentarily forgot how to form words. Usually I can completely retune every string while telling a witty story, but usually there aren't four TV cameras staring at me. I managed to finish and do the next song, a ballad this time, about a friend who'd had stomach surgery. I didn't do too badly with that one, only stumbling on one or two chords.

* * *

It was time to retune. Why did I have all these blasted songs in different tunings? I tried to talk some more and again, it was a jumbled mass of words. Geez. I got to the tuning as fast as I could and jumped into "Grace." I felt a catch in my throat as I reached one of the high notes in the first chorus. Uh-oh, that sometimes means a…cough. During an interlude without words I turned my head away from the mike and coughed, hoping that was it. But the catch haunted me, chasing down every note with threats that sometimes burst through. In my haste, I forgot one of the verses in the story song. I ended on a fairly strong note, the hacking not far behind. I bowed quickly at the applause and got my ass offstage. I hoped the song still made sense without the missing verse.

As I bolted backstage, Malcomb kindly asked how it went. In a rush I said that I had a coughing fit and forgot a verse, then quickly added that the audience was great. With a sympathetic look, he said he was sure it was fine.

Panicked about the ending song, I ran through it in the green room while Martha's Trouble was onstage. Pulling the words from some long-ago memorization, I tried out the new key and it worked well for my voice. It was a little low but would give me some room to do some improvisation at the end. I went back into the audience and caught Martha's Trouble in their last song. I really enjoyed their great energy with percussion and guitar. Jen's voice really shone, like a clear-voiced Janis Joplin. Malcomb was up next and as I suspected, he was a Tom Waits kind of folksinger. Quite a personality onstage, like an old blues guy you'd see at some roadhouse.

Ed was on next. Closing my eyes, I lowered my head toward my lap and let his beautiful music carry me someplace else, the lazy notes hanging so perfectly in the air. I was so taken by it that when I looked at my watch and realized the time, I had to jump up and rush backstage to grab my guitar. I was expected back for my second set, and I hadn't even checked my tuning yet.

The stage manager tapped my shoulder. "There you are," she exclaimed, "you're on now!" I walked briskly onstage, furiously turning the tuning pegs so that in the end, I didn't make a sound that would make dogs howl. The emcee was commenting that I'd fill up the stage, so I spread my legs and arms, eliciting chuckles from the crowd. After he said my name, I started my song with the reoccurring line, "Ain't nothing wrong with me a little chocolate won't cure." The audience chuckled in the right places. They were warming up to me.

I introduced the next song by saying it was an assignment and one they'd probably connect with. It starts, "Better than chocolate…" perfect for following the first song, the first verse ending in "I think you should know, I'm talking 'bout public radio." Well, how could I go wrong with a bunch of people who were there because they love public radio? The song got some big laughs. I remembered all of the lyrics even though it was the first time I'd performed it. I wasn't even through the whole song before they started applauding. All right!

The catch in my throat was gone and my knees finally stopped knocking, so I thought I was in the clear for the next song. But an alien took over my vocal chords again and the clever song intro to this last song was turned into some confusing short speech about whether or not it was true. Oh shut up, Jamie, and just do the next damn song. I think I may have even said that out loud before I sang "Your Mama Scares Me." They laughed, I smiled and zoomed offstage, happy to give it up to Martha's Trouble.

The rest of the performers took their turns. Somewhere in there I ran through "Angels From Montgomery" with Martha's Trouble backstage while two teenagers, the sons of one of the crew, were discussing music. I didn't tune into their conversation until we'd finished singing, and I heard one of them explaining to his friend what an LP was. "It's like a CD, only bigger, and you put it on this big flat disc that spins around." I grinned and interjected, "My first album was an LP, that's how long I've been at this." They looked at me with this slack-jawed expression that kids use when at museums—a mixture of coolness and boredom.

All too soon, the emcee was saying the credits and we were walking onstage for the final number. I prayed to the goddess RememberWordsia and started "Angels from Montgomery." One by one, the other musicians joined in. We were a little hesitant getting into the groove, but as the song went on, a harmony was added, then a drum, then Ed played this tasty but mournful slide guitar. Oh yeah, baby. Malcomb did a verse in his gravelly voice, perfect for this song with the aching lyrics. Ed did another solo. Then we broke it down on the next chorus, with only the voices and percussion, a little hushed, then blasted back the with the guitars, full voices and kickin', with the audience clapping along. For the last verse, I let loose a gospel kind of riff, doing my best Bonnie Raitt. All those times I sang with her album, alone in my room, and here was my chance to channel her. We ended on a bluesy wail, the audience jumping to its feet before the last chord had begun to die away. All of the musicians gathered together, our hands around each other's waists, and took a big bow. A big ol' grin stayed on my face a long time.

They lined up four deep around the CD table, the credit card machine practically smoking as I swiped cards and filled out the forms. There were many smiles, lots of compliments and requests for the last number on CD. No, we've never sung that together before. Eyebrows flew up and mouths formed big O's.

With the tech crew packing up and the last audience members leaving, it was time for me to gather my stuff and roll out. On my way out, I caught a couple of the radio staff talking about their station and the time Jeb Bush came to visit. He promised to tear the station down brick by brick because it was perpetuating some commie plot. He hadn't been back since and no one was crying about it. I smiled and thought, well now, here are the commie public radio people and the big lesbian folksinger, all gathered together.

I should send Bonnie Raitt a thank-you note.

CHAPTER THIRTY-SIX

Who Booked This Gig? Oh Yeah...I Did

In 2003 I was booked in a bar on the East Coast with Donna and Liz, two other singer-songwriters who do a lot of comedy. Taverns aren't always the best kind of venue, but this one had a lower level that was set up well for live music. Also, we had free housing just a few doors down.

The first clue that all was not well was when no one answered the door at our housing. I'd arrived in the afternoon, when I said I'd be there. I shrugged and decided to walk around town a bit. I couldn't leave my truck for too long, though, since it was packed with my valuable instruments and laptop. Just as I came back to the truck, Liz pulled up. We walked around together, and then I checked the door again. There was still no answer. She sat in her car answering email, and I sat in my vehicle, listening to public radio. When the van with the sound equipment arrived, I knew I should check inside the club. I pulled my guitar and gig bag out of the truck and walked a few doors down to the venue.

I looked around at the loudly talking men sucking down drinks and a TV over the bar that was blaring a football game. A radio blasted out some bad seventies pop number. I noticed the big wall dividing the bar in half, and saw no stage. Where would we stand? "Over in front of the pool table," was the answer. About then, the producer showed. The sound crew got busy setting up equipment.

After singing over the bar radio, dealing with squealing feedback and a bad monitor connection, we finished the sound check as the bar filled up with people. Since our housing host had appeared, we dashed to her place for a quick meal of lukewarm pizza.

The half of the bar where we were to perform was crowded and as she promised earlier, the producer ushered the nonpaying members of the audience out of the venue and closed down the pool tables. The emcee introduced us, starting with Donna. The three of us are seasoned comics and we know which lines in our songs are good for a sure-fire laugh. Her first song was about being spaced out on cold medication and talking with someone for five hours—the kind of conversation where you reveal all sorts of personal information, then don't remember it afterward. The punch line comes in the first line of the chorus, "I have to kill you now." A sea of grim faces greeted that phrase. A table of my fans sitting near the front talked loudly through most of Donna's songs, while a noisy bunch in the back did the same thing. She struggled through the rest of her set, getting the same tepid response to most of her funny lines. Liz was next, doing four songs for the almost dead audience, and then it was my turn. Treasuring the few smiles I got, I still felt like I was bashing my head against a very hard wall. They did laugh at my parody of a right-wing institution's theme song, with a nod to Disney, especially where I sing "We have small minds after all," but that was about all. I ended the first set and the three of us rushed over to the opposite side of the bar where our CDs were displayed. We had one of those quick conversations you have when you don't want someone across the room to know how you really feel—smiling broadly, in low tones we grumped, "What's wrong with these people?"

The second set was about as dismal as the first but at least we performed most of these songs together. A male stripper revue had cranked up on the upper level of the bar, sending their booming bass vibrating through the ceiling. I made a few jokes and asked if someone could get them to turn it down. Almost immediately it stopped and I thought that was the end of the problem. No, it was only a pause before the next pounding dance number. We struggled gamely on, throwing out more sure-fire comedy lines to a few grins and not much more.

At one point, I looked out at the bar in the back and noticed that the TV was still on. Several perky cheerleaders in sparkly costumes were jumping around. Ironic, since Liz does a satirical piece about cheerleaders. Near the end, as she sang another one of her songs, a guy I'd seen earlier slumped over the bar began clapping loudly. I wasn't sure if he was applauding because he thought the song should be over or if he was attempting to keep time. We sang the last song and escaped. Thankfully, when we took our lonely outpost over by the CDs for sale, a couple of fans came over to talk with us so we wouldn't look like total losers as the rest of the room filed out. We waved goodbye as we engaged ourselves with the folks who liked our show, looking gratefully toward a good night's rest that night.

At our housing, I stayed in a room upstairs while Liz and Donna were ushered to the basement depths of the old house. I think my bed had clean sheets, although I found a long silver hair on one of the dark pillowcases. The floor hadn't been swept in a long while, gray fuzz tucked into the corners and dust coating most surfaces but hey, I was there to sleep, not admire the view. In the better light of morning, the place looked worse, with magazines and books cluttering every available surface. The bathroom sink and shower were coated in beige scum. I quickly brushed my teeth and skipped a shower. The day before, our host had talked about spending thousands of dollars on a remodeling project. A housekeeper would've been a better choice.

I was awake first. I sat in the living room, catching up on email and talking to my girlfriend on my cell. Liz got up next, then Donna. We made polite conversation with our host, and then made excuses to leave. We followed each other a short drive down the interstate and pulled over for lunch. With just the three of us, I found out about their bottom-floor accommodations. Putting her hands up around her face Macaulay Culkin style, Liz exclaimed that the bathroom sink was so coated with grime that she had to wipe off the faucet handles before using it. She also didn't shower, choosing not to describe what she'd found there, given that we were eating lunch. Add that to the dead audience and the small amount of pay in our pockets, and it was my turn to do the Culkin routine. Donna asked if I was the one who'd got them that gig. I sheepishly answered yes. I wonder if "I'm sorry" made it right with them?

CHAPTER THIRTY-SEVEN

Winning the Lottery

It was a gig in a small military town, just a short drive from home. I'd played there once before. I drew about twenty people then, so I wasn't expecting a big audience this time. The pay wouldn't be huge—just a percentage of the small door charge.

The drive was pleasant, a refreshing summer breeze coming in the open car window and some vintage Neil Young on my MP3 player. I sang along as I drove.

At the door of the small church, Lana met me with a brilliant smile and a warm hug, exclaiming how good it was to see me again. It wasn't long before Annette burst into the room with more of the same.

I set up my CDs for sale and tuned my instruments as they put out trays of fresh veggies, cubes of cheese and packets of chips. Three ice chests were filled with ice and a variety of soft drinks. Signs were put up advising folks where to put their recyclables and what doors to use. Earlier in the day, they'd set up rows of chairs and moved tables. A table near the door held gifts for everyone who attended—trinkets probably picked up at Target and maybe a few things from Lana and Annette's home.

After I finished my work, I sat and talked with Lana. A white board hung in the area where she worked. "Prayer List" was written neatly at the top. Under it was a column of names and reason for the prayers. I joked with Lana that I'd like them to pray that I win the lottery and offered to generously share the winnings with them.

As Annette breezed around putting up signs we talked about the joys of yard sales. I bragged about a recent sale where I scored three T-shirts and a pair of pants for only three dollars.

The door opened only a couple of times before the concert was due to start. Each time, I'd anxiously look over and then check my watch. At the start time, there were only eight people, including Lana, Annette and Lana's mother. (Her dad came in later.)

At fifteen minutes past the hour, it was obvious that no one else was going to come. I pasted a smile on my face and started the first song. I was greeted with easy smiles and tapping feet. I relaxed and stopped worrying about the numbers. Their open faces and attentive manner made the show easy and so much fun. They laughed loudly at the funny songs. One woman cried at "My Dad Loves to Sing." I ended with "I Wanna Be a Straight Guy," urging the only guy there, Lana's dad, to sing because that was his theme song. That got a huge laugh. Everyone sang along, including him.

Afterward, almost everyone bought a CD, including Lana's mom.

When we set up this gig, I agreed to do a jam session after my show. Only two of the audience members brought instruments, and I thought, Why should I do what will feel like another show, especially if I'm not making much money? But I'm not one to go back on my word, and besides, they were looking forward to playing music. I didn't want to be the party pooper.

We had a great time with classic rock tunes, country and folk. We ended with a rousing "Proud Mary." If I left then, I'd get back around midnight, so I made my excuses and packed up. As I got into the car Lana handed me an envelope and apologized for the small turnout. "Ah well," I responded, "we had fun."

I arrived at home, dropped my CDs and guitar on the floor, and then set my purse on a chair. I turned my weary body toward the bedroom then thought I'd check that envelope. I opened the flap, expecting about fifty dollars, and pulled out ten neatly packed twenty dollar bills. I'd won the lottery after all, in more ways than one.

CHAPTER THIRTY-EIGHT

Crazy Bitch

With a booming beat I felt in my chest, a rapper repeated "crazy bitch…crazy bitch" as a dancer rotated her hips in a suggestive circle. The cocktail-sized tables at the edge of the dance floor in this cavernous lesbian bar not far from my home in 2008 were occupied by cheering lesbians eagerly leaning forward to catch the dancer's every nuance. She turned her back to the audience, quickly looked over her shoulder and dropped down into the splits just as an audience member in a ball cap, a beer dangling in one hand, galloped up with a wad of dollar bills and threw them over the dancer's head. "Crazy bitch…crazy bitch" the rapper continued. Her fellow dancers gyrated around her, breasts barely contained in sparkling bras or tight tops slashed in just the right places. I sat a few yards away, my mouth open like a freshly caught trout and wondering what the hell this middle-aged feminist-lesbian folksinger was doing on the same bill with a group of loose-hipped dancers in four-inch "ho" pumps.

My band had played just before them. I finished my set with a song about bellydance, shyly including a few shimmies and turns with a veil. Later, backstage, one of the dancers brightly exclaimed, "My mom was a bellydancer."

Mom. You'd think that performing for My People in a lesbian bar would be a great crowd, but to these young dykes I was Mom. Albeit, a weirdly funky mom, but all the same, someone born before 1960.

I'd rather play in a folk coffeehouse, but then I get all the gray-haired guys in beards blinking rapidly as soon as I do my first lesbian song. I don't always sell CDs in a place like that, as if having the recording of an out queer would brand them. "Oh yeah, I wonder about *him*. I saw a Jamie Anderson CD sitting on his coffee table."

But I digress…back to the bar. What was I doing there? Well, it was Durham and my band needed a place to play. Another lesbian band that does a lot of gigs in the area offered to organize the performance and at the time, it seemed like a good idea. After arriving, setting up and looking across that football field expanse of empty dance floor, the smattering of women huddled at little tables filled with empty beer bottles, I changed my mind. By then, it was too late.

The bar owner sauntered up and inquired, "One more song?"

Huh? We hadn't even started playing yet.

Her lips formed a hard line, her brows pushed together. She repeated, "One more song?"

It was then I realized that she was the DJ and wanted to know if she should play one more song before we performed. "No," I replied, "we're ready."

I quickly walked to the bar and asked for a glass of water. The twenty-something year old bartender grinned and said, "I can give you a bottle."

Oh yeah, no one drinks tap water anymore, even in a bar. I grabbed the frosty bottle and hurried back to the stage. The rest of my band assembled around me and I counted off "Her Problem Now." My drummer crashed and banged behind me and my guitar roared out through the monitor speaker, nearly knocking me over. I felt like I was in the middle of some crazy mega-decibel stereo, the bass guitar and electric violin swirling around in a frantic whoosh of sound. My fingers automatically went to their places and we finished one song. I said something witty, and then we started another song.

After three or four more, I played one of my most popular tunes, "Dark Chocolate," a quiet ballad I wouldn't normally do in a huge dance bar, but then, I was playing for lesbians and it's a love song to a woman. They would've been happier had I played Katy Perry's "I Kissed a Girl." (I hate that song. A girl who tastes like cherry Chapstick? I'd rather have a girl who tastes like dark chocolate or, as I told the crowd later, good beer. That's me, always ready with a good bar joke. I don't even drink beer.)

The high point of the evening was getting to borrow Laura's electric guitar. She played with the two other bands on the bill and generously offered to let me play her beautiful Strat. I've never owned an electric guitar—I am such a folksinger—but if I did, I'd want one like hers. It groaned and rumbled like it should on songs like "Yoga Teacher," where we ended with a parody of "Smells Like Teen Spirit."

I rushed through the rest of the gig like my hair was on fire. Finally, with the last stroke of my pick, it was over.

I returned Laura's guitar, then carefully put my two thousand dollar acoustic guitar back in its case. I could've been playing a sixty dollar K-Mart special for that crowd, and they wouldn't have noticed.

After a gig like that, I needed to drink. I settled on a bench with my vodka tonic, hanging out with my band until they drifted home halfway through the next band's set. How I longed to be in my warm bed with a good book, but since I was the band leader I thought it'd be best to stick around to support the other bands.

I enjoyed the tight Indigo Girl-like harmonies of the next group. I knew almost no one in the bar, though, and sat by myself feeling like I was under a huge neon sign that blinked "LOSER." Occasionally I'd glance at the table where my CDs were displayed for sale. Earlier, I'd told the crowd I was giving away one title for free because I was so overstocked. In spite of that, it was like I had a snarling pit bull stationed in front. I took some solace in noticing that the other two bands weren't selling (or giving away) any discs, either.

After the second band, the dancers came out again. Some of them actually had some dance training, one of them doing an impressive pirouette with pointed toes. The crowd whooped with excitement, some of them strutting up to tuck dollar bills into tight costumes. Their exit was heralded by more joyful hollering as the DJ informed us that the girls were available for body shots, only five dollars!

The next band cranked up and blasted through several rock numbers. They were good but that imaginary loser light was still blinking above my head, it was past midnight and my middle-aged eyes were threatening to close. I said goodbye to the leader of the other band. She promised to mail me a check for my portion of the door. I hoped it'd be enough for a couple gallons of gas. I dragged my sorry behind out to my truck.

Next time I'm bringing pasties.

CHAPTER THIRTY-NINE

Beware of Middle-Aged Folksingers
in Pickup Trucks

One of the things that made dating a Canadian different was crossing the border. It usually took a few minutes, long enough for the official to glance at my passport then ask me where I was going and why. In 2009, crossing from Canada to the U.S., I didn't expect anything out of the ordinary. After handing my passport to the U.S. border guard, he asked me the usual questions. When I answered that I'd been in Ottawa to see my fiancée he smiled and commented "I'll bet he was happy about that."

Without hesitating, I firmly answered, "She."

He showed no response, just tapped away at his computer. After a minute or two he asked "Ever been inside?"

I'm thinking, Inside? Inside what? The Big House?

"Do I *want* to go inside?" I asked, a confused look on my face.

"No, I'm *not* asking," he replied, looking slightly peeved. He then told me that I'd been selected for a random check—one out of every two hundred vehicles was stopped. He kept my passport and directed me over to the side, where I was to park. Another guard asked for my keys and pointed me toward some double doors. The poker-faced guard inside instructed me to sit down.

The room was crowded with agitated travelers who looked like they'd rather be getting a root canal than sitting in that stuffy little room. A French Canadian family of four stood at one counter, the woman in tears, as an official explained in English why the little boy with the expired passport was not allowed into the United States. A portly man reeking of cigarette smoke was crammed into the seat beside me, muttering under his breath about having no time for this.

Feigning nonchalance I pulled a magazine out of my purse then realized it was the *Utne Reader*. Great, now they'll really think I'm some wild-eyed liberal hippie chick. I couldn't concentrate on the page, thinking about all the things in my truck that would raise eyebrows such as the stack of U.S. cash in small bills (earned at gigs a week ago) or the prescription drugs that were all mine, but in an unmarked container. I heard a deliberate "Anderson" from one of the officials so I affected a casual look and strolled over to the counter.

The guy in uniform, a stern look on his face as he tapped away at the computer keyboard, asked, "Do you know why you're here?"

"A random check...um, 'cause I'm attractive and you want to give me lots of money?" No sooner was that out of my mouth then I thought, Crap, you're not supposed to joke with these guys. Beat one...beat two.

He chuckled and said, "Are you kidding? I work for the government." My shoulders relaxed as he asked me a bunch of questions and had me fill out a customs report. He instructed me to sit down while they searched my truck. Fortunately, it was parked around the corner where I couldn't see it. Otherwise, I probably would've freaked out as they moved my instruments and unzipped my suitcase.

After a couple of minutes I was called back to the counter, handed my passport and informed that I could go. I went out to my truck, retrieved my keys from a grim-looking guard, got in my truck and sped away. At my first stop I peeked in the back of my truck and saw that the tarp covering my instruments hadn't even been disturbed. I could've smuggled in a whole hockey team.

A couple of days later my journey took me back to Canada, this time through a different border crossing. Peering through the rain on the U.S. side, I could just pick out a guy in a dark uniform directing me between two rows of orange pylons. He put up his hands, told me to stop, then instructed me to get out of the truck. He stopped a line of cars behind me and asked them to get out too. We darted through the rain and under an overhang. I asked a lady next to me if this crossing was always like this and she said no, her brows furrowed.

We waited in the chilly air as a large pickup truck slowly cruised up one side of the cars and down the other. I'm guessing they had some kind of sensing equipment and were looking for drugs or weapons, but no one ever told us. After a few more minutes they let us back in our vehicles.

They stopped me on the Canadian side, too, but I expected that since I had a house concert in Canada. I had the correct paperwork so I wasn't concerned. The border guard, after staring at my papers and his computer screen, looked over the top rim of his glasses and inquired, "They *hired* you?"

"No," I was tempted to reply, "I just break into random houses with my guitar, let loose with a song and they pay me to stop." Instead, I simply nodded yes. He let me go after running out of his highly intelligent questions.

Was that the end? Oh no. A few days later, traveling back through that first border crossing, I was stopped on the United States side. They asked the same questions and again, when the guard used the male pronoun I corrected him. In a déjà vu moment he asked if I'd ever been delayed at the border.

My eyebrows must've gone up when I answered, "Yes, last week."

He asked if I knew why and while I wanted to say 'Cause I'm a big lesbo, I politely answered, "A random check."

He laughed and said, "Well you've been selected for another random check." What? Is this Delay a Lesbian at the Border Month?

I knew the ropes. I pulled over to park and as I got out of the truck the guard jokingly thanked me for spending time with them. I walked the now-familiar path into the building. When my name was called I sauntered up to the counter. The guy looked at me, glanced at his computer screen then looked at me again and said, "You look familiar."

"Yep," I informed him with a smile, "I was here just last week."

He told me he was going to skip the usual questions because he was tired and it was the end of his day. After he was sure I wasn't hauling explosives or anything else nefarious, he let me go.

I wish these middle-aged lesbians in pickup trucks would stop transporting hockey teams and drugs across the border. They're ruining it for me.

CHAPTER FORTY

Singing for the Stars

It started innocently, with an email in 2010 from my friend Nedra Johnson, asking me if I'd play guitar for her at the Michigan Womyn's Music Festival…on the night stage. Oh I don't know, let me check my schedule.

Hell, yes.

It was part of a show with many different musicians called Chix Lix, featuring songs from the seventies, and she was asked to sing Cris Williamson's "Joanna."

"I can't get that fingerpicking thing," she explained. "You can do it, right?"

I had Meg Christian's 1975 songbook that contained it, so I thought I could learn it.

"Joanna" is one of the songs that Meg discovered back before Olivia started, when she was looking for songs by women for her own show. When she found a Cris Williamson LP in a bargain bin, she bought it. Totally taken with it, she learned her songs and performed them so much that when Cris came to town, women packed the place and sang along, totally surprising Cris. I knew all that history when Nedra contacted me and I was honored to perform it with her.

She also asked if I knew Ferron's wonderful "Testimony" and would I play that with her band on the day stage for her regular set? That was another "Hell, yes," from me.

Using the songbook, I acquainted myself with "Joanna." Meg has a classical background and some of those chords looked like physics equations. I simplified a few and smoothed out my rough edges, ending up with a guitar part that sounded pretty close to Meg's. I've taught the Ferron song to a couple of students so I already had those chords. I practiced both until they were sneaking into my dreams.

Every year, Nedra and I do a concert in town the night before the festival gates open. It's always a blast and a great way to start the festival experience. At that show, she casually asked, "Do you also want to play mandolin in my band?" She told me the songs she thought would sound good with it. I nodded affirmatively. Inside, a little voice was screaming, "Holy crap." I'm a guitar player who dabbles in the mandolin and I'm going to get up at a major festival and play in a band totally new to me in just a few days? Who did I think I was? Robin Flower?

The next day, while sitting in the car in the long line to get into the festival, I put on Nedra's CD and played mandolin with those two songs, hitting replay over and over again. I wasn't sure what chords I was playing, but they worked. By the time I reached the gate, I was having fun with the songs and acting like I play with Nedra all the freaking time.

A couple of days later, I rehearsed with her group of wonderful musicians. My acoustic guitar part for "Testimony" was similar to what Ferron played. The band added a cool groove and an ethereal electric guitar part. When we added Nedra's soulful vocals, it was heavenly. I couldn't wipe the grin off my face. As the last notes faded, I heard a rough but friendly voice say, "Sounds good, guys." I turned around to see a woman ambling away. I could only see her back so I looked questioningly at Nedra. She grinned and said, "That's good—Ferron liked it."

We ran through the songs with the mandolin, too. We were ready for our day stage set the next afternoon. I don't remember much about the performance except it felt like flying, especially when that awesome electric guitar kicked in.

A day or two later, I showed up at the night stage for our "Joanna" sound check. This was the big mama of all three stages, with enough room for a huge band. It was just Nedra and I, though. As I walked up with my guitar, I saw Holly Near sitting off to the side. She beamed and said, "Jamie on the night stage. It's about time." She gave me a big hug.

Onstage, I plugged in my guitar as Nedra took her place at the center mike. I started the song, her voice joining me a few measures later. About half way through, the smooth notes of a violin joined us. I turned and there was Barbara Higbie.

That evening, I took my place backstage about an hour before we were to perform. Pacing while I mentally ran through the song, I hardly heard what was happening onstage. Before I knew it, the stage manager was giving me a little tap on the arm and saying, "Okay, you're on."

As I walked on to the darkened stage, I thought I saw twinkling lights, like stars in a clear night sky, only it was several thousand women, waiting in anticipation. Someone called out my name. I grinned as I connected my guitar, stood up, willed my hands to stop shaking, and looked over at Nedra. She nodded. A yellow spotlight found her. I felt my left hand form an A chord, and my right hand start picking out the opening bars. Nedra sang the song a little slower than Meg did and with some syncopation that made it uniquely beautiful. I love her voice. Halfway through, Barbara's sweet violin tiptoed in. Toward the end of the song, I stopped playing for few seconds, Barbara followed me, and in those moments there was only Nedra's expressive voice and the near-quiet of thousands of women. I came back in gradually with an ascending bass line, and the violin joined us, as Nedra finished the last couple of lines. It was over way too soon. The joyful cheer from the crowd rang in my ears for a long time afterward.

The next day, I ran into Cris Williamson on one of the paths. She warmly commented, "I liked the way you did my song. You could include it in your show anytime."

If there'd been a ceiling, I would've needed help to get back down. On the other hand, it was kind of nice up there.

CHAPTER FORTY-ONE

Never Assume

I like playing at conferences because they're indoors and I usually get a set fee, no matter how many people are there. The planning for this one in 2005 had been a little strange, though, so I wasn't sure what to expect. The producer, a lesbian, was disorganized, and her conversations with me were blunt and not exactly friendly. At one point, she asked me if I'd enjoyed my vacation in Sri Lanka and Thailand. I wondered what she was talking about—I'd never been to either place—then realized she was making a joke because they'd recently had a tsunami. Don't quit your day job, babe.

Fortunately, this conference wasn't in either place, but in a pleasant resort area in the US.

When I arrived at the hotel, I was given no conference program, I couldn't find a registration table and when I phoned the producer, I got her voice mail. I had no idea where in the hotel my show would be, but I could check into my room, so that's what I did. My producer called not long after that, informing me, "Your sound check is at three p.m. You can go back to bed now."

It was noon and she thought I was in bed? Ah yes, the glamorous life of a touring folksinger. Or maybe that was another joke.

A few minutes before three, I picked up my guitar and gig bag, and then headed for the floor with the ballrooms. I'd forgotten to ask the producer which room it was and I couldn't reach her on the phone. After wandering around a little, I found the biggest room and looked inside. No one was there. I returned at three thirty and still, no sound equipment. The producer was there, though. "Oh," she said while waving her hand, "They said they'd be here between three and four."

Be here? When I told her it would take a while for them to haul the equipment up to the second floor and set it up, she replied, "Well, the hotel said it would take no time at all."

Right.

I checked the room at four thirty and the sound company still hadn't arrived. I called the producer. "Don't get too excited," she snapped, "they'll be here around six thirty." I asked her to call me when they arrived, then dragged my stuff back to my room.

All this time, I could've been doing something far more fun than hauling my guitar and gig bag all over that huge hotel.

Around six, I got a call from the front desk. "Your sound guy is here and he needs to know where to set up." As politely as I could, I told the clerk that it was the producer's responsibility. I knew the room, but I had no idea where she wanted the stage.

The clerk answered, "She went to take a nap and said you'd take care of it."

Okay, then. I picked up my stuff and trudged downstairs to meet the sound tech. He smiled and reached out his meaty hand to shake mine, apologizing for his late arrival, and saying that another show had delayed him. He was a middle-aged guy, a little round through the middle, dressed in a worn denim shirt and jeans. He could've used a shave. At first I thought, great, an older half-deaf rock dude with his band's ancient equipment. I was wrong—he was a middle-aged rock guy, but he had been a professional sound person for many years and there was nothing wrong with his hearing or his PA. With the help of his teenage daughter, they swiftly set up the equipment. I did a quick check and they made me sound like a million bucks. His daughter settled in on the far side of the room, focused on her phone. I sat next to the guy and asked him about his daughter.

He smiled. "She's adopted," he replied. "I teach at a local school where she was a student. She came in one day, covered in bruises. I looked into it and found that her father had been using her as a punching bag. My wife and I didn't have any kids so we found out how to adopt her." He was teaching her to run sound.

We had some time before the show, so we talked more. He had great stories about the stars that hired him. I asked about favorites and he said he always enjoyed the country performers because they were so polite. He loved working with Martina McBride and with some rock acts, like Melissa Etheridge. One tour in particular stood out. It featured k.d. lang, the Indigo Girls, Tori Amos and Sarah McLachlan. (It sounded like Lilith Fair although he didn't say that. How I would've loved to have been at one of those shows.) After a long tour in hot weather, the crew was getting pretty tired. During one of the last shows, Tori ordered lots of icy Gatorade for them. It was a kindness he never forgot.

Of course, I had to ask him about the difficult artists. He laughed as he recalled a rock singer who smacked him across the face because her monitor kept feeding back. "I wasn't running that speaker," he said. "My board wasn't even on."

The concert went great that night. I was well-received—they laughed at the funny tunes and listened closely to the quiet songs. Afterward, I told the producer that the sound company had done a stellar job. "I hope so," she answered, "they cost more than you did."

I have a song, "Never Assume," and sometimes, I need to remind myself of that. It's not always the lesbian who treats me well. Sometimes it's the grizzled straight rock guy.

CHAPTER FORTY-TWO

Maybe I Should Learn
"Somewhere Over the Rainbow"

I love talent shows like *America's Got Talent*, so when I heard that a Canadian version was starting, I was excited (since I live in Canada now). I knew better than to try to compete with adorable kid singers, so I decided to enter as a comic. Comedians never get far in the competition, but that's okay with me. Getting a little face time on national TV was my goal, and if it meant being sandwiched between an eight-year-old warbling "Somewhere Over the Rainbow" and a guy who stuck nails in his nose, then so be it.

After registering on a website in the fall of 2011, I was instructed to go to Montreal the following week. (There were no auditions in Ottawa where I lived because you know, it's only the nation's capital.)

As someone who's toured for many years, I've negotiated many a big city street. New York City? No problem. Los Angeles at rush hour? Easy. Montreal with lots of construction signs…in French? Dial 911. I didn't know if those blinking signs were telling me to merge left, stop, yield…or get the hell out of Quebec. I elected to follow the traffic and to listen to the soothing voice of Marcia, my GPS.

The problem? Marcia didn't understand French. When I entered the address of the downtown convention center where auditions were held, she kept telling me, "Address not found."

I yelled, "Of course the address exists! It's the freaking convention center!" If Marcia could help me navigate the mean streets of Rockford, Illinois and Cincinnati, Ohio, why not Montreal? (I'm kidding about Rockford, but Cincinnati? Who designed that town? I didn't know they had crack in the 1800s.)

I thought maybe Marcia didn't like "rue," so I entered "street." Another error message mocked me. I entered the address of the parking garage instead of the convention center. Still, "address not found." I tried the postal code. That was a language she could speak, and immediately her soothing voice instructed me to "follow the highlighted route."

Good thing. I don't know if I could've negotiated the dizzying array of highways without her. Left exits, one-way streets, drivers yelling at their kids while periodically stomping on their brakes for no reason, signs only in French…Marcia saved my English-speaking ass.

When she intoned "destination on left," I shouted a little hallelujah and parked. Fortunately, the convention center is large and hard to miss. As I entered the enormous structure, I noticed the small TVs hanging from the ceiling with the bold red *Canada's Got Talent* logo instructing me to turn this way, then that way, then up to the second level, then turn again…it was like being spun around just before you whack a piñata. After a while I had no idea where I was or where to go next. There was no bat, no candy and no cheering group of friends. However, I spotted a group of little girls in pink spandex accompanied by a couple of women fussing with their hair and pulling up costume straps.

I asked one of the adults about the audition. I didn't just get directions to the main room—I got a rundown of how the auditions work. "You go up that escalator, then get in line, then move to another room and another line, then you register…" She was still talking when I thanked her and headed off toward the escalator.

I stepped off the escalator and as I rounded the corner, I saw a huge room with a long queue snaking back and forth and a sea of young hopefuls with their parents. I took my place in line and decided to get to know my fellow auditioners. With the exception of a dance troupe, they were all singers. The preteen girl dressed in jeans, frilly blouse and heels who stood behind me was going to sing her favorite Alicia Keys song. The young blond-headed gentleman in a blue suit beside me was singing, you guessed it, "Somewhere Over the Rainbow."

His parents confided that they hadn't wanted him to audition because, you know, they weren't *those* kind of parents. "He bugged us and bugged us, and we kept saying no," the mother commented, "but then when he told us what he wanted to do with the money, we said yes."

"And what was that?" I inquired.

She named a nonprofit that feeds poor African children.

Yeah…after mom and dad pay off the house and buy a Ferrari.

A lot of those waiting knew each other, mostly from other talent shows. They talked about how long those lines were and who advanced in each show. I listened in silence, wondering if I should get my middle-aged ass out of there but no, I hadn't muscled my way through busy Montreal streets just to give up.

"You're a singer?" they'd ask while eyeing my guitar.

"No, a comic."

"Oh," they'd nod, "you sing funny songs?"

No…I just carry it around. Mostly, I use it to whack people who annoy me.

We stood in line an hour or so before a guy with a megaphone strode into the room and blathered on about how much talent was sure to be there. Then he gave us directions. The doors would open soon. Those auditioning would go to the right, their guests to the left. There'd be another wait. After that you'll be directed to a table where you'll register and then you'll take a seat until they call the range of numbers that includes yours. From your group of thirty you'll be divided according to your type of talent.

The doors opened and the line moved swiftly. After we separated, I ended up in line in front of Nicolette, a young woman dressed all in black. She had dark eyeliner surrounding her eyes with extra "eyelashes" drawn in at the edges. Glitter twinkled from her eyelids and under her eyes. Thick black dreads cascaded down her back. At first glance I thought "hard ass," but with her brilliant smile, it was clear she wasn't. She showed me photos of her three adorable sons and told me she was a Kindermusik teacher. I knew

I'd found a kindred spirit. Sure, she was born after I graduated from high school, but at least I wouldn't have to explain a rotary phone to her.

We had an easy conversation about our families, our hometowns and what we were doing for our auditions. She was singing a Boyz II Men song. Bold for a woman singer but then, she was wearing glitter and as she informed me, her grandfather was a stripper. I asked if she thought that would help her win and she giggled and said no, it was just fun to tell people.

I told Nicolette that she should win because she looked like a rock star. She looked at her feet and quietly replied, "You haven't even heard me sing yet."

After an hour or so, it was my turn to check in. I walked up to the long table where several clerks were seated in front of laptops. After answering a few questions, I asked if I was the oldest contestant that day. The twenty-something-year-old woman thought for a minute and replied, "We had someone who was fifty-four."

I was fifty-three. Just put "grandma" on my audition form.

I was issued what looked like a bumper sticker with a huge number on it and instructed to put it on my front. I looked down at my breasts and thought, no, not there, then decided to put it just below, across my belly. I took my seat in the enormous room along with a hundred or so other hopefuls.

I sat next to the kid in the suit and his folks. Again, his mom told me that he was donating his money. I got that, thanks.

Behind us a camera crew was interviewing people. The parent next to me leaned over and said in low tones, "The kids shouldn't know this, but one of the camera crew told me that they're interviewing the people who are going through to the next level. You're an adult, so I thought you could handle the information."

You learned that without a secret decoder ring?

We lounged in the hard plastic chairs, sipping water and mentally going through our auditions. A dance troupe ran through its moves. A girl sang into her pen, like a mike. Parents hovered and slicked back cowlicks. I tuned up my guitar and strummed through a few chords, just to warm up.

Another hour went by before they called my group of numbers. I gathered up my purse and guitar, and then scurried to the front of the room. A young woman with a headset and clipboard instructed anyone who wasn't a singer to step up closer to her. Three acts moved forward. She looked at my guitar, tilted her head and scrunched her eyebrows together. "I'm a comic," I explained.

"Oh," she replied with the weariness of someone who's already seen a couple hundred people with guitars that day. After some dialogue with a colleague about where to send me, I was told, along with a dance troupe and a skateboard artist, to follow her. The rest of our group, twenty-seven singers, all kids, were told to go in another direction.

I was never so grateful to be a gray-haired comic. I can't imagine sitting in a room for eight hours and listening to nothing but Alicia Keys hopefuls.

After waiting a few more minutes, our little group was ushered into a small conference room. Half of the room was covered with a portable wood dance floor, like the kind you'd rent for a wedding reception. In an opposite corner was a long table where a pleasant-faced woman in glasses sat before a computer. Next to her was a crew member behind a huge camera. I knew the film wouldn't be shown on TV, because there were no additional lights. I had assumed that earlier and was glad it was confirmed, because I hadn't worn anything special, just the patterned jeans, white T-shirt and purple Chucks I'd put on that morning. I looked down at the Chucks, wishing the left one didn't have a huge stain. The judge looked at me and started to open her mouth. "I'm a comic," I said. She mouthed, "Oh."

We huddled in the corner as the friendly judge explained that she'd call each act for their audition. First up was the dance troupe. Dressed all in black and with silver makeup covering the top halves of their faces, they made a striking picture. The judge started in French and laughed, probably making a joke about her language skills, then changed to English. The group looked confused but with some pointing and giggling, the judge and their spokesperson came to an understanding. Their leader held up their number and in a heavily accented voice said the name of their troupe and that they were from a small town outside of Quebec City.

The judge hit "play" on their MP3 player and they sprang into action. The twelve of them stomped and backflipped through their hip-hop routine. I stood as far away as I could, clutching my precious guitar. Fortunately, none of them ended up in my lap.

They finished with a flourish as we applauded. They joined the rest of us in the back of the room.

My name was called next. Immediately, I had tumbleweeds blowing across the desert of my mouth. I gripped my guitar with white knuckles and took my place on the "T" taped to the floor in front of the camera. I apologized about the guitar hiding my number. The judge smiled and asked me to take it off my shirt and hold it up in front of me. "Don't put it on your guitar," she quickly added, "because you won't be able to get it off."

I laughed and said, "It's a two-thousand-dollar guitar. I know better than that."

Looking straight into the camera, I spoke with authority. "Jamie Anderson, Ottawa." I hoped the smear of liner around my left eye wasn't too prominent. (I'm legally blind in that eye, so I apply makeup by feel. I've stabbed myself many times. I wonder if there's a special ER code for that?)

"You can stand on the dance floor if you want."

I looked behind me. "I haven't figured out the dance portion of my act yet."

She chuckled. Yay! I'm already making her laugh.

She asked me a few questions about where I was from and when I told her I'd recently emigrated from the States, she wanted to know what brought me here.

"I married a Canadian. Can I help it if you're all attractive and intelligent?"

Again, the judge laughed. The skateboard girl giggled but the dance troupe sat in stony silence.

The perfect comedy crowd.

I introduced my song by saying that it would explain a few things about moving here and then sang:

Thirty below, snow and ice, people look at me and they try to be nice
Then comes the question I dread, they look at me like I'm not right in the head
Yes, I could be in the U S of A, eating cheese in a can every day
Doing without that stuff isn't hard, I moved to Canada for love…and a health card

I sang a couple more verses then ended with a flourish, holding the last note out and raising my right hand in the air like a victory salute. The judge let out a loud guffaw, the skateboard kid giggled and the troupe just looked at me, a blank look on their faces. I added, "Merci y'all!"

I smiled and strutted off the stage.

* * *

Glad that my audition was over, I relaxed into a sitting position on the floor near the dance floor. I couldn't get to my guitar case because the troupe was standing in front of it. I gently laid the guitar on the floor in front of me.

The skateboard kid took her place in front of the camera. The music started and she jumped on the skateboard, scooted a couple of feet, jumped and missed the board, sending it skittering off into the side wall. I felt sorry for her as she missed trick after trick. For her grand finale she attempted a flip and caught only the tip of the board, sending it zooming off the stage and like an arrow to a target, directly toward my guitar.

I lunged forward, ready to throw my body over the precious instrument. Before I could there was a loud clunk. The judge immediately asked, "Is it all right?"

Like a paramedic checking a car accident victim, I quickly looked it over and with a huge sigh of relief, answered, "Yes."

The skateboard kid was mortified, apologizing several times. Out loud, I assured her that it wasn't her fault. In my head I was screaming a different response. It's good no one in that room was auditioning as a psychic.

Just before filing out of the room, we were given a sheet of paper telling us that we'd hear from them in a couple of months if we were selected for the next level. No congratulatory letter ever arrived in the mail. A dance troupe (not the one in that room) won the competition.

Next time, I'm working on the dance portion of my show.

CHAPTER FORTY-THREE

It's Not the Battery

"It's the battery," he said emphatically, his eyes narrowing.

I pointed to the light on my guitar. "No. If the battery was dead, this light wouldn't be on."

He started to say something, threw up his hands and stomped away. This was going to be a long night. Most of the sound technicians I work with are great. They work long hours for little pay and if it wasn't for them, people wouldn't be able to hear me. So, that's all good. But once in a while I get someone like Mr. Important.

In 2012, my band and I were at this Ottawa restaurant and onstage at the appointed time. We pulled instruments out of cases and set mike stands where we needed them. A harried waiter rushed up to us and blurted, "I've still got a couple of tables to take care of. I'll back in a few minutes to set you up. Do *not* touch the board." He was referring to the amp where we would plug in our instruments and mikes.

We finished setting up what we could and waited. He walked quickly up to the stage, announced that he had twenty-two years of experience in "sounding and engineering" and scurried over to the sound board. He must have started as a fetus, because there is no way he'd been at this that long. The other guitar player muttered under his breath that he had underwear older than that guy.

My band member strummed his guitar. No sound. He checked the connections and strummed again. No sound. The sound guy strode over to him and said, "Your battery is dead."

"No it's not. I just bought this guitar this morning, plugged it in at the store and it worked."

"Well, it's dead," the sound guy announced, tilting his chin up to emphasize his point. He picked up a mike that was near and shoved it in front of the guitar.

Then it was my turn. I strapped on my guitar, strummed it and heard nothing. That's when we had the argument about my battery. He grabbed a mike and set it near my guitar. When I strummed it there was a loud booming noise, close to feeding back. I told him it was the A string. Experienced technicians know that when that kind of sound is associated with a particular note that there is a certain frequency they need to adjust on the board. This guy stood at the board, turned a few knobs, wiggled some connections and turned back to me. "I could adjust the 1K," he informed us, "but that isn't possible."

Huh? The 1K? Neither I nor the other guitar player knew what he was talking about.

"Just listen," said the other guitar player, "forget about the frequencies."

"Is the sound in the house the same as what I'm hearing in the monitors?" I asked.

"The house sound is off," he said, chopping off the ends of his words. "I'll make quick adjustments during the first two minutes of your first song."

"Why? We're doing the sound check now."

He waved his hand as if what I had to say wasn't important.

Meanwhile, the restaurant stereo was blasting some progressive rock tune. When the sound guy said he had trouble hearing us because of that, I asked why he didn't turn off the stereo. He looked like I'd just asked him to set his head on fire. He repeated slowly, as if I were a toddler, "I'll make the adjustments during your first two minutes."

He tested the bass. We could barely hear it and told him so. "I'll turn it up later. I have the volume down now." I'd stopped asking him why. He was living in some parallel universe I didn't understand.

The fiddle player bowed a few notes. It sounded great. At least something did. She asked him about muting the sound so she could unplug her instrument. (If it's not muted, it makes a loud clunk sound that can sometimes damage equipment.) "I always mute the instruments then," he pompously informed her.

"Okay. Can you do it after we play the song we're checking?"

"Of course!"

We played a song all together, the two guitars sounding like the boom of a faraway car stereo set to hip-hop. I stopped. "Can you fix that booming sound?" I asked.

He threw his hands up in the air, got inches from my face and said, "I've never had trouble with a band like this before."

Yeah, it's our fault.

"I went to school for five years to learn this," he says, as he stomped back to the sound board to do yet another adjustment. Five years?

We played all together again. The bass was at such a low volume that it was a mere suggestion. The fiddle was clear and loud. I couldn't hear my guitar and the other guitar player's instrument was low, but could be heard. My vocal sounded far away so I asked to be turned up. I hadn't even finished my sentence before he turned his back and started turning dials. At this point, I turned to one of my bandmates and said, "I'm going to fucking kill him."

The other guitar player offered to make some adjustments.

"I know what I'm doing!" the sound guy retorted.

Sure you do.

Next, we tried my mandolin. I could hear it but when I asked into the mike, audience members shook their heads no. Again, I asked for the volume in the instrument mike to be increased. I don't think he was even listening at this point.

A minute or so later, he strode over to the table where my partner and the fiddle player's parents were sitting to complain that my battery was dead, but I wouldn't listen to him. Complaining to our families is really going to further your cause.

We started the show. I couldn't hear my guitar and as I found out later, neither could the audience. My mandolin was absent in the mix, too. The bass was only a low buzz. The sound guy ran over to the board a few times, but the sound never improved.

Halfway through the first set we ceased to see him. Even if the sound sucked, at least we didn't have to endure any more of his lectures.

At the end of our set, we looked around for him so he could mute the violin. I even called for him through the mike and still, no harried self-important sound guy/waiter appeared. The other guitar player did the forbidden and touched the board and muted the right channel so the fiddle player could unplug.

The second set wasn't much better. We were hesitant to touch the board. We certainly didn't want the management to blame us for any problems.

After he got home, the other guitar player tried out his instrument and indeed, the pick-up had crapped out. My guitar, on the other hand, worked fine when I plugged it in at home. How about that? Twenty-two years of experience does teach you something. Maybe in the next twenty-two he'll learn that when the light is on, the battery isn't dead.

CHAPTER FORTY-FOUR

Clogging, a Harp and Holly F***ing Near

In June of 2012, I was on tour in North Carolina. As I headed to the airport in the quiet morning, anticipation mounted because I was headed to one of my favorite music festivals in the whole world, the National Women's Music Festival. They were the first big festival to book me, back when I was an unknown folksinger from way out in Arizona, in '90 or '91, and they've been kind to me ever since. Some women miss being out in the woods, and while I love me some green, there's nothing like this indoor festival with live music in a nice hall, with no worries about the weather, and sleeping in real beds after the last late-night jam.

If only I'd thought to put the hotel information in my itinerary. After retrieving my luggage, I went to a bank of phones and called the number for one of the hotels listed on a big sign in the little Madison, Wisconsin airport. I asked if this was the place that hosted the women's music festival. I was relieved when the woman at the other end of the line answered yes. She said their shuttle was otherwise involved, but I could take a cab and they'd cover it.

The cab driver answered "Huh?" to most of my polite conversational questions so I quit trying. He dropped me off at the front door and I strolled up to the counter and gave them my name. Eyebrows knitted in concern, the clerk said I wasn't listed.

"Maybe it's under the festival's name?"

"No." She looked sympathetic.

"You don't have others from the festival here?" I added. Again the answer was no. It was then that I looked up and read the sign above the desk—Radisson. The cab driver misheard me and brought me to the wrong hotel. A young man in a Radisson uniform offered to take me to the right hotel, bless his heart.

As soon as I walked into the lobby of the Marriot, it felt like home. In the few feet between the door and the front desk, I heard several delighted greetings and received a couple of warm hugs. Now we're talkin'. After a quick check-in, I headed to the elevators and coming the other way was a smiling face I remembered from long ago—my first-ever girlfriend, Lois. We were together in the seventies and after many years with no contact, had found each other again through the miracle of the Internet. After a hug, I headed upstairs to my room, but didn't stay long. Lois and I and our friend Deb grabbed a quick dinner, then ducked into the room where a concert was already in progress.

It was great to experience the festival through Lois and Deb's eyes. Neither one of them had ever been to a women's music festival before. Often I'd sneak a look at them as they stared wide-eyed at all the happy women.

That first night I heard some really fine jazz from Lynette Margulies and Jane Reynolds, a great set of drumming from Sister Ngoma and half a set by the charming duo Nervous But Excited. I would've stayed for more, but getting up at five thirty that morning suddenly whapped me upside the head. I was very disappointed to have missed Ladies Must Swing, the act after them, especially since I adore swing dancing. The only dancing I'd witness that night would be counting the sheep sashaying across my brain as I dropped off to dreamland.

The next morning, the breakfast area in the lobby was hopping. I table surfed, had a little conversation here, a little conversation there. I sat with musician friends and dished about tours. I talked with fans about the book I'm writing. I had coffee with Holly Near. In fact, I saw Holly a lot. We don't know each other well, but she always has a friendly word for me. At one point we were walking down the hall as yet another fan stopped to compliment her. She graciously smiled and thanked the woman, then continued walking with me. I told her she should change her name to Holly F***ing Near. Fortunately, she gets my humor and laughed.

One morning at breakfast, I was introduced to Kay Gardner's daughter Juliana. Not only does she look like her mother, but oh, that voice! It was like talking with Kay. Tears sprang to my eyes. Juliana was there because her late mother's work, *A Rainbow Path*, would be performed on the Saturday night stage.

Soon it was time to meet my band for a rehearsal. I knew I had a great group—Kara Barnard on mandolin and guitar, Phyllis Free on percussion, Jamie Price on vocals and Martine Locke on vocals—but I was nervous about me. I usually perform solo. When I hear a hot guitar solo or sweet vocal, I'm likely to stop because I'm listening to them. Then I realize, oh yeah, I'm supposed to be playing the guitar. During my new song "Mamaw's Roses," the backing vocals were so gorgeous I started crying. Who'd have thought that bad-ass rocker Martine would call up some inner angel and sound like that? Or on another song, that Phyllis Free could pound on a giant plastic bucket and get beats so tasty I could eat them with a spoon? Don't even get me started about Kara's effortless accompaniment or Jamie's complementary vocals.

Immensely satisfied with the practice, I sauntered down the hall to the day stage for my first emcee gig and checked in with my old friend Retts Scauzillo, who was stage managing. We went over some details and I sat down to write out some intros. I thought about what I'd say to entertain while the set changes were going on behind me. I was assured that everything would go quickly, but I'm always ready with a funny tour story because you never know when a cranky amp will refuse to work or a mike will get plugged into the wrong input. Aside from my stories, I can always take off my shirt and that's good for a minute or two of cheering. (No, I'm not *that* kind of entertainer, but I'm always wearing a pretty bra that makes it real handy to do a quick little bellydance. Costume? I don't need no freakin' costume. And before the rumors start, my bras aren't any more revealing than the average bathing suit.) One time at that festival I was onstage for a half hour talking about my dog, my home, my partner…I was about to recount what I'd had for breakfast by the time they tapped me on the shoulder and said, "We're ready."

Leela and Ellie Grace were on first. When I introduced them, I said that when I saw their names on the festival publicity my heart did a little flutter, and I really meant it. Their old-timey-flavored set of banjo, mandolin and guitar ended with a riotous burst of clogging.

Stellar songwriter Chris Collier was on next, and last, the energetic Summer Osbourne. I don't know what she puts on her cereal in the morning, but I'd like some too. During her set, I saw a familiar face rounding the corner into the backstage area, her arms out and wearing the biggest grin. My partner, Pat, had just arrived after a two-and-a-half day ride on her motorcycle from our home in Ottawa. It'd been over a month since we'd seen each other. I don't know how long we hugged, but I think Summer got through two songs before we drew apart.

I got to relax in the audience that night, listening to Melanie DeMore, Emma's Revolution, Holly Near and Sugar Beach.

Saturday morning I had a quick sound check, then tried to nap. My brain was buzzing with anticipation though, so I sat up, grabbed my guitar and ran through a few of the songs I'd be singing that afternoon. If nerves got the better of me while I was onstage, I wanted to make sure my hands and voice would carry on without me. There have been times during a show when I looked down at my strumming hand in awe, like an alien had taken over my body. Yeah, that's it, I was training the aliens.

I needn't have worried. The aliens came through for me. My band was awesome. My songs felt solid and the competent sound crew made me sound wonderful. At one point, I looked over at Kara on my right. She raised her eyebrows, a smile filling her face and silently I replied, "Yeah. Freakin' yeah." (Well, it was another F word but my mother may read this book.)

That night an orchestra—strings, wind instruments, percussion and harp—awed us with *A Rainbow Path*. I was transported. Big Bad Gina followed and although I loved their high-energy set, I couldn't keep my eyes open. I shuffled up to my room to catch some shuteye. I could wake up in time to hear Toshi Reagon who was on next. But oops. Never underestimate the lack of sleep in a middle-aged musician. I overslept and only made it back for Toshi's last song.

She wasn't the last on that night. One of the highlights of this festival is the performer jam on Saturday night. Musicians from every stage show up and each does one song with others jumping in to help. I'd had a power nap. Y'all watch out.

We started with a traditional tune, "Whiskey Before Breakfast." With musicians like Kara Barnard and Leela and Ellie Grace, it's national law that you have to do some bluegrass. The drummers cranked up—who says traditional acoustic music can't have a djembe or two?—and the rest of us sang or played guitar. Leela and Ellie closed with some fine percussion accompaniment a la their feet. Our thirty-part harmony continued for many songs.

Sharon Katz told us she was going to rock it Zulu style and laid down an upbeat guitar riff. Melodie Griffis cranked out a groove on the bass, the drummers amped up and girl howdy, we were rockin'. Big Bad Gina ripped out a rollicking blues tune and Holly Near sang the inspirational "Mountain Song."

Somewhere in there it was my turn. I started my medley of classic women's music with Therese Edell's "Emma." Immediately, Holly Near jumped up to join me. It was all I could do to keep focused. C'mon aliens, don't fail me now. As I segued into other songs, various performers onstage accompanied me. The audience sang, too. On Maxine Feldman's "Amazon" I saw hands go up in the air and heard their voices joyfully rise with mine. The medley gathered in energy with Cris Williamson's "Song of the Soul" and to end, Holly's "Something about the Women." I levitated with happiness. It's for these moments that I do music.

We ended the round robin with a lively "Will the Circle Be Unbroken." Kara Barnard tore the top off her guitar ripping out a great solo. Guitars, banjo, drums and mandolin rang out with the audience on their feet, singing along.

Now that's a jam, baby.

The energy continued in the hotel lobby, because some of us weren't ready to quit. After a couple of songs the management politely asked us to move. What, people were trying to sleep at midnight? We traipsed into a room where we could shut the door and jam some more. We sang everything from Martine's "Hallelujah" to rounds learned in Girl Scouts. Around two a.m. I finally ran out of gas and floated back to my room.

I woke up way too early on Sunday morning. Damn hormones. Some women get hot flashes, I wake up at oh-dark-thirty every damn morning. Maybe the energy from the previous night would continue to fuel me, I theorized, and besides, now I could go to breakfast and hang with everyone some more. I listened in on a conversation about Africa between Holly Near, Sharon Katz and my globetrotting wife (who works for a humanitarian organization). At another table, I talked with a woman who asked how she could further support women's music. I moved on and laughed with performer buddies about all that had happened that weekend.

After a quick trip to the crafts area, I hightailed it to the main stage for my second emcee gig. My batteries were certainly low at this point, but I managed to sound somewhat coherent as I introduced the drum chorus, the festival choir and the WIA's (Women in the Arts) Got Talent finalists, Ginger Doss and Barb Neligan. Hilarious comic Dana Goldberg was on after that. I introduced funny woman Julie Goldman after her, but couldn't stay because my flight was leaving soon.

As I sat at the airport, my brain ran a happy festival movie—a pastiche of lovely music, laughter and beautiful women, including that amazing performer jam.

Holly Near sang with me. I can die now.

CHAPTER FORTY-FIVE

NERFA Has Nothing To Do With Toys, But Playing Sure Helps

The New England Regional Folk Alliance conference is all about folk music and in the fall of 2012, I was excited to go. It'd been awhile since I attended one of these orgies of music and I figured it was about time, especially since this event centered on happenings in the Northeast US. As a proud new resident of Ottawa, Ontario, it was time to meet My People. Or at least, My People-who-lived-nearby-who-might-book-me-for-their-venue. As a bonus, I'd get to hear a bunch of live acoustic music and that can't be bad, unless it involved out-of-tune accordions.

The Catskills resort was packed when I arrived on Thursday afternoon. A seething mass of humanity, many armed with guitars, stood shoulder to shoulder in the huge lobby, a roar of happy conversation rising to the ceiling. Some were in the long line for the registration table, others were in clusters, drinks in hand and laughing with their fellow folk junkies. The line to the hotel front desk was short so I opted for checking in there first.

I quickly got my key from the efficient desk clerk, and then made three trips back and forth to my car, trudging across the lobby, into the elevators and to my room on the fifth floor. It would've been easier had I brought a dolly, but my small rental Nissan didn't have space for that. The hotel luggage trolleys were elsewhere—not surprising since everyone and their bass player were trying to get piles of instruments and other equipment to their rooms. I had two instruments, a couple of suitcases, two bags loaded with snacks and promo material, and four folding chairs. I was sleeping in a showcase room, so I needed all that stuff.

Showcase room? Chairs? Yep, at this conference, performers move the furniture, set up folding chairs and offer live folk music in their hotel rooms. In addition to these guerrilla showcases, there were also the conference-sponsored showcases in the bigger rooms and theaters downstairs. We hope that the booker for the Philadelphia Folk Festival will catch our act and insist that we headline their next event. Or at least, a house concert organizer in Poughkeepsie who's looking for one more musician for the year.

Right away, I posted fliers advertising my shows. Even though we were supposed to stick to approved bulletin boards, there were pieces of paper everywhere, all shouting, "We're great! Come to our showcases! Book us!" Every surface was spilling over with brightly colored piles of paper. The insides of the elevators were covered. I even saw posters in the bathrooms. The conference gave us a comprehensive directory of all the showcases, but at several pages, who could actually use it? Maybe these fliers helped some stand out from the crowd. Or maybe we were needlessly killing a lot of trees...neon orange ones.

It was fun to wander from room to room and hear the scheduled live music. It was even more fun to discover a great late-night bluegrass jam in a stairway or a lone pianist in the lobby, playing beautiful ethereal instrumentals at six a.m. Sometimes I'd join them and sometimes, just listen. On Thursday night, the first evening, I fell in with The Tres Amigos, a great trio from New York City. These young guys seemed to be everywhere at this event and always wore matching vintage cowboy shirts, with embroidered red roses and pearl snaps. "Makes laundry easy," one of them joked. We played through some folk and bluegrass, even though my only cowboy (Cowgirl? Cowperson?) shirt was hanging at home. (Surprised I own one? My mother wore it in the 1955 Phoenix Rodeo Day Parade. It's black with white leather fringe—a thing of beauty. Find my 1992 album *Center of Balance*, and you'll see me wearing it.) I joined in with their lively accordion (in-tune), acoustic guitar and saxophone. Ah yes, the traditional folk saxophone.

I woke up stupid-early on Friday morning and couldn't go back to sleep so I stumbled down to the lobby. My roommates hadn't gone to bed until the wee hours and they didn't need me banging around the room.

Ah, roommates. One was my friend, Bernice Lewis, an amicable singer-songwriter from Massachusetts. Having a bad time with Bernice is simply against the law. To save money, we had a third roommate, a woman I'd never met before. Bernice doesn't sleep well when she shares a bed so I volunteered to sleep with the stranger. Not the first time I've ever done that. (Mom, cover your eyes.) We did our best not to cross that invisible middle line one draws in such situations. She kept much later hours than I. It was halfway through the second day before we actually met.

So on Friday morning, I was in the lobby without much to do. It wasn't long before I'd borrowed a guitar, gathered around the piano and jammed with several others on "City of New Orleans" and more. One of the jammers, a skinny long-haired guitar player, knew an endless array of old folk songs. Later on, I realized that he was a guy I talked to many times over the years because he runs a coffeehouse on the East Coast. He'd never booked me, though, because he required a live recording of a show as an audition. I have terrible luck with live recordings—either the equipment fails or I do—and never had anything to give him. Now, I thought, I don't have to give him a CD. We jammed for over an hour. Surely he had an idea of how my show might go.

I contacted him after the conference. First, he apologized for missing my showcases.

"But we jammed on Friday morning," I reminded him.

"We did?" he responded.

* * *

There were lots of workshops and panel discussions. After touring for many years, there isn't much this old dog needs to learn. What I really needed was a workshop about how to go back to my twenties and learn to be a better guitar player. I'm all right now, but only because I worked my ass off in middle-age. Perhaps that's not so bad. I plan to live to be a hundred, so look for me in the old lesbian home. I'll be the one stopping strangers in the lobby and excitedly asking, "Wanna hear my new song?"

There were no time travel workshops, though. I did, however, attend the house concert peer group. While I've played at house concerts for years, I've only started presenting them and was eager to bond with others doing the same. (House concerts are just what they sound like. It's a great intimate venue that most musicians and audiences love.) Unfortunately, the facilitators, a Canadian couple, let a few people go on and on. That's what happens when you put Canadians in charge. They're too polite to pull out the big hook when someone is in the middle of their *War and Peace* recitation. (It's a stereotype that Canadians are overly polite. But there's a shred of truth, definitely—when you need to turn left into traffic, they actually let you in. Try that in Los Angeles.) By the time everyone introduced themselves and said something about their house concerts, there was little time for discussion.

The program specifically said the group was only for house concert presenters. Still, there was a small group of performers present. Granted, I'm a musician too, but I wear two hats. Most of the musicians were very respectful, so I don't have much to complain about, however, the young musician who sat next to me droned on and on about his experiences at several conferences, actually bragging about how good he was and by the way, he was doing a showcase there and blah, blah, blah. I feigned interest in the carpeting. I wasn't the only one examining its worn threads. When it was my turn, I got as far as saying my name and that I present house concerts, when one of the organizers interrupted with, "We need to make time for everyone." Huh? We let Caesar here go on about conquering Rome, but I can't finish my sentence? Obviously, these were not the Canadians who would let me turn left. They must be from Montreal. (That's a little joke for Canadian readers. We love to make fun of Quebec drivers and we can, because assault weapons are illegal in Canada.)

Throughout the conference, I ran into a few people like Caesar. At dinner one night, I sat near someone who helped organize a concert series. At first, I thought, great, I can schmooze this guy. After his fifteen-minute speech on the wonders of every performer who'd ever played his venue, I turned my attention to the musician on the other side of me, someone who actually knew how to participate in a conversation. After the meal, I asked a friend about the first guy and she commented, "Oh, that's Harry. Even the people who work with him avoid him." I thought she was kidding until I saw him at a couple more meals, sitting alone at a table meant for eight. I felt sorry for the man. Not enough to sit with him, though. I'm going to hell for that.

On Friday night I attended the traditional music jam offered by a group from New York. I happily mashed through sea shanties, old folk songs, rounds, and whatever else people wanted to sing. As a singer-songwriter, you wouldn't think I'd know many of these tunes, but I remembered a lot of them from Girl Scouts. We played John Prine's "Paradise" even though it's not a traditional folk song. It sure sounds like one, though, and we all knew the tune.

When someone started "Cruel War," I felt the tears come. It's a passionate song in a minor key about loving someone enough to enlist and go to war along with them. I hadn't sung it since I was a teen in scouting. It reminded me of my dad, too, who I lost just a month before. He didn't sing that kind of music, but it made me think of the times my family would all sing together. The guy leading the song saw my tears and joked, "Hey, I don't sound that bad, do I?" I elected not to smack him. Instead, I kept singing and wiping my eyes.

I also stopped at the room proudly displaying the red and white maple leaf because another reason for going to the conference was to meet Canadian musicians. And you can never have too many friends who'll let you make a left turn. Only a handful of people were there, but I got to play one of my funny songs about Canada and folks seemed to enjoy it.

Over the four days, I performed at a couple of guerilla showcases and pressed some palms. However, I quickly realized that with five or six hundred musicians and maybe a couple hundred presenters, including every tiny house concert from here to Maine, it wasn't going to be a gig-getting bonanza.

I made sure to attend some official showcases so I could hear acts in a real theater setting, not just sitting on a bed in someone's hotel room. Most of what I heard was very good—I especially loved singer-songwriter Zoe Lewis's quirky songs and Suzie Vinnick's excellent bluesy guitar work—but was disheartened to see one performer who shouldn't have been there. Not only was her band far from folk, but her singing was a tad off-key and her songwriting, too simplistic. Most of her lyrics were repeated phrases, like what you'd hear in a dance club, and certainly not appropriate for an audience used to rich metaphors and long story songs. ("Wreck of the Edmund Fitzgerald" anyone?) She was African American and it was a mostly white crowd, and I hoped that had nothing to do with her getting this choice showcase.

I've always loved Vance Gilbert's approach. He wasn't at the conference but I thought of him because he's one of the few well-known African American singer-songwriters who's popular on the folk circuit. In the early nineties, I heard him at the Folks Festival in Colorado. He spied a white sheriff standing guard on a cliff near the audience. "What?" he quipped, "are you waiting for the black guy to do something illegal?"

At eleven thirty p.m., I facilitated a women's song circle in the Local 1000 room. (Local 1000 is a special union for touring musicians. I love being a member.) Normally I'd be asleep at this time of the night, but like a good conference attendee, I'd taken a nap. Proudly dubbed a showcase-free zone, it was a chance for us to make music together without having to worry about impressing a booker. We had a wonderful time. With musicians like Tret Fure, how could we not?

Over the weekend, I often hung out in my own room. My roommate, Bernice, organized kick-ass showcases there that always had a full house. I got to hear her, too. I love her well-written songs and clear, lovely voice on her solo work and as a part of the duo, Ladies Auxiliary Ukulele Orchestra. And of course, she had the good taste to book me. Really fun shows, but it meant that I couldn't go to bed until after the showcases were done at two a.m.—hard for a morning person. (I'm not a Real Musician. If I could do all my gigs between nine a.m. and noon, I'd be happy.) I was lucky. Some of the showcase rooms went on much later.

The conference was organized well—surprising since it was almost entirely volunteer-run. Even the hard-working director, Dianne Tankle, was unpaid.

Some didn't like the somewhat-tired resort where it was held. I thought it was just fine. As you've seen in other chapters, I've definitely seen worse. The hotel fed us and again, a few folks didn't like the food, but I appreciated the variety. (However, I was the weird kid in the grade school lunchroom who ate everyone's peas, so you might want to take that with a grain of salt.) They even had soy milk at breakfast and a gluten-free option at dinner. Lines always moved quickly. The waiters were graciously efficient and so were the other hotel employees. The maids deserved combat pay for all the trash we left behind.

It was great to see friends like Martin Swinger, who offered an ear and a shoulder when the lack of sleep and constant promo got the better of me. He's one of the few out gay men in folk music. Besides him, I can only think of two more. When someone tries to tell me that the folk music world isn't homophobic, I think of Martin and wonder why there aren't more like him. I admire his talent and his spirit. And he gives amazing hugs.

On Saturday morning, near the end of the conference, Bernice inquired brightly, "Want to take a walk?" I jumped at the chance to get some exercise and to get away from the constant frenzy inside. As we walked out into the sunshine, I realized that it was the first time I'd been outside in two days. We strolled in the crisp fall air and chatted about recording new albums, our families and our music. We're about the same age and had been at this performance thing a long time. We found a river, stood on its banks, threw back our heads and sang "Down by the Riverside" in harmony, with no one to hear us except the rushing water and the nearly bare trees.

Back inside, I realized there were people at the event that I seemed to run into everywhere, like the woman who was always dressed in spandex, expensive jewelry and nose-bleed-high heels, exclaiming to everyone that she was recently divorced. The first time I heard her story, I listened politely because, hey, she ran a venue and it might mean a gig. It didn't take me long to realize that she'd book an out-of-tune accordion player, provided he was male and single, before she'd even listen to my audition CD. There were also folks I wanted to see and never did, like the New York City musician that I'd connected with over email beforehand. It was crazy, with musicians thrusting fliers at everyone and jamming happening everywhere. (I mean, *everywhere*. At a similar conference a few years ago, there was a jam circle in a janitor's closet and a fiddle player in the elevator.) It mixed into this stew of joy and desperation, sometimes savory and sometimes sour.

By the time Sunday morning rolled around, I felt like I'd run a marathon on a rocky mountainside in my bare feet. My hormones awoke me at the usual too-early time of six a.m. My roommates were just dragging in, raving about an all-girl jam they'd been at most of the night. How I wish I could've joined them. I knew I'd have a long drive that day, though.

At that hour, I was able to get a hotel luggage trolley, so I loaded it up with everything for one trip. As I pushed it through the lobby, a woman came from seemingly nowhere and offered a hand. When I asked why she was up that early, she gave me a warm smile and replied that she'd been up all night listening to music and figured going to bed would be useless. We laughed as she helped me pack my little car. I still had one functioning brain cell and it told me to ask her who she was because after all, she might be the booker for the Philadelphia Folk Festival. As it turned out, she did book a small venue in Connecticut. She didn't grimace when I handed her my card and instead, wished me a safe drive home, folded her hands, bowed slightly, added, "Peace," and disappeared as quickly as she appeared.

I travel better on a full stomach so I grabbed a quick breakfast, sat in the lobby, and listened to a ragged trio that had been playing all night. One of them, a haggard-looking young man in a wrinkled shirt and worn jeans, sipped from a whiskey bottle as he slumped over a guitar and sang the oddly appropriate "Sunday Morning Going Down" by Kris Kristofferson. I added a harmony to the last line before I headed off into the quiet morning. Thank God for dark chocolate mint M&Ms and a large latte from Starbucks, or I never would've made the seven-hour drive home without crashing into a bridge abutment.

Was the conference worth it? I don't know. I really enjoyed the live music and loved jamming. It was a lot of money to spend, though, and the gigs I snagged as a result won't pay for everything. As a cranky middle-aged musician, I'm not sure about staying up all night just because there's a good jam. Maybe this whole experience will be like childbirth. I'll forget about the pain, remember the joy and want to do it again. Perhaps I'll just learn to sing and sleep at the same time. Or keep schmoozing and loading my car at the same time because the woman who helped me on Sunday morning gave me a gig, and I didn't even have to play "City of New Orleans" with her.

CHAPTER FORTY-SIX

The Lord of Beginnings

It was the type of motel where their idea of landscaping was a little gravel and a lot of dandelions. Painted orange with accents of deep maroon, this Econo Lodge rose like a modern-day brothel on a small hill just off I-81 in central Pennsylvania. I didn't see any ladies of the evening but I could just hear a consultant advising them that these colors would be noticed by weary motorists. It worked for me. I often stay at budget motels painted in garish colors and even have my favorite chains, but I don't usually stay at Econo Lodges since they tend to hover around the one-star rating and that's being generous. This one looked pretty new, though, and anything built after 2010 is more likely to be without permanent rust rings in the bathroom or huge carpet stains you hope aren't blood. This was May of 2013, and generally rust stains take longer. Yes, I am an expert.

It had been a long day of driving. I dragged my exhausted behind in the front door. The entryway sported several large plastic plants, including an undecorated Christmas tree. I took a few more steps and noticed the small kitchen to the left, with groupings of tables and chairs, a big hand-lettered sign in front proclaiming "Breakfast six a.m. to nine a.m." To my right was a front desk of faux marble and veneer oak. On the other side of this counter sat a middle-aged guy, comfortable in an overstuffed chair, reading a fat book with a picture of Ganesha, a Hindu god sometimes known as the Lord of Beginnings, on the cover. I smiled to myself, thinking that this was a good sign. The man looked up over his reading glasses, sighed, hefted himself out of the chair, took two steps forward and looked at me expectantly.

"I'd like a room."

"Nonmumblemumble?"

"What?"

Looking directly at me and talking louder, he enunciated, "Non-smoking?"

"Yes."

He shoved his hand forward, palm up and mumbled again.

"Pardon me?"

"Card."

I handed him my credit card. He tapped on the keyboard in front of him.

"Dmumble mumble?"

"Excuse me?"

"Driver's license."

I handed it to him and waited. He finished his paperwork, printed out a receipt and slid it across the counter with my credit card, license and a plastic credit card-type key. I signed next to his X, turned and headed down the hallway to my room.

Why someone decided that a pink floral bedspread looked fetching with a brown striped carpet, I'll never know. The rest of my room's décor included nearly-colorless beige walls, except one that was the same maroon color as the door. Completing it all was a watercolor print of a quaint fox hunting scene. The bathtub had no rust stains, but there were several long cigarette burns. Ah well, I didn't come here to photograph it for *Motel Beautiful*. The sheets looked clean, the room was cheap and the carpet wasn't sticky, so I was good to go.

The Wi-Fi was fast enough to watch a few videos before I fell asleep to the lullaby of an idling diesel.

The next morning, I got dressed and made my way to the lobby for some of that free breakfast. A warmer held links of sausage sitting in pools of yellow oil and perfect circles of what I think were scrambled eggs. I elected to get the cold cereal and milk at the other end of the table. I got some orange juice out of the dispenser. It had an odd bitter taste. (When was the machine last cleaned? Never mind…sometimes, it's better not to know.) The coffee wasn't bad with a lot of milk and sugar. I carefully balanced the bowl and two cups and headed back to my room. I gently set one cup on the ground, fished the key out of my pocket and slipped it in the lock. It flashed red and the handle refused to turn. I pulled out the card and tried again. Same thing. I set the rest of my breakfast on the floor and headed back to the lobby. My friend at the front desk was back in his chair, only this time he was reading a newspaper. His outfit of plaid pajama bottoms, flip-flops and T-shirt told me that he hadn't been up very long.

"My key won't work. There's a red light."

He grunted, thrust his hand out, grabbed my card, punched some numbers in a machine, ran it through the side slot, and handed it back. I walked back to my room and swiped the card. Again, I got a red light and a still-locked door. I returned to the lobby.

"It still doesn't work."

He sighed, grunted, mumbled something, then turned around, grabbed a shirt, thrust his arms in it and buttoned it just before heading off in the direction of my room. I followed.

He stuck the card in. The lock flashed red.

"Huh. Red light."

"Um, yeah."

He shoved it in a few times, each time trying the handle, like some miracle was going to happen. Where was the Lord of Locks when you needed him? He muttered something about it being locked from the other side. I informed him that no one was in the room.

He grunted, then headed off down the hall. I wasn't sure if that meant, "Stay here, I'm trying something else," or, "You're screwed, good luck getting into the room."

A few minutes later, he returned with a screwdriver and a key. He pried a small plastic disc off another lock, inserted the key and after two tries, opened the door. I thanked him but since he was already halfway down the hall, I doubt he heard me.

Another long day of driving awaited me so I quickly ate my breakfast and packed up. I opened the door and leaned a chair against it because the clerk hadn't given me another key and I couldn't take any more of his warm customer relations. I quickly loaded the car. As I motored away, I wondered if there was a Lord of Endings. Just to be sure, I muttered a quick "Thank you" to him.

CHAPTER FORTY-SEVEN

Chasing Hallelujah

It was 2013 and one of those gigs I never should've taken. I thought the crowd might be noisy and inattentive, but I was already in the area and this popular café in Carrboro, NC, was bound to have some walk-in traffic. A bonus was that I was doing the gig with my friend Wes Collins, a really great songwriter and one of the nicest guys you'd ever want to meet. If only the Indigo Girls weren't playing in the area on the same night. I knew where most middle-aged lesbians would be. Heck, if I didn't have the gig, I would've been at their concert, too. I do have fans that fall outside of that demographic, so I was hopeful.

Wes arrived just before I did. "They want us to set up there," he said, pointing to a dark corner of the cavernous space. I remembered the place as having a small stage and lighting, but either they'd taken it out or I was confusing it with one of the thousands of other gigs I'd played. I looked up and saw a lone lamp swinging above our heads. It would have to do for stage lighting. We moved a huge scratched-up table and pushed back a couple of chairs, set up the equipment, did a quick sound check and waited for eight p.m.

The place was almost empty except for a few people hunched over laptops, huge cups of coffee beside them. To my left was a table of folks talking and laughing. A straight couple slumped against each other on a worn couch in the middle about halfway back from the stage area. Two beat-up, sagging brown leather chairs hunched in front of them. Scattered about the room were mismatched tables and chairs, as if a truck from the Salvation Army had backed up and disgorged its contents. The floor was cement, painted what was once a glossy maroon, now patched and faded into several colors. Behind our stage area was a mysterious giant pool of water. At first I thought someone had spilled a drink. However, it seemed to grow as the night progressed. Wes and I carefully avoided it.

As I stood off to the side, a woman stepped up to me, grinned and said, "Remember me?" I didn't, but then she reminded me... Oh, yeah, she'd organized a show I did in the area last year. And she wasn't an Indigo Girls fan. Bless her, she brought a friend. They settled in at a small table to the right of the stage. I sat with them, friendly conversation flowing easily about many topics, including some of the different housing situations we'd been in. One of the women was staying with a friend who was into flamingos. Also an Elvis fan, memorabilia from him crowding every available surface not taken up by flamingo kitsch.

It got me talking about some of the places where I'd stayed. We laughed about the Wi-Fi in the house where I was currently staying and how the only way I could get online was if I stood right next to a certain window and even then it only worked in thirty-second increments—not so good for someone who's trying to finish a book and an album. It didn't rattle me too much because I knew there was a Starbucks a couple of miles away. But after making the trek I'd found that indeed, they had Wi-Fi, but it was so weak I kept getting kicked off. My laptop showed that there was a signal from a store across the street. It had been hard to give up the comfy chair and the soft music of the Starbucks for that hard wooden chair at the Krispy Kreme, a refrigerator loudly humming to my left. Their Wi-Fi was strong, though and, as one of my companions laughingly pointed out, at least their doughnuts were good (especially in the morning when they're warm and fresh). We also giggled about the fact that we were all wearing the same color of shirt, a dark pink.

Wes went on first. I love his work, so it was a treat to hear his contemplative songs, including one called "Chasing Hallelujah." It's got what we call in the business a hooky chorus. When I listen to his album, it's the one song I hit repeat on a few times. He introduced the song by telling a story about waking up in the morning and sleepily avoiding the toys his daughter has left throughout the house. However, it could be taken as a metaphor for gaining awareness in your life and not quite getting there, hence "chasing." This gig felt a little like that. Hallelujah was close, but just out of range and frankly, I didn't feel like running.

I sang harmony with him on that and a couple of other songs.

Wes and I have written a song together. We were part of a songwriter's circle for a while that met monthly. One month, we had an assignment—take the lyrics of someone else's song and write a new melody. Wes drew my song "Drive All Night." The next month, he returned with a great new melody and arrangement for my words. While my version is an upbeat love song, his is moodier with a cool fingerpicked guitar accompaniment. That night Wes did his version of "Drive All Night" and I followed up with mine. It was wonderful to hear them back to back. The audience seemed to enjoy it, too. Ah yes, the audience. While there were pockets of interested folks, including my sisters in pink (who hung on every word and laughed loudly at the funny lines), mostly I was looking at empty chairs. In back of them was a bank of huge windows. I could see a busy bar across the street, their small outdoor patio packed with happy customers. Next to it was a Wendy's. I had a clear view of the drive-through, busy the entire night, headlights of cars steadily gliding out like some crazy freeway where you could only drive five mph and at the end, you get a bag of hamburgers. As night fell, part of the sign out front lit up. "Wen" it proclaimed. I contemplated this Zen message as I played.

My friend Paula took the tip jar around. We joked that her six-year-old should've been there. Kids always help you get great tips. Paula can be quite adorable, though, and she turned on the charm.

I don't usually take jobs where I'm paid with tips because too often, I end up with a jar of change and a few one dollar bills. Ever the optimist, when I booked the café a few months ago I remembered that one coffeehouse in Ohio where I got a couple hundred dollars in the tip jar and also, I didn't know about the Indigo Girls' show. (It's not the first time that kind of thing has happened. During one Midwest tour in the nineties, I was following Melissa Etheridge's tour around. Either she was on the same night or women had already blown their budget on her show and couldn't afford mine. I should've sent her a bill.)

People filtered out as the night progressed. A former student of mine and his wife came in later. He's a banjo player who favors old-time folk so I was sure to include a couple of my folkier numbers. As it neared time to close, I looked up at the bright red light across the street shouting "Wen" and thought, now. I finished with a funny tune and slipped offstage.

Wes and I said goodbye to the handful of people still there at eleven p.m.—at least, the people who weren't focused on a laptop screen, earbuds firmly in place. As I packed up equipment, Wes went through the tip jar. "Wow," he exclaimed, "we got more than I thought!" He smiled and handed me my half, $23. He recently started his performing career and is still at the stage where he can't believe he gets paid for playing songs. I just grinned.

After loading our cars, we stood outside in the warm summer night and excitedly talked about our new albums, both recorded at the same place and with some of the same musicians. It was midnight by the time we exchanged warm hugs and parted. I wearily opened my car door, settled inside and turned the ignition. Maybe hallelujah would be at the next gig.

CHAPTER FORTY-EIGHT

Plinky-plink and Skippy-skip:
The Recording of *Dare*

"Remember this as the time when you still like the songs," intoned Jim Henry, the CD producer for my 1999 release, *Drive All Night*, on our first day in the studio. It may seem like a mean thing to say, but it was a joke we both understood. By then I was on my fifth album and I'd learned that during the recording process we'd hear the songs so many times that by the end, I could barely listen to them. It's necessary, though. Through practice and then recording the layers of instruments, each song could be heard forty or fifty times. Also, unlike a live performance that goes by quickly, a recording is permanent and every musician wants to be remembered for that great guitar solo or that perfectly executed harmony vocal, not that off-beat drum hit in the first chorus of the second cut. That kind of excellence doesn't come with one quick take.

I was beyond excited to record *Dare*, my tenth album. Sounds ominous, doesn't it? Back when I toured full-time I put out a new album every two or three years. While I still tour, teaching is now my main source of income, so I need to stay home more for my students. That and moving to Canada derailed me for a while.

Anyway, there I was, making a new album, my first one of all-new material in eight years.

All albums start with a lot of planning. This is the boring part—putting together a budget and thinking about logistics like what songs to include, where to record and what musicians, photographer, graphic designer and duplicator to hire. I've got a group of professionals who've done a great job on my earlier recordings so, mostly, that's who I went with this time. If it ain't broke, don't fix it. I chose Chris Rosser to engineer and co-produce this project because I recorded a couple of songs with him three years ago and loved it. He's fast, creative, affordable and he gets a great sound. And, he's one of the nicest guys on the planet. If I'm going to work with someone that intensely, and see them for that many hours, it better be someone I like.

Raising money for albums is often difficult. My first release, *Heart Resort*, was financed with money from a fan who heard me at an open mike. I cut every corner I could, including hiring my musician friends for free and booking the cheapest studio I could find. The next project was funded by a loan from a wealthy friend and some presales. It was recorded in a much nicer studio with musicians I could afford to pay. The next few recordings were funded by fans. I'd make appeals from the stage for presales and loans and after a year, usually had the money I needed. *Dare* wasn't as hard for me because a family member gave me a good amount of money. I added a few dollars earned from teaching, plus some money from a crowd funding campaign.

Albums aren't cheap. While *Heart Resort* cost $1,500, it was released only on cassette at a time when gas was under a dollar a gallon. Subsequent releases cost a lot more. The budget for *Dare* was $8,000. I could spend a lot more, especially on promotion, but was still able to put out a quality recording. My most expensive album was probably 1999's *Drive All Night*. I spent $25,000 on it. I was touring full-time then so I was able to sell enough to make a profit. Still it was a gamble, especially for someone who sometimes didn't even make $25,000 in a year. After making my first professional album, 1989's *Closer to Home*, I watched in wonder as the Yellow Freight driver delivered a pallet of LPs and I thought, I could've bought a car with that money. (Not that I would, of course, but you get the idea.) Fortunately, I sold enough of those albums to pay back the investor and make money. (In fact, I did so well with it that Reggae, who worked for the distributor Ladyslipper, had to reorder it several times in just a few weeks. During one call, she laughed and said in an exasperated voice, "I don't order this often from all of my suppliers.")

I know this all sounds like a ton of money, but it's peanuts compared to what major labels spend. Eight thousand dollars could be their latte budget for one afternoon.

I recorded *Dare* in Asheville, North Carolina because that's where Chris and some of the musicians were. I planned recording in June of 2013, a time when I needed to be Durham, about a four-hour drive east, for teaching and performance gigs a few days of the week, so Chris and I scheduled Mondays and Tuesdays in the month of June. By the end of the month, I'd have a finished recording.

I never quit writing songs in the years I didn't release an album so I had a lot of songs to consider—twenty-eight of them, way too many for one recording. Some of those were good for a concert or two, but certainly nothing I'd put in a permanent form. Still, how to decide? I enlisted the help of several friends and sent them rough recordings. I also got input from my partner and I did a concert in Ottawa where the audience got ballots. They all gave me great advice, helping me to narrow it down to fourteen songs. Some pieces were a surprise, like "The Lucky Ones," a solemn song about war that I'd never performed in concert. Almost everyone said I should include it. My friend Kara said that "Run," a tune inspired by my Facebook friends, was the funniest new one I did, so I chose that one, too. (Some people post photos of their breakfast. My Facebook friends get to help me write songs. See how much fun I am?)

Once the groundwork was laid, it was time to get on the road. The drive to North Carolina was on two beautiful days in late May, the trees a bright green, topped with the bluest sky and cottony clouds. I was in a great mood, contemplating all that lay before me.

You can't just walk into a studio and play. Lots of practice needs to happen. I'm a pretty good player, but even musicians at my level need to polish up their work. Everything is played to a click track—a simple beat—so when the different layers of music are added, all of the musicians can start and end at the same time, playing smoothly and cohesively. That means my scratch vocals and guitar—the first things recorded—have to be right on the beat.

I practiced each song several times with a metronome before I left town.

For my first visit to Asheville, I stayed with friends in their beautiful home. Before heading out to the studio on that Monday, I found a comfortable couch bathed in morning sunlight, set up the metronome and played through every song, sometimes more than once. I was ready.

I walked in on that first day and instantly felt at home in Chris's little home studio, soothing light green walls surrounding me, like the greenery outside. Chris bent his six-foot-seven frame down to hug me, smiled and asked how I was doing. We chatted for a few minutes and then got down to work. He'd already set out a chair and two mikes—one for my vocal and one for my guitar. There's a science to mike placement and where in the room the musician sits. For my *A Promise of Light* album, I sat in the hallway of an old farmhouse because the acoustics were good there. Kiya, my engineer, sat in what was a bedroom. Chris's studio was only one room, but there was one sweet spot where he put everyone to record.

His computer screens showed the recording program, all ready to go. (I'd include more technical stuff here, but it all looked like the cockpit of a space shuttle to me.) I recorded my scratch vocals with an instrument, usually a guitar. These are the tracks that every song is built on. Later on, I'd replace those tracks with something more refined. I recorded the scratch for fourteen songs in three and a half hours. Chris said that was some kind of record and of course I demanded a prize. We spent the rest of the time listening to what was recorded while Chris wrote up detailed charts for the musicians. I had charts, too. They only had the words and the names of the chords, though. He wrote out something so thorough that the band could play it well on the first run-through. Ah, the beauty of having a very knowledgeable musician as your engineer and co-producer.

I record on my stomach. When I'm in a studio for seven or eight hours, I need energy, and mine came from roasted nuts, fresh cherries and these wonderful fig-raspberry bars that I found in the whole foods section. Record…eat…record…eat…my kind of job.

Day two was spent laying down percussion tracks. Like many drummers I've met, River Guerguerian has endless energy. He often has a serious look and with his wire-framed glasses he looked like some hip librarian. River's a very skilled drummer, though, with experience on everything from Turkish oud music to American jazz—perfect for someone like me who doesn't settle in just one genre. He intently listened to my scratch tracks, read Chris's charts and recorded his parts. For some songs, he got it in one take, but we did two, just so we'd have a backup. Some required a bit of discussion—should "Menopause Mambo" have congas or a drum set? (We chose the latter.) Would a cymbal sound good over the bridge of "Hold Me?" (Yes.) Would a "hot for teacher" beat sound good on "Yoga Teacher?" (Definitely.) Should "Black and White" be "swishy" and not "backbeaty?" (Yes. That's all drummer talk, by the way. I *think* I understood River and Chris.) He didn't have just one shaker, he had a whole bag, all with different sounds—some that were subtle enough for the quieter songs, and some brighter-sounding ones that were perfect for the bigger numbers.

River told me my rhythm was so good on "Dare" (the title song) that we should keep the scratch guitar track. That's a high compliment from a drummer. None of my hats will fit anymore.

I love what River did. At the end of the day, "Bellydancer" had a wonderful dance beat, with doumbek (Turkish hand drum), riq (Turkish tambourine) and cajon (wooden box drum). "Yoga Teacher" had a solid rock back beat and "Menopause Mambo" had a lively Latin feel.

River and Chris are a crack-up. They're old friends and the banter back and forth had me in giggles a lot of the time. At one point, Chris had to stop recording because a loud plane was flying overheard. River looked up and said in a matter-of-fact way, "I was just thinking about Amelia Earhart." We joked about a lot of things, including combining genres—pop/folk became "polk" and folk/jazz was "fazz." All day, there was a running joke about *Planet of the Apes* that I never understood, but the incongruence made me laugh every time.

After "Carla Williams Kissed Me," River quoted some of the words: "Some tasted like candy, some made me want to run." Chris teased, "You've played with me for years and you don't know any of my lyrics." It's true—most of the drummers I've worked with don't focus on the words, just the feel. That's okay because I don't hire most of them to sing.

I took notes and during a break, Chris jokingly warned River, "Be careful what you say, she's writing a book."

"Just make Chris look good," River replied with a straight face.

Partway through the day, the computer gave an error message, so Chris had to spend a few minutes rebooting it. We joked that it was because it was overwhelmed from the egos of so many musicians in one room. That couldn't be farther from the truth—rather, there was a spirit of cooperation and respect.

At the end of that day, Chris made me a copy of what we'd recorded so I'd have something to practice with. On the following Monday, I'd record my permanent guitar work. It needed to be spot-on, matching River's beats. If we had to spend extra hours fixing my parts, it would come out of my pocket.

I journeyed back to Durham to do some teaching. The following week, it was time for day three in the studio. I was so amped to lay down my permanent guitar tracks that I was afraid I'd play everything double time.

You might be wondering why we're recording the instruments one at a time instead of getting everyone together in the studio. Back in the day, that's how recordings were always done and while that sometimes worked, more often than not, the bass player or someone would make a mistake and everyone would have to play the song over. The way we were doing it (and the way most modern recordings are made), if anyone made a mistake, they were the only ones who had to play it over. Also, you get more control over the individual elements and don't have to worry if you can hear the drums through the vocal mike. Or the drums through the guitar mike. Pretty much, the drums through anything because they can be damn loud.

I did an album a few years ago where we did some of the tracks live—i.e., with several instruments at once—and while we got a cool live sound, we ended up with mistakes that we couldn't fix. I'm not so anal that I have to take out every string squeak, but I don't want to have to deal with that prominent vocal clam, just because there was too much of the drums in the mix for us to adjust the mistake. (If you can hear the drums in the vocal mike and you turn down the vocals to hide that bad note that was sung, you're also turning down the volume of the drums and surprisingly, sometimes that makes them too soft, at least for that second.)

For my 1995 album, *Never Assume*, we recorded the mandolin at the same time as another instrument. We put Orville Johnson in a utility closet so the other instrument sounds wouldn't creep into his mix. And of course, after he was done, we had to make a big deal about him coming out of the closet.

For *Dare*, I listened to the drums and scratch vocals in headphones as two mikes recorded the guitar. We couldn't use speakers because the mikes would record that, too. The mikes were so sensitive that if you listened to my guitar tracks alone, you could hear me breathing. If it was a soft breath, it was no problem. (I am reminded of a classic Meg Christian album where you can hear her sigh just before the start of the song. It makes me feel like I'm right there in the studio with her.) However, if it was a bigger breath, it could be distracting (as would the guitar brushing up against my shirt or the tapping of my foot). And if you add the other musicians' gulps of air, sometimes in a brief lull in the music, you'd wonder where I got that band of asthmatics.

Every once in a while, we'd have to stop and turn on the air conditioning. It couldn't run when we were recording or the mikes would record its hum. Since it was North Carolina in June, it could get pretty steamy. Sometimes Chris and I would talk, but during one break, I felt like I was in the lounge of some classy restaurant because he pounded out a happy melody on the piano keyboard attached to his computer, grinning goofily as he finished with a flourish that sounded like a band at some mad circus. It felt good to laugh, especially after the focus of recording.

By the afternoon, I'd finished all of my instrumental parts. Mostly it was guitar but I also recorded a mandolin for "The Dream" and a ukulele for "The Boy Who Wanted to Fly." I played my dad's ukulele on the latter because it's about him and in the song I mention that he played the ukulele for his friends when he was in the air force. It didn't sound bad for an instrument that's at least fifty years old and full of scratches and cracks. It can sound a little off-key, though. Usually I'm very particular about pitch, but for this, I chose to believe that this peculiarity made it sound charming.

My hotel was in the quaint downtown of Asheville so for a late-night dinner, I had my pick of restaurants. It was such a beautiful spring night that I chose one with an outdoor patio, the Mellow

Mushroom. I enjoyed the food. However, I was dismayed at the demonic hippie jam band music playing on their stereo. Distorted guitars and strange lyrics don't fit with my vision of something with "mellow" in the name. Being in a studio gives me supersonic hearing so I doubt the other patrons even noticed the music. Or maybe they liked it and I was just too middle-aged to appreciate it.

The next day, it was Eliot Wadopian's turn to sweat behind the mikes. He's got a medium build that leans toward round, short graying hair with a beard, and a ready smile. He's one of the finest bass players I know. It was fun listening to Chris and him discuss the songs. "Play plinky-plinks," advised Chris for one song (pluck single notes as opposed to using the bow).

Eliot's string bass added a lot to several of my songs. On "Bellydancer," he played a samba beat on a song that already had Middle Eastern percussion and a Spanish-flavored guitar, written and sung by a folksinger. And yup, it worked.

He had to retune to play with that charming ukulele. Chris called it "ukulele standard tuning." As he turned the keys of his bass, Eliot commented, "With bass, you have four excuses to be wrong. With guitar, there's six." (Or four, if you're playing a beat-up ukulele.)

After he finished most of his acoustic bass work, we took a break and turned on the AC. I got him talking about the famous people with whom he's worked. He had some great stories. Unfortunately, I can't repeat most of them. However, he did say that Judy Collins was a sweetheart and he'd work with her again in a heartbeat. Great to hear nice things about an artist I admire.

During some of the breaks, we stepped outside. It was satisfying to stand barefoot in the grass, with just the sound of the birds, and remember that there was a world outside of the studio. One time, during the recording of *Never Assume*, I walked outside just in time to hear the faraway sound of a train whistle. I had just been working on "Sound of a Train."

Also at that studio were a group of friendly cats who hung around the building. My favorite was a battle-scarred orange tom named Cooter. He had a purr like an old motor boat and holding him in my lap really helped to ground me. When we recorded "When Cats Take Over the World," I wanted a purr at the end. We considered making Cooter a recording star. Instead, we settled on a sound effects CD with a recording of a real cat. It was much easier than corralling a squirmy feline who would probably rub up against the mike.

After a few minutes, Eliot got back to work, finishing one song on the acoustic and then switching to an electric bass. He sat in a half lotus position, rocking back and forth with the rhythm, his expressive face changing with the tempo and complexity of his part. We turned on the air because this bass was recorded directly into the computer (no mikes) and wouldn't pick up the AC hum. By this time it was afternoon and poor Eliot needed cooling down. Not only was he playing some hot parts, but this is a man better suited to life in a colder climate. (Funny, we started the day talking about Canada. He'd really like to move there. I offered to marry him, but remembered I was already married…and a lesbian.)

Chris and Eliot are also old friends, often calling each other "brother." Sometimes it was in a joking manner, but other times, it was sincere. It's nice to see that kind of connection between men.

It was interesting to share a small studio and bathroom with two guys. I had to put the toilet seat down. I've got three brothers, so I know the score.

By the end of the day, Eliot recorded fourteen songs. Two of the tunes were alternates, though, in case I ran out of time or money and could only release twelve songs. When I told him "Menopause Mambo" was one that might not make the cut, his face fell. "I'll record that one for free, just put it on the album," he informed me, smiling.

I was tired so it would've been nice to end the day that way. I sat on the couch the whole time, but all that intense listening can really sap your energy. It was my turn again, though. After Eliot left, I recorded lead vocals until Chris and I ran out of steam.

I'd started at ten a.m. and didn't haul my tired body out of there until ten p.m. I was so exhausted, I zoomed through a red light. I tried to find some late-night dinner, but gave up after finding that even the grocery store had closed. The dark chocolate bar I'd left in my room had to suffice.

The next day, as I drove back to Durham, my throat started to feel raw and by Thursday, I was so congested I could barely speak, much less sing. I canceled a Friday night concert and the album photo session because I looked like W.C. Fields on a bender. I holed up at the place where I was house-sitting, eating so much chicken soup that I started dreaming about armies of angry chickens charging after me.

We were tightly scheduled for the album so it had to go on. The long drive back to Asheville a few days later was hard. I was still coughing and very tired. The music pulled me through, though. There were times when I was sitting on that couch in the studio and was so damn happy about the musicians and their parts that I felt like I was floating. On days five and six, with Kara Barnard and Tory Trujillo, I had several of those levitating moments. And also, finally, some musicians who wouldn't leave the toilet seat up.

Day five started with more of that strange musicians' language. Kara sat behind the mikes with her acoustic guitar and commented that she had a lead part in mind for the skippy-skip notes I was playing on the mandolin for "The Dream." That's musician-speak for "harmony line on the mandolin solo." After completing the instrumental break in "Carla Williams Kissed Me," she asked if her guitar part should be ballsier. I asked for ovaryer. On "For Love," a song about moving to Canada, Chris asked her for Canadian riffs. (Parts of "Oh Canada"? Neil Young licks?)

I sent her a few instructions ahead of time and for "Yoga Teacher," I said simply, "Make me sound like Nirvana." So, in the studio, she dutifully replicated a short section reminiscent of "Come as You Are" and also borrowed two notes from "Smells Like Teen Spirit." Not everyone will get the musical jokes. Sometimes it's just about amusing us. I still laugh when those licks come around.

After each take, whether it was Kara's guitar part or someone else's, there'd be a moment of silence. You don't want any sound to show up as that last note fades. It also felt like we were honoring the part, holding our breath and relishing that very last sound.

Kara played guitar on a bunch of songs, and also added mandolin to a couple. I love working with her. She's been on my last several albums. I wish she could've stayed longer—she's a friend and we don't get to see each other very much—but she needed to get on the road and besides, I had more work to do. It was time to finish my vocals. I'd done most of them the week before, but still had four songs to go. Fortunately, I was only hacking up a few hair balls by this time. If I collapsed in a coughing fit, Chris could take out that part and I could record just that portion again. Oh, the beauty of the digital world.

At one point, I heard a weird humming in my headphones. I took them off and asked Chris about it. We discovered a neighbor weed whacking his yard. We stopped for a couple of minutes, and thankfully, he wasn't at it too long. When you're working in a small home studio, the outside world doesn't always cooperate. For the album *Drive All Night*, I recorded in a home studio too. We had to quit every afternoon at a certain time because a school bus would rumble by. Even in a big studio, weird sounds can interrupt recording. For one of my earlier albums, there was an amorous cricket in one of the ceiling tiles. We never did find him, but if we banged on the ceiling, he'd quiet long enough to let us get a good take.

Back in Chris's studio, I sang the end of "Menopause Mambo" many times. There's a high note that's hard to sing when I'm healthy. I sang in a faux operatic way—it's a funny song, obviously—and while I didn't have to be Maria Callas, I needed to hit the note. After a few takes, I finally got it. Where's my medal?

Chris was not just the engineer and co-producer, he's also a wonderful musician. He played a beautiful keyboard part on the jazz-flavored "Black and White." "Too Norah Jones?" he asked. I assured him it wasn't but then, I like Norah Jones.

That night, Tory Trujillo arrived in town. She's a beautiful woman with sensual curves, dark eyes and a gorgeous smile that looks like she's hiding a little mystery. We've performed together a few times and I love how our voices blend. She's had little studio experience, though, so we were both a little apprehensive when we started out the next day. I prioritized the songs so if we had to spend extra time on her parts and ran out of time for some, I could let them go. Fortunately, we didn't have to do that. She sang well and offered some great arrangement ideas.

That high note I sung on "Menopause Mambo"? After experimenting with harmonies below that, Chris asked Tory if she could sing higher than me. She responded with, "I'll try." (That's one of the things I love about her. She never answered "no" to any of our suggestions, it was "sure" or "I'll try.") She nailed a note above mine. I swear it's a note only dogs can hear.

We took a few breaks and had some great conversations. I joked with Chris that everything he knew about menopause, he learned from my song. (That's me—the great educator.) Tory and Chris realized that they knew some of the same musicians, which is remarkable, considering that Tory lives in Michigan and Chris, North Carolina. Sometimes, it's a small musical world.

As usual, there was a running joke and for the last few sessions Chris had been planning his scat singing solos which, of course, would be on every song. I promised Kara a saw solo. (The kind you get in a hardware store. Played with a bow, it sounds like something out of a fifties science fiction movie.) Next album, Chris and Kara, I promise. Oh God, I put that in writing.

There are a couple of songs on this album that I feel especially close to. One, "Mamaw's Roses," is for my maternal grandmother. She passed away about thirty years ago and it took me almost that long to write the song. Hearing Tory sing the lovely backing vocals, I felt the tears come to my eyes. I wish Mamaw could've heard it. Likewise for my father and "The Boy Who Wanted to Fly." When Tory sang, I thought about Dad and how much he would've liked the song. I have another one about him, "My Dad Loves to Sing," that I put on an earlier album. He used to put it on for friends and cry while it played.

To prepare Tory for "For Love," Chris ran what we'd recorded earlier, but forgot to use the final vocal and instead played another one. I sang, "I moved to Canada for love…and a health card," and then went into a coughing spasm. For a half-second I thought we should keep that version.

After Tory recorded the vocals for "Carla Williams Kissed Me," I decided on the spur of the moment that as the last chord fades, it needed a kiss, so I ran up in front of her mike and made a kissing noise with my mouth. You can hear it on the recording, along with us laughing hysterically and me asking, "Did that sound like a kiss?"

Tory recorded backing vocals for twelve songs, and then had to dash back to Wilmington, a six-hour drive away, to catch a flight out. She had a gig in New York.

Chris laid down a few more keyboard parts and then pulled out one last instrument, a cumbus-oud for "Bellydancer." It's an instrument sometimes heard in bellydance music so we thought it'd be perfect. Even though the song is in a sharp key, the instrument has no frets and it uses different scales, Chris figured out a part for the song and recorded it, all in thirty or forty minutes. A guy that quick and smart should run for office. I'd vote for him.

Suddenly, we were done recording all the parts. I don't know when I've recorded an album so quickly. It's what happens when you hire professionals and have a strong sense of what you want.

I journeyed back to Durham the next day. On Thursday, I met with photographer Monika Shakinovsky in her home studio. I had some ideas for the album cover as well as this book. I thought *Drive All Night* should feature me holding a steering wheel so a few days before, I googled "junkyard" and found a place fairly close to my housing. At the front counter stood a skinny guy in a plain T-shirt and baggy jeans. I explained that I needed a steering wheel. "What make and model?" he inquired.

"Uh, it doesn't matter. I'm using it for a photo shoot."

"Okay."

"And I don't want to keep it. I just want to rent it."

He smiled and explained, "We don't get the part for you. You have to go out there," he said, pointing toward the yard, "and take the part off yourself. It might be kind of hard if you've never done that kind of thing before."

My puzzled look told him everything.

He shrugged. "I've never seen a lady go back there and not get help from one of the men."

"Um," I replied, looking down at my sweat-stained T-shirt and baggy shorts, "I'm not exactly dressed in my 'get men to do things for me' outfit."

With a blank expression, he shrugged again and said, "You might find a steering wheel just lying around out there."

I ventured into the dusty lot with rows of junked cars, carefully lined up according to make and year. I peered inside a few vehicles. Most still had the wheel and steering column attached, some had nothing in that spot, a clump of wires and plastic parts barfing out of the hole. After a little wandering around (and questioning one guy who didn't offer his help—maybe it was the baggy shorts), I found not one, but two, steering wheels. I chose the most complete-looking one. I was charged the hefty sum of twelve dollars and told that I could bring it back for a full refund after I was finished. I didn't need the "get guys to do things for me" outfit after all.

So, I had the steering wheel. Monika and I got to work. I adore working with her. She's a calm professional who's great at getting the best from me. You can see how relaxed I am in the photos. I played a little music for some of the shots, including making up a goofy little song on the ukulele. We laughed a lot. She joked about wearing the wrong sized pants. She'd take a photo, pull up her pants…take a photo…pull up her pants.

The album is called *Dare* so for the cover photo I thought it'd be fun to have me perched on a cliff. There aren't too many of those around Durham, so my graphic designer said we could photo shop one in. Monika took a few photos of me balancing on one foot, like I was about to teeter into an abyss, and some of me crouched down, like I was on an edge.

Finding a good photographer is so important. You can see the rapport in the facial features and the posture of the subject. The photoshoot for my 1995 album *Never Assume* was tough. I'd chosen a fashion photographer because he had a lot of portrait experience. We spent hours getting the right shots. "Turn your head right… no, not that far…now tilt up your chin…that's it…now move your right hand up slightly…good…" I wanted to scream that I wasn't Cindy Crawford. We finally got something that worked, but I never want to do that again.

Before I knew it, it was back to Asheville for the last two days with Chris, this time for mixing. This is the process where we check the volume and quality of sound for each instrument. Is the guitar too loud? Does the bass drum need more "thump?" Will the doumbek sound more present with some high-end added? Is that smooching sound at the end of "Carla Williams" really that funny or should we remove it? Lots of decisions needed to be made.

Each track on each song required a careful listen. Some instruments had more than one track. There were nine tracks for drums on "Dare"—two on the bass drum, two on the snare, etc. The acoustic guitars were recorded with two mikes, and thus, on two tracks.

We also fixed some mistakes. All musicians make them—it doesn't matter if you're Barbra Streisand or Jamie Anderson, although I suspect that Barbra doesn't have a tendency to sing flat at the end of phrases like I do (or make other errors…I should've chosen a singer for that example who's more on my level, someplace between Neil Young and Cheryl Wheeler). There was also the occasional bad note played by one of the musicians. On one song, my guitar didn't quite line up to the drums, so we had to move some of my strums around. It's really cool to watch the process. Each instrument and voice shows up as a sound wave. Chris can blow it up so that all you're seeing is that split second where I made the errant strum. He put the cursor on it, clicked and moved it a fraction to match the drumbeat, also showing on the screen. If I sang a little flat, he could boost that one note with a similar method. You have to be careful with this process, especially with voices, or it'll sound robotic. We've all heard that sound, usually on some dance diva's vocals. My voice is good, we just needed to change a few notes. (If it wasn't pretty good, I'd have no business singing for a living. Don't get me started about all those stars who got their job simply because they had the right look and not because they can, I dunno, sing or play an instrument.)

Like the rest of the recording process, there were times of intense concentration and times when we got damn silly. Chris kept insisting, with a straight face, that "Menopause Mambo" needed a bass vocal.

Another thing that's done during this process is to place the instruments. When you hear a band live, you'd hear the bass coming from the side where the bass player's amp is located. The singer's voice comes out of the middle since they are often standing there and also, because they need to be more prominent. In mixing, we sometimes try to replicate that live sound, so if you're wearing headphones, you might hear an instrument a little better on one side while the lead vocals will be heard equally on both sides. Chris and I joked about how on some songs, the musicians must've been standing on each other's shoulders, since all of the sound came from the center.

Then there's reverb—that cool effect that can make a voice sound like it's recorded in a big cathedral or a small intimate club. It's one of the reasons we sound so good singing in the shower—all of that tile and glass makes your vocals sound more full. Chris had a million reverb settings, from "large room wood" to "small room tiled." Not only did we add reverb to the vocals, but also to the drums and a few other instruments. It can really enhance the blend of instruments and voices.

After we got a satisfying mix, we listened to it on two sets of speakers. The three-thousand dollar set gives a glorious sound that could make you sigh with pleasure. However, most of my fans don't have that kind of equipment. So, we also listened to it on a cheap speaker that Chris joked came from a 1979 Camaro. Suddenly, the bass dropped out and the higher sounds, like my voice and the high notes on the guitar, sounded like they were miles in front of the rest of the band. We had to shoot for the middle so it would sound good on a variety of devices, from MP3 players to ten-thousand-dollar stereos.

Finally, twelve songs were done. All of that intense listening had left me with numb ears. Chris was fried, too. After working a long day, we decided to call it quits with two more songs to go. (I ended up having the time and money to record those two alternate songs. Eliot will be pleased that "Menopause Mambo" made the cut.) Chris would mix the last couple without me. Meanwhile, I needed to listen to the mixes several more times over the next few days, in case there was anything else that needed to change.

It was a bittersweet moment as I stepped out into the cool summer evening dotted with dancing fireflies. I was happy to have the recording almost done, but sad to be leaving the studio. I'd gotten used to the satisfying routine of going to work in a studio with all those wonderful musicians.

The next day, I made my way back to Durham. That night, I taught a bellydance class. Because of a big storm, only one student showed up. I took her through some moves, and then asked if she wanted to hear my new album. She brightened and said, "Yes." I put on "Bellydancer" and watched her face light up as she followed the rhythm with her body, shaking her hips for the drum rolls and doing a playful step during the verses, using the moves I'd taught her and making up some of her own. I also had an ulterior motive and that was to listen to it on yet another system, this time in a huge dance studio. After she left, I listened to the rest of the album. I wasn't crazy about how some of the songs sounded, however, I doubt that many of them will get played through tiny speakers mounted in the ceiling of a big room lined with enormous mirrors. (Do you think there's a reverb setting called "huge room with mirrors"?)

The next night, I took the CD to some musician friends' house and we listened to it on their stereo. They gave me some great feedback, often confirming changes that I wanted to make. Also, they're rock musicians and listened to the songs differently than I, advising me to turn up the electric guitar solo in one song and the drums in another.

The following day, I emailed the suggestions to Chris and he made the adjustments. He also sent me the final mixes for those two remaining songs.

A few days later, the album was mastered. This is the process where a few more technical changes are made and the songs are put in order. In the coming weeks the graphic design would be finalized, the liner notes and lyrics typed and placed on my website, and the promotion planned and implemented (including ad placement and sending them to DJs). *Dare* was released in August of 2013. It was a lot of work and definitely worth it. And you know what? I still like the songs.

CHAPTER FORTY-NINE

She Leads Too Well to be Straight

There's always been something about shaking my booty that appeals to me. It started with Miss Poston's ballet classes, a time in my life when I was asked not to shimmy, but sedately glide around the floor—very hard for a wiggly five-year-old. Mom did the neighbor's ironing so she could pay for my classes in the storefront with the scratched wood floor and huge mirrors. I was disappointed when I was told that only the big girls with more experience got to wear tutus for our recital. I worked hard, placing my feet in fifth position, and with classical piano pouring out of the stereo speakers, carefully followed Miss Poston's direction to flutter my hands upward, plié, bring my hands down, and do it again. If sweating like this got me into a tutu when I reached the ripe old age of ten, I was going to do the best pliés ever seen. I don't remember much about the recital. I got to wear lipstick, though, and that was almost as good as a tutu.

I was a busy kid and had too much else going on to continue with ballet. At school and church dances, through grade school and high school, I satisfied myself with the same steps and hip thrusts practiced by my peers. Even now, the first strain of the Jackson

Five's "ABC" sends me into a hip thrusting frenzy, which is kind of embarrassing if I happen to be on the elliptical machine at the gym.

In Phoenix, sometime in the late seventies, I started hanging out with a very funny comic, Slique Callahan. She put together a comedy act, The Sliquettes. Decked out in silky lingerie from Goodwill and sporting sexy red lipstick, we sashayed across a small lesbian bar's stage, lip-synching to Patti LaBelle's "Lady Marmalade." This was supposed to be a one-time thing to help a friend celebrate a birthday, but we ended up doing several performances. It was quite the radical thing, given that this was during the time when most lesbians we knew dressed in a uniform of flannel shirts, jeans and earth shoes. Fortunately, our audience got into the theater of it, waving their hands and screaming, acting like we were LaBelle in the flesh.

Shortly after that, Slique put together "Swan Dyke Lake," a tennis shoe ballet. Since I was the only one who had any ballet training, I taught everyone pirouettes and tour jetés. I still didn't get to wear a tutu. As the evil Phyllis von Schlafly, I wore a dark costume and an enormous black cape that flared around me as I did my dramatic turns. It was filmed and I hope that whoever owns it has buried it deep in their backyard—else the ghost of Miss Poston will find me and make me do pliés in fifth position for all of eternity.

In 1992, I journeyed to the West Coast Music Camp near San Francisco. For a whole week, I dedicated myself to daily music classes, from songwriting to bluegrass guitar. Every night there was a concert or a dance. If the latter, the instructors would form an ad hoc dance band and hot damn, they were good. It was the folk equivalent of bringing together Led Zeppelin with Heart. None of my dance partners had two left feet. Who else could keep a steady beat with the right steps, but a roomful of musicians? While I danced with a lot of the men, one of my favorite dance partners was Kristina Olsen, a really great musician known on the folk circuit in several countries and as it turned out, an amazing lead partner. When the band started a swing tune, she grabbed my hand and whirled me around. I happily hung on and tried not to trip on her feet. Later, I was inspired to write a song, "You Lead Too Well to be Straight." She is, though.

I've danced with a lot of women in my time. When a handsome woman confidently strolls up to my skirt-clad self and assumes she's going to lead, she has another think coming. Just because I'm wearing lipstick doesn't mean I'm following. Unless it's Kristina. She can throw me around a dance floor anytime.

At a gig in Portland, Oregon, fellow musician Anne Weiss asked if I wanted to go out afterward to a Latin club to dance. I wasn't very well versed in those styles of dance, but she assured me I'd have fun, so I gave her an enthusiastic "yes." When we pulled up in front of the bar with a big sign advertising karaoke, I thought she was pulling my leg. We walked through the bar crowded with white people, as someone onstage massacred "Feelings." I turned to Anne and said, "Great joke!"

"Just wait," she encouraged.

We walked to the back of the bar and descended a long flight of steps, opened a door at the bottom, and salsa blasted out at us. We stepped into a scene very different from the upper floor. Music with a polyrhythmic Latin beat pounded out of the speakers. Disco lights merrily sparkled as couples swung each other around the crowded dance floor. There were few white folks and even fewer women. Anne leaned forward and said in my ear, "Don't worry, the men are respectful. If you don't want to dance, just tell them no."

I said yes almost every time. Most of my partners didn't speak much English and my knowledge of their language was limited to bad restaurant Spanish and, "*Mi nombre es Jamie.*" We weren't there to talk, anyway. Like dancing with Kristina, I simply held on. I picked up some of the steps and laughed with my partner when I didn't. No one held me too close or tried anything inappropriate. One older well-dressed gentleman asked me to dance several times. Toward the end of the evening, he got a little more insistent, telling me in broken English that he was much better than my boyfriend. (How do you say "lesbian" in Spanish?) Anne shook her finger at him and said something in Spanish. He smiled, shrugged, and backed away.

Anne and I stayed until the last song. As we were leaving, the older gentleman came up beside me and hooked his arm in mine. I could smell the alcohol on his breath as he started in again about "my boyfriend." Anne fired a response at him in Spanish, telling him that I'd said no and he should have more respect for women. At least, I think that's what she said. Or maybe she was telling him my boyfriend just got out of prison. At any rate, he went on his way.

There are no drunken men at women's music festivals and festival-goers always have dance opportunities. When Maile and

Marina made country line dancing at them fashionable, I could usually be found in the front row, boot-scootin' away. I loved Marina's outfits—high cowgirl chic with flouncy skirts and lots of sparkles. It's probably her fault that I bought a pair of pink cowgirl boots a few years ago. I've also taken salsa and swing lessons at festivals.

In the late nineties, when I lived in Tucson, I was introduced to bellydance. It might seem like an unusual thing for a feminist-lesbian like me, but I was really attracted to the positive body image and warm women's community that it provided. Women of every size, shape and age can bellydance. It's great low impact exercise and a lot more fun that sweating away on a treadmill. Plus, I get to wear lipstick and something even more engaging than a tutu. People sometimes confuse bellydance with that other kind of dancing, but we don't take off our clothes and the music's better.

In 1997, just six months after starting classes, I decided to bellydance on the main stage of the National Women's Music Festival. Bedecked in a glittery costume given to me by a friend, featuring a silver bra dripping with sequins and a full magenta skirt with a fringed silver hip sash that sat low on my hips, I stood backstage, awaiting my cue. The normally serious festival producer, Mary Byrne, looked at me with eyebrows raised and mumbled, "You're wearing that?" I laughed and answered that indeed, I was. I took off my glasses just before the first strains of music cascaded through the speakers, then glided onstage, my hips shaking in time with the drums. I carefully danced in front of the curtain, about three feet of floor between it and the orchestra pit several feet below. From the darkness of the audience came hundreds of camera flashes and a roar of approval. I felt like Madonna. I stopped in the middle of the stage, turned my back as I did a figure eight with my hips, then gracefully bent back to see the audience… and remembered that the edge of the stage was within inches of my feet—my blurred feet because I'd removed my glasses. Somehow I righted myself, finished my routine and got my sequin-clad ass off the stage.

It wasn't too long after that that I started teaching beginning bellydance at festivals. You haven't lived until you've taught fifty giggling women to shimmy. My classes at the Michigan Womyn's Music Festival often had a group of women watching that I jokingly called the butch gallery, and a few times I convinced them to dance, too. Hey, why should bellydance be relegated to those of us who like to wear lipstick?

One year at Michigan, temperatures soared into the nineties and I was scheduled to teach a three-hour dance class that was only half in shade. I started the workshop by saying that my goal was to have no one die during class. They laughed. I was serious. We stopped several times so women could line up at a spigot and get hosed down. Teaching fifty wet giggling women to bellydance was even more fun.

Another year, I taught a class for the women in DART (Differently Abled Resources Tent). Bellydance is done with every part of the body, so if you have mobility issues, you can focus on another part. I taught them a choreography that could be modified in different ways. The women who couldn't stand long (or at all) did movements with their upper body while seated, while the rest of us danced in a circle around them. One woman, who used crutches, grinned widely as she told me that it was my workshop that prompted her to come to the festival. That's the reason I taught bellydance. I want women to be proud of who they are, no matter what the rest of the world sometimes tells them.

A couple of times I got to dance for the Sunday night candlelight concert. A spiritual event organized by priestess Ruth Barrett, it featured solemn presentations of poetry, song and dance, with only candles and torches to light the stage. I'm about as far from spiritual as you can get, but dancing in this celebration seemed like fun, so I asked to be a part. The first year, I did a veil dance—an interesting endeavor on a stage crowded with seated participants and a lot of fire, especially when you're holding a huge piece of silk and your depth perception stinks. (Never let me parallel park your Subaru, especially if it's near a large flaming torch.) Even though I had visions of becoming a spinning fiery top, I finished without the fire department being summoned. Full of that accomplishment, I volunteered again a couple of years later, this time carrying fire with me and dancing with candles. At one point, I balanced a candle on my head and turned. It flew off and landed upright with a clunk not far from my feet. I swiftly bent down, scooped it up and continued. No one was scorched that year either. I quit dancing on that stage after that, deciding to tempt fate in other ways.

Most of the dance performing I've done has been with my classes at student recitals or solo at women's festivals. I had no desire to dance in a restaurant, shimmying my heart out while some guy buried his face in his hummus plate. (I wasn't interested in dancing for men, anyway, unless they happened to be at a student performance.) For one student recital, they asked the teachers to do a solo, so I prepared one to Teresa Trull's wonderful "Sway of Her Hips." It wasn't even close to the Middle Eastern music that most danced to, but I loved the lyrics about a beautiful woman and her powerful hips. And who says you can't bellydance to R&B? (I'm not the only one with this attitude. I've seen dancers do routines to everything from techno to country. If it has a beat, we can shimmy to it.) I had a huge grin during that whole performance. The audience really loved the song and a couple of dancers asked where they could buy it. I got a kick out of introducing it to straight folks. Teresa Trull was on the Olivia label and is well-known to many who attend women's music festivals, so it's mostly lesbians who know her work.

I ran into Teresa not long after that and asked if I could dance with her to that song the next time we played the same festival. She smiled and said, "Sure." In 2007, at the Ohio Lesbian Festival, I had my chance. Bedecked in a glittery costume I did my best hip swaying as I made my way around the stage, over cables and around instruments. I couldn't use a veil or I would've taken out one of the musicians. I found plenty else to do.

At that same festival, I emceed and for part of that I wore the costume because it gave me something to talk about. I also did a short little routine during a set change. As I danced, I laughed when audience members eagerly approached the stage, waving dollar bills. First, the stage is about five feet tall—my back bend's good, but not that good. Second, I hate having people shove dollar bills into my costume. I'm not that kind of dancer. I once went to a great Lebanese restaurant in New York City where the dancers were never touched by strangers—adoring audience members simply went up with dollar bills and threw them over the dancers. Yeah, do that…especially if those bills have a lot of zeroes on them.

In February of 1997, I had a gig singing at the Superstition Mountain RV Resort in Arizona, a community consisting mostly of retired lesbians. After my concert was a dance. I asked if they wanted me to put on a costume and do a little shake, rattle and roll. They thought that was great. So, about halfway through their dance, the DJ put on my song. I came out with a veil, spinning and shimmying across the huge dance floor. Immediately, a woman rushed up with a bill in her hand. I put my extended index finger in front of my hip and shook "no" to dissuade her. Never say no to an eighty-year-old lesbian. Finally, I pointed to my hip sash and asked her to put the money there. Then I moved quickly across the dance floor, hoping the veil would create a zone around me. No such luck. I ended the choreography in a near-run as the women chased me around. Some of those women were in really good shape.

There were other times when I let strangers tuck money in my costume. In the nineties, the National Women's Music Festival was having financial issues. At one of the evening concerts, an announcement was made asking for support. It was like an old-fashioned tent revival, with women standing to testify how important the festival was for them and ending with a request from organizers to donate money after the show. As the audience came streaming into the lobby afterward, comedian Vickie Shaw started collecting dollar bills for the festival, inviting women to stuff them in the top of her bra. We laughed about that and I thought, well, I could do that too, but I felt like I should do something more than just ask, so I took off my shirt to reveal a modest and plain black bra. I pushed my skirt down below my navel (but still covering the important parts…have I mentioned I'm not that kind of dancer?) and voila! Instant costume. I stepped out, threw out my arms and started a shoulder shimmy. I think there was a drummer or two around, so I got some music too. A line formed as women rushed up to tuck money in my bra strap and skirt band. Even the festival producer got into the fun. Vickie and I raised $580 for the festival that way. I was glad to do it.

I did something similar at a more recent Virginia Women's Music Festival. I don't think I raised much more than a hundred dollars (there weren't many women at the stage that day), but it was a hundred or so that the festival didn't have before.

I've also had the great pleasure of playing music for bellydancers. At many of the local haflas (a gathering featuring bellydancers), there'd be a band, mostly made up of the dancers' husbands and boyfriends. I knew most of them from these dance events and one night I asked if I could join them. I thought I'd just tap a little on a Turkish hand drum. I'm not a drummer, but I've got a good sense of rhythm and know a few bellydance beats. I was surprised when one of the guys handed me a cumbus, a Turkish instrument that looks like a banjo with extra strings. He knew I was a guitar player and I guess he figured that a stringed instrument would be more up my alley. Feigning confidence, I sat down with the band and quietly figured out a scale, tentatively tried a melody, played it louder, repeated it, then proceeded to jam my ass off. The guys joined me on drums. How absolutely amazing it was, seeing the colorfully dressed dancers shake and sway to the music we were playing. After that, the guys let me sit in with them several times.

But you know how musicians are—our tiny brains crave attention. It wasn't enough to jam with the band. I wrote a song about bellydance and asked one of my favorite dancers, Shahzadee, to perform it with me. I played it on my guitar as one of the guys beat out the rhythm on a doumbek. It was as big a thrill as riding a great roller coaster, only I couldn't scream. Shahzadee danced beautifully and the audience was appreciative.

Oh the pleasure
Whisper to your soul
A thousand secrets
Only the dancer knows

Since then, I've played that song for other dancers. It's always a thrill.

I took a fun hula class once. Some of the hip movements were similar to bellydance, so I found them easy to do, and I liked that the graceful hand movements told a story. The teacher commented that I must've done Hawaiian dance before. I replied, "No, but I'm a bellydancer." She nodded and smiled. I added, "Some of the movements are alike, but we don't tell a story with our hands…well, we do, but it's X-rated." (There I go, perpetuating a stereotype. While the dance is sometimes sensual, it's a variety-packed style, sometimes based on folk dance. Some believe it has spiritual roots.)

The other day, my Zumba teacher was leading our class through a few stretches. She asked that we turn our feet out, then bring them together, placing one in front of the other. My feet automatically went into ballet's fifth position.

That's it—I'm wearing a tutu to the next class.

CHAPTER FIFTY

Do You Like Me Yet?

I hate song contests. There's that bug-eyed moment of short breath when I'm onstage, a line of stern judges with clipboards in hand before me, when I wonder if this is really the best route to instant stardom. I can reflect and relax afterward, realizing it's not so bad, especially if there's vodka nearby—a vat of vodka.

The competition that set the standard for me was in 1974, my first public performance for a large crowd, my high school. For a couple thousand other teenagers, my friend Val and I played cheap acoustic guitars and sang John Denver's "The Eagle and the Hawk." As I looked out over the crowded gym, my knees shook violently and I squeaked out the words with a mouth dry as sand and hands that felt like they were carved out of wood. We cranked out some kick-ass harmonies, though, and we must've done okay because we placed third, tying with a modern dancer. We were beat by a group of football jocks who pulled T-shirts over their heads and with painted faces on their bellies, "lip-synched" to a song.

Fast forward to 1994—I was very excited to be chosen for the song contest at a popular festival in the West. At the tiny airport I found my suitcase, but no guitar. Panicked, I talked with the only airport employee I could find. With a reassuring tone he told me not to worry, that they didn't have room for it on this flight and it'd be on the next. "When was that?" I asked. He named a time long after the contest ended.

Not only was this an important festival, but it was my first big music event that wasn't a women's festival. I labored over my clothing choice, not wanting to appear too dykey, so I chose a bright flowered dress with pink cowboy boots.

I was the only woman in the contest who wore a dress.

I borrowed a guitar from another contestant and went on for my slot. I jokingly thanked the airline for losing my guitar, then sang my song as I fingered the unfamiliar instrument, feeling like a beauty contestant forced to wear someone else's gown. The guitar had a rounded back and the strap was set too long, so it kept sliding down my front like it was trying to escape offstage.

I figured that since everyone else was singing serious ballads, I'd stand out with my up-tempo, funny bluegrass number. I could see the judge, a songwriter known for his insightful ballads, frown as the rest of the audience laughed. He sat there with his arms crossed through my entire performance.

Catie Curtis won that year, and without wearing a dress.

I still had a good time at the festival, palling around with some of the other friendly folks from the competition, especially Richard Berman, a gentle-voiced folksinger from New England. When we showed up together for yet another song circle (like singing around a campfire but with no fire), one of the guys said in a jokingly accusing tone, "Oh, there's Jamie and Richard *again*."

I cracked, "He's married and I'm a lesbian…I think we're safe."

At another West Coast festival contest a couple of years later, I heard one of the judges lean over to another judge and stage whisper, "The women just aren't as good as the men."

I'd just performed.

Next time, I'll borrow a penis.

One of the judges at another competition helpfully told me that "there'd already been too many songs about dogs," and that's why I didn't win. Maybe he was a cat fan. I do have a song where I imitate hacking up a hair ball. I would have done it, but too many people were eating.

In my recent past, I ran a song contest. Seeing things from the other side really opened my eyes. It's a hard job, sifting through all those entries and choosing the best ones. Some are easy to turn down, like the song about tampons or a CD imprinted with the artist in a bikini. Oh, the arguments we judges had about some of the others. Usually we'd get it down to about twenty entries, and then pull out the boxing gloves to determine the finalists. In the end, it's art. Some people like a bright abstract that dominates the living room, while others prefer a muted watercolor that matches the sofa.

So far, I haven't won any contests although I've been chosen for many, including three times at one festival. I think I have it now—no dress, no song about dogs and most importantly, bring a penis.

CHAPTER FIFTY-ONE

Driving For a Living

If I ever decide to stop touring, I'd make a great semi driver, because I can drive for long periods of time, I like country music and I'm good at spotting cops. I'd rather stab myself, though. Driving is not my favorite part of touring.

I used to travel with a radar detector until I got a ticket with one. The first thing the officer did was poke his head in my open window, look at the detector and drily say, "Didn't work, did it?" I was tempted to retort, "Actually it did until I topped that hill and saw you. Otherwise, you would've clocked me at eighty-five instead of seventy-five."

In 2003, I got another ticket the same way in rural Minnesota, only that time I didn't have a detector, I just saw no reason to go fifty-five in the middle of the prairie. I should've remembered about cops and hills, though, and as I flew over one, a patrolman caught me going seventy-two. I paid the ticket, thinking nothing more of it until I got home to find a stern letter from my home state of North Carolina. It said I should put my driver's license in an envelope and mail it to them. Huh? Apparently, if you're a N.C. resident you can't go more than fifteen mph over the speed limit *anywhere* in the United States. If you're caught they could suspend your license. It's legal to bury your relatives in the front yard—make sure Grandma is really dead—but if you drive too fast, watch out!

At the end of the letter was an option to make an appointment with a hearing officer. Since it's hard for me to get a ride to work (So, can you give me a lift to Texas tomorrow?), I opted for the meeting. I thought it'd be easy since I was home for nearly a month—unusual for me—but the only available time was on a day when I had a gig a couple thousand miles away in Denver. I made the appointment as early in the day as possible, allowed myself two hours to get to the airport and crossed my fingers.

I consulted with an attorney about my meeting. I told him about the contracts that I'd have to break if I couldn't drive to gigs. "She doesn't care about that," the lawyer told me, "she'll want you to show remorse."

So, I trudged in on the appointed day, transformed into an earnest Meryl Streep ("I am *so* sorry"), and got to keep my license, provided I didn't get a single moving violation in twelve months. For an entire year, I drove exactly the speed limit everywhere I went, regardless of how fast everyone else was going. I hoped that if someone slammed into me on I-95 in Connecticut, that my family would have the sense to sue the state of North Carolina. "Yes, judge, she was told by the state to drive that speed."

Like all good singer-songwriters, I turned the experience into a song, "Felon":

A sunny day in Minnesota
Just me on the two-lane, on the prairie
Flashing lights in my mirror
Deputy Fife was after me
(He said) Ma'am, in this part of the country
Of criminals we take a dim view
The speed limit here is fifty-five
I clocked you at seventy-two

(Yeah) I'm evil, reckless, a villainous outlaw
Just to name a few
A folksinger in her Toyota
You never know what she will do

For that whole twelve-month period, I was afraid to do the song in North Carolina, just in case the hearing officer showed up at one of my gigs. After the year was up, I was tempted to send her and Deputy Fife a CD.

Back when I was living in Arizona, a similar thing happened to me. I neglected to pay a speeding ticket in a timely manner. I got it in Washington State, so I didn't think it'd matter. Frankly, it pissed me off that I even got the ticket. The first question the cop asked was why I hadn't changed my license plate yet. "Huh?" I replied, and then flashed my Arizona driver's license to show him that I wasn't a recent Washington resident trying to avoid new registration charges. I could hear his mental wheels turning as he firmly replied that he was writing me up for speeding.

Speeding? People around me with Washington plates were breaking the sound barrier. I was only visiting your fine state. I felt so welcome.

I grudgingly put a check in the mail, but not until I was home. Only a day or two later, I heard from a collection agency in Washington and from the state of Arizona. I trotted down to the DMV, pleaded my case, and got my license back from a clerk who, while sighing and rolling his eyes, said they had a lot of trouble with the state of Washington. I marched home and fired off letters to the mayor of the city where I got the ticket, the chamber of commerce and the daily paper. The paper printed my letter, along with an angry response from the judge who handled my case. He called me a scofflaw. I didn't even know what that meant. I had to look it up.

Okay, so I'm not so good at spotting cops.

People at toll booths could sometimes be interesting. At one in New York was a hand-lettered sign that said, "No smile, no receipt." True to his word, the toll taker made me smile before I got a receipt. (What would "Bite me" get?) At another toll booth, this one in the Midwest, a toll taker saw my purple Teletubbie toy on the dashboard of my truck and commented, "I don't know why there's all that fuss about him. He's my son's favorite one." (At the time, Jerry Falwell was blathering on about how the purple one was promoting homosexuality.)

I've been lost in every major city in the US. Heck, I've been lost in minor cities. I've gotten directions that ranged from "turn left at the red mail box, not the blue one," to a turn-by-turn breakdown with the exact number of miles between, and naming every landmark. Back before GPSs, good directions were gifts from God. Bad directions usually contained the phrase "you can't miss it," because, inevitably, I did.

One time, I asked my host for directions to her house and she started off with "I'm not very good with directions." I should've asked her to stop right there, but it was in my early years of touring and I didn't know any better. She ended her litany of turns by saying, "Whatever you do, don't end up in East St Louis."

I ended up in East St. Louis. That's exactly where her directions told me to go. I knew where I was as soon as I started seeing rows of boarded up buildings covered in graffiti and groups of young men with seemingly nothing else to do but stare at my truck with the out-of-state plates. I quickly made a U-turn, drove until I found an open gas station without any groups of kids or broken windows, pulled out a map and figured how to get to her place on my own.

Sometimes, I can't even find my way out of the venue and to my vehicle. After a university gig in New York in October of 1999, I headed out the door to my truck. None of the students who organized the show had stuck around so I was there by myself, toting a guitar, a heavy gig bag and my purse stuffed with the cash I'd earned that night. I thought I knew where I was going, but I hadn't paid close attention when I arrived earlier. It was late, the nearly deserted campus wasn't well lit and many of the buildings had no signs. I wandered about the maze of buildings for an hour, my bags seemingly gaining weight with every step. Every time I came to a parking lot, my heart would leap, only to realize my truck was nowhere in sight. Finally, I slapped my forehead and remembered that I had my cell phone with me. (It was huge, as those early phones were, so I didn't always carry it.) I pulled it out and started digging for the phone number of my producer. After some searching, I found it. Fortunately, she worked on campus and knew it well so with the phone to my ear, she guided me to my truck.

I've been in traffic jams in every major city—Los Angeles, New York, Chicago, Denver and more—as well as quaint spots like in rural Ohio, where the vehicle behind me was an Amish buggy.

Sometimes it's not the amount of traffic, but the roadways that frustrate me. Boston is the most confusing city with its twisting one-way streets. If there's a one-way street going north, there should be one going the other direction a block away, right? Not if you're in Boston.

I lived in Durham, N.C. for eleven years, but I still had to pull out the GPS to find the most mundane things, like the post office. There are three streets called Chapel Hill. At one point is the intersection of Chapel Hill and Chapel Hill.

Next door to Durham is the city of Chapel Hill. They have a road called Durham.

In the San Francisco Bay Area, there's a point where I-580 and I-80 join and is the same road. Signs say "I-580 East/I-80 West."

I also get a kick out of the gas stations and diners common along interstates. While some are impersonal and boring, others have quirky things that make a weary touring folksinger giggle. On the door of a restaurant in Quartzsite, Arizona was this sign: "No Loitering, No Soliciting, No Firearms." Damn, I've gotta put my AK-47 back in the car. At a rest area in the Midwest, I stopped for a dish of frozen yogurt. I asked the cashier for a receipt, joking that I was going to convince the IRS that it was a meal. He laughed and offered me the whole roll of receipts so I could claim that I'd taken all of my mythical clients out for dinner at TCBY. IRS agents please take note: I turned him down.

Folks assume I hate driving in big cities, and while I don't love it, they aren't all bad, especially Western cities with their nice straight streets and big street signs. I don't even hate driving in New York City. As soon as I learned that honking was simply a method of communication, and how to best get in and out of Manhattan, I was okay. It's parking I don't like to do there. Or rather, it's parking I can't find there. Why anyone would live in NYC and have a car is beyond me. Unless they're musicians, that is. It's hard to carry all that crap on a bus or subway.

Cabs are expensive, although when my girlfriend lived in the city it was our best method of transportation, since she had a whole drum set to carry. (I once saw a guy with a huge dolly loaded with an entire drum set on a Brooklyn subway. I don't recommend it.) For one gig, we piled as much as we could in the trunk, and then crunched three people into the backseat. The trunk lid didn't close all the way and every time the taxi stopped for a light, we could see the trunk lid bounce up and down. Realizing that anyone could help themselves to anything in the trunk, we darted out each time we stopped, gradually pulling almost everything in with us. When we arrived at the gig we had a snare, cymbals, their stands, a couple of gig bags loaded with hardware, a guitar, a garment bag and three people crammed into the backseat.

I've owned four pickup trucks and a car since I started touring, racking up about 500,000 miles. It's inevitable that there'll be a few tickets and other mishaps. Maybe I should write a bunch of truck driving tunes and tour truck stops. I look good in a feed cap.

CHAPTER FIFTY-TWO

Death-defying Roller Coasters, a Tree Stump and Chunky Monkey

I had recently arrived home after a long tour. Unpacking was done, but as usual, it took me a while to ground myself. A friend came over, plopped on my couch and listened politely as I went on and on about tour fatigue, then shook her head and said, "But you get to travel!" Yeah, and Des Moines is nice. It's not Paris in the springtime, though, and wherever I went, if I wasn't working, I was eating food covered in canned gravy in a small-town dive or making some long boring drive on a flat interstate. However, there were times that I got to do a little sightseeing. I loved the beaches in Hawaii, visiting Shaker settlements and seeing the glaciers in Alaska. There were other places I got to experience, also.

I did two gigs in Ithaca, New York, before I realized there were waterfalls there. When I finally had some time off to visit, I had a great time walking along them and admiring their beauty. I've been to Niagara Falls twice while on tour. I love standing just a couple of feet away from that powerful water. (It's amazing how close you can get, even with the fencing.) In one year, I saw the Mississippi River, the Ohio River, the Gulf of Mexico and the Atlantic Ocean. That's a lot of water for a woman who lived most of her life in the desert.

In fall of 1996, I had the pleasure of going to the Rock and Roll Hall of Fame in Cleveland. How exciting it was to see Jimi Hendrix's handwritten Woodstock set list, Janis Joplin's car, and Lead Belly's guitar. I watched film clips, including one of Ma Rainey singing "Prove It on Me Blues." That was the only lesbian representation I could find in the whole place. I even watched a clip of a female fan going on and on about k.d. lang, but never actually saying a word like "lesbian" or "queer." I left the museum, dreaming of a place where we could see Maxine Feldman's 1970 forty-five, Cris Williamson's Carnegie Hall set list and Kay Gardner's flute.

I've been to Graceland twice, even though I'm not an Elvis fan. The first time I visited because of a dare from a friend. She said she'd pay for the ticket if I got a photo of myself outside. Hey, it was free and I had a day off, so why not? I kind of enjoyed the tour, especially the Jungle Room. Amazing how small the house is. The second time I toured it, I was traveling with my mother and she's a big fan. She stood at his grave with tears in her eyes.

My girlfriend met me on a Florida tour once where we went to Disney World and Epcot Center. I was disappointed in the rides at Disney World. I'm not big on theme rides. I love huge scary roller coasters and Space Mountain was so tame, I could've done my nails while on it. I much preferred the roller coasters at Six Flags, near Chicago. I rode one coaster where your legs dangle free, twice. I would've ridden more, but none of my friends would get into line with me again. I did a gig in Wisconsin that night and could barely sing because I'd screamed myself hoarse that day. Maybe that was the real reason my friends didn't want to ride with me anymore.

After my gig in Kokomo, Indiana, my hosts took me on a tour where I saw...a big tree stump. Next to it was a stuffed steer. In small town Indiana, sometimes you have to reach a little.

Sometimes the drives were beautiful. I made the trek on I-10 through southern Arizona and New Mexico many times. I loved the far-off mountains that changed color with the day, from deep violet to dusty reddish brown. One of the rest areas along this route in Arizona is in Texas Canyon, a place that looks like some giant hand had casually stacked a bunch of rusty colored boulders and topped it with a vivid blue sky.

I'm not a big shopper so huge malls never attracted me. However, show me a good bookstore, and I'm there. If I had time on tour, I visited the local women's or LGBT bookstore. Tucson, where I lived for several years, has a great one, Antigone, which I still visit when I'm in town. (Thankfully, they're still open. Too many have closed in recent years.)

The mecca for booklovers is Powell's Books in Portland, Oregon. Covering an entire city block, it carries more than a million new and used books. I could spend days there. On one disappointing West Coast tour, my spirits were lifted when I found *Lesbian Culture* there. It had a chapter about me. As I was buying it, I exclaimed to the cashier, "I'm in this book!" He smiled and nodded. I was just another nutso book fan on a usual day in the world's biggest bookstore.

I love eating local food wherever I go. When I'm in the Southwest or North Carolina, I eat Mexican food until my hair ignites. In Memphis, I make sure to have barbecue and during a trip to Montreal, it was French food. One of the reasons I love New York City is for the variety of food. Where else can you get excellent Korean food at midnight? In Vermont, I toured the Ben & Jerry's factory. I still have an affinity for Chunky Monkey, the flavor they were handing out that day. In Buffalo, my friend Leah took me out for buffalo wings, to the place that lays claim to making the first ones. My mouth waters thinking about them.

If you ever want to make me very happy, take me to a faster-than-the-speed-of-light roller coaster and after I'm done, give me a carton of Chunky Monkey. Make sure it's in that order.

CHAPTER FIFTY-THREE

Housing from Heck and Some Far From Heck

While I occasionally have the luxury of staying in motel rooms, more often than not I stay with strangers. Most of my hosts are gracious, sometimes giving up their entire home for the night or doing other nice things like packing me a lunch for my drive the next day. There are other housing situations, though, that remain embedded in my skull. Maybe that's why I get migraines.

I've stayed in macrobiotic households, where most of the food consisted of rows of jars with uncooked grains, and in households where they lived on frozen dinners. I'm not a picky eater and can often find something to munch on, but it wasn't long after I started touring that that I began carrying a food box stocked with soup, dried fruit and tea. As long as the sheets were clean, and a slobbering basset hound didn't jump into bed with me at two a.m., I was golden.

Traveling with food didn't guarantee that every housing situation would be stellar. I should've carried clean sheets and towels. Hell, a bedroom suite would've been great, but that wouldn't fit too well in a Toyota truck.

One night I was asked to sleep on a couch while a loud party roared in the next room. It was still better than what I got on a

New England tour, where I slept in a teenager's room in a bed with sandy sheets. (Even after I bluntly, but nicely, asked if the bedclothes were clean.) At a Midwest stop, I had sheets so encrusted with dust and cat hair that I washed them myself before my host got home. After I stripped the bed, I found a huge vibrator wedged between the wall and the mattress, still plugged in. At an apartment in the South, I was offered a towel and told it'd only been used once.

In 1998, a hippie coffeehouse in the Midwest offered me housing. Green Day's "Good Riddance" was popular (as much as I don't like to admit it, I do listen to mainstream radio occasionally) and it was probably running through my head as I arrived early at the venue for my sound check, and met the pregnant teenager who would be my housing host. Not even she could muster a positive description of her digs, so after thanking her I lied and told her I'd made other arrangements. I approached a friendly group of lesbians who had arrived early for the show and asked if any of them had a place where I could stay. One of them volunteered to take me home with her, explaining that she lived with her mom who would probably be asleep by the time we got there. She'd be glad to make up the fold-out couch in the living room of her duplex. Would that be okay? The mattress was comfortable and the sheets smelled freshly laundered. I slept like a baby that night, grateful for her offer.

In another city things started out well with a dozen fragrant red roses in my room and a box of chocolates on the bedside table. I unpacked then wandered into the next room to have a cup of tea with my host. She regaled me with stories about how she spoke many languages, used to drive a race car and had a dungeon in her basement. Would I like to see it? Fortunately, I know how to say "no thank you" in several languages.

On a West Coast tour I had a host who insisted on cooking me every meal, even refusing to let me pour my own cereal in the morning. She followed me around, asking questions about everything. I couldn't even make a phone call without her listening in. I managed to send an email to a friend who was housing me at my next stop and asked if I could arrive at her place a day early. She kindly replied that I could, so I gave my current host an excuse and made a break for it.

At a Southern festival, while I was indisposed in a bathroom, an enormous scorpion sauntered across the floor inches from my feet. I was just about to see if I could scream and pee at the same time when the scary bugger squeezed into a crack in the wall opposite me. And speaking of critters, another place I stayed had a mysterious rustling coming from the walls that kept me from a good night's rest. When I asked my host about it the next morning, she casually said, "Oh those are the mice."

Maybe one scorpion would've been better.

In April of 1993, at housing in the Midwest, there was a flood. (Is this starting to sound biblical?) My bedroom was in a finished basement. While sitting in the living room on the main floor with the woman who lived there, she commented in an offhand manner, "Oh, the basement sometimes leaks." I didn't think anything of it until I went to bed that night. Sure enough, there was a half-inch of water lapping around my suitcase. I dragged everything upstairs and spent a restless night on her couch. I swear I heard creaking hulls and seagulls in my sleep. For years, that suitcase sported water lines, like some flood marker in a riverbed.

For another gig, I stayed for three nights in a house at the end of a runway, the planes so close they rattled the windows. I learned to fall asleep before midnight. It was easier to doze off in the quiet one or two hours before the red-eye flights started taking off.

Sometimes even the hotels scared me. I arrived at one in eastern Colorado (the only place to stay for miles around) that sported a bold banner in the lobby exclaiming, Welcome to Cattlemen for Christ! I kept envisioning weird initiation rites that included a Bible and a side of beef. I could've introduced them to the woman with the dungeon.

Another time, at a Folk Alliance conference in a nice hotel, I got locked in a stairway. After checking every door on several floors while trying not to hyperventilate, I finally found one that was open. I took the elevator the rest of my stay, even though I'd already been trapped in one once during that weekend. At least the elevators had phones.

After a gig in Ohio, I stayed in a motel that sat right next to railroad tracks. I don't mean that in a metaphorical way. If I reached out my window, I could touch the train. I put in earplugs and drifted off to sleep, trying hard not to think about derailments.

There was no train at a hotel on a later tour, but there was a mysterious rolling noise coming from the roof, like God was bowling. I kept expecting a loud commanding voice to yell "Strike!" After a restless night of sleep, I asked the clerk about it on my way out.

"Oh, there's been something loose up there ever since the tornado," she said in a matter-of-fact way.

It was probably just the body of a customer.

At another hotel, I was sleeping soundly after a long day of driving when at midnight the people in the next room awakened me. A young kid was singing loudly out of tune as the adults laughed. I banged on the wall to no avail. When I got up at six a.m. the next morning, I phoned them. I'm not proud of my behavior, but it sure felt good to hear that groggy "Hello?" on the other end of the line. I should have sung for them. At least it would've been in tune.

In other places, fire alarms have gone off in the middle of the night, once when there really was a fire. Fortunately, it was a small one in a room far from me. I couldn't get back to sleep, so a couple of friends and I went out for breakfast at four a.m. in our pajamas. When you've got beautiful purple satin sleepwear, why keep it hidden?

I've stayed in countless other cheap motels with sticky carpets, peeling metallic wallpaper, leaky toilets and lopsided beds. One hotel had a ringer heard all over the motel that went off every time someone called the office. At a place in central Pennsylvania, I was offered a room with no key. I clearly remember a motel in El Reno, Oklahoma. The blue bedspread clashed with the brown carpeting, a big crack ran down one wall and an opposite wall was peeling, like they'd painted over wallpaper. There were two nails in another wall, with a square of grime outlining where a picture used to be. Judging by the Kmart style art that still hung in the room, it was probably good that someone stole that one. (But why did they want it?) The ugly black vinyl chairs were slick, like someone had sprayed them with Armor All...I hope it was Armor All. Two hapless beetles had lost their life in the bathtub and an orange stain dominated the sink. The TV worked, though, and the room only cost thirty dollars. After a ten hour drive, it looked better than a nap in the front seat of my small truck.

I learned quickly to never stay at a motel that said "clean rooms" on the sign—if they have to advertise, they aren't—had strings of beads instead of curtains, or anyplace that offered an hourly rental option.

The clerk in a New England motel near a military base asked if I was military. I replied, "Far from it. I'm a folksinger." I joked that my bumper stickers might make the rest of their guests uncomfortable. He laughed and said he was in a metal band. We had a brief moment of bonding.

I've stayed in some wonderful hotels, too, including the Anderson Inn in Minnesota. (No relation that I could tell—it's just that Andersons breed like rabbits.) It was a beautifully restored place filled with antiques. It was especially appealing to me because every room came with a cat. After checking in, you simply visited the room where the felines were housed and picked out your companion for the night. I chose a big Siamese with a purr like an idling motorboat who kept me up half the night. I didn't care since he provided a little piece of home.

I've spent the night in accommodations where there was no indoor toilet, usually at outdoor festivals, and that doesn't generally bother me unless it's winter. One of my friends has a thermostat in her outhouse. (Can pee freeze on the way down?) None of that concerned me as much as the house with indoor plumbing but no bathroom door.

Another place had no bathroom issues, but there were several clocks in every room. Most of them didn't work. Every surface—tabletops, counters and even the toilet back—was piled high with sloppy stacks of newspapers, junk mail and overflowing ashtrays. The only one who did the dishes was me, and the floors were so dirty my white socks turned black within minutes. The poor resident kitty was so wracked with fleas that she had scratched bald spots into her fur. I'm sure I took a few bugs with me, since she spent a lot of time in my lap. I felt sorry for the poor critter.

At a city on an earlier tour, a woman graciously gave me her apartment for the night. I counted eleven Janis Joplin pictures in the bedroom alone. After a while, it felt like some weird ride at Disneyland where I'd have to drink a few shots of Southern Comfort and sing "Piece of My Heart" before going from the bedroom into the kitchen. At least her cat didn't have fleas.

After a Midwest gig, I stayed with a Christian woman. Normally, I don't notice anyone's religion unless they're at my door pounding on a Bible, but the way this place was decorated, there was no question. In the room where I slept, there were two pictures of Jesus, a photo collage of a garden featuring a statue of Jesus, a plaque that said "Lord" and along one wall, a wooden contraption that I concluded was for praying—it had a padded plank along the bottom, and a board farther up for your elbows. It was topped with lace. Above it was a foot-long print titled "The Crucifixion." The rest of the house held a lot of religious objects, too. Even the bathroom included a sampler that proclaimed, "Life is fragile, handle with prayer." I wanted to exclaim, "Oh Lord," but that felt so wrong. My host was very nice, even if we didn't share the same taste in décor.

As I said earlier, I've had some wonderful places to stay. One of my favorites was with a delightful woman in southern New Mexico. In her eighties, her eyes sparkled as she told me about her journeys. It was her goal to visit every country on the planet. So far she'd been to 148 of them, including a recent trip to Iran. She told me how wonderful it was to talk with the women there. They'd stop her and ask about her husband and children, and then were very sad when she told them she didn't have either. It was assumed that all Americans were rich and wore cowboy hats. Men didn't stop, as it was forbidden for them to talk with a woman not related to them.

She liked to eat the native food wherever she went. As she made me a delicious omelet, I asked her to name the weirdest thing she ever ate. She thought for a minute and said a fish eyeball. It was a delicacy, and as an honored guest, it would have been rude for her to turn it down. She grinned and commented, "It was salty but not bad."

She and her brother built the bright and airy house. In her sixties at the time, she could lay about 140 adobe bricks in a day. Each one weighed thirty-four pounds.

The cozy house had no central heat or cooling. She explained that in the winter, the adobe holds the heat from the day's sun, as does the colorful Mexican tile on the floor. I commented that she must get quite warm in the desert summer, and she replied that no, there were no windows on the side of the house where the summer sun shines the most. She simply opens up the doors on the front and back of the house to let the breezes blow through. Sometimes that was supplemented with a fan.

As I was shuffling off to bed, she told me not to flush the toilet. I puzzled over the comment until I saw that she had a composting toilet. There was no way to flush it.

In the morning, the thermostat in the hallway said seventy, in spite of it being December in the high desert. Never underestimate the warmth of adobe, Mexican tile and a wonderful woman.

I also enjoyed staying at a spacious B&B on a college campus in Ohio. The caretaker said that after I arrived in my Toyota pickup, the next guest showed up in a stretch limo. The week before, she housed three Tibetan monks. I have no idea how they arrived, maybe floated in on the ether.

I often stayed with my friend, Toni, in Chicago. She has a penchant for creepy things and the décor in her house reflected that. In the entryway was a coffin (empty...I think) and on the walls were posters from cheesy scary movies. The guest room had bookcases stuffed with vampire books. Plastic skulls added to the ambiance. I'm not complaining because really, it was just an extension of her interesting personality. I always enjoyed staying with her. She lived in the Andersonville neighborhood which not only has a great name, but was within walking distance of the women's bookstore, Women and Children First, as well as a great hippie coffeehouse, Kopi. They have the best Mexican hot chocolate—perfect on a chilly day for this homesick traveler. In the other direction was Lake Michigan. I never had to find a gym when I stayed with her. I'd simply make the long trek to the lake, and then walk along it for miles.

Another wonderful place to stay was with my friend, Mosa Baczewska. She had a tiny trailer—a former circus wagon—on a beautiful wooded lot at the end of a dirt road in the Ozarks near Springfield, Missouri. I slept on the floor because there was nowhere else, but she made it comfortable with a foam mat and bedding. Every morning, I woke up to the melodic sound of birds and nothing else. At night, Mosa would ask what I wanted for dinner, and then we'd go to the garden and pick it. She made the best grain burgers—not from a mix, but with a variety of chewy grains and spices. Electricity came from solar panels and was stored in marine batteries under the wagon. Since it was a precious commodity, we avoided using it, except for a few things like a light and the boom box. We spent our time talking, playing Scrabble and making music. When the weather was nice, I'd walk around in the woods or hang out in the swing on the big walnut tree nearby. The air smelled great, like freshly mown grass.

I love staying with my friend Kara, too. She has a little cabin in the woods in Brown County, Indiana. There's a big front porch that's perfect for enjoying good weather and watching the colorful birds that gather around her many feeders. She's got a beagle that always welcomes me with happy squeals. Hot and cold running cats, too.

Another host wasn't a friend and the stay, not so pleasant. I shared his big home with a couple of other musicians. The homeowner was a guy I liked at first because he seemed friendly and easygoing. He loved to talk. After a while the nonstop chatter about his family, his house, his work and his hobbies had me climbing the walls. The only way to participate in this mostly one-sided monologue was to wait until he took a breath, then rush in with a comment or question. Often he didn't even hear me, just picking up where he left off. It wasn't until another one of the performers walked in that I could make my escape. I scampered to my room and closed the door so I could get some shuteye for the night.

The next morning, it was more of the same only this time he directed all of his comments to the other musician. That was fine with me except that even when I said something, he'd look at the other musician, like she was the one talking. (I asked her later what she thought was up and she said maybe it was because I was a lesbian and he felt he couldn't flirt with me.) A break in the conversation wasn't ever going to happen so I interrupted him and said it was time for me to hit the road. He followed me out to my truck, telling me three or four ways I could get to the interstate, all involving a myriad of turns I wasn't ever going to remember (and this was before GPSs were around). Since I was fairly sure I could simply retrace my route from the previous night, I tuned him out, trying to graciously make my excuse to leave in the brief seconds when he stopped to take a breath.

I crawled into the back of my truck, explaining that I needed to repack a few things, and still he chattered on about directions. As I pulled a small plastic bag of tampons out of a box to put into my suitcase, he mumbled something and left. I busied myself with the reorganizing, and then got into the cab of the truck to leave. I kept thinking he'd come back out of the house after getting maps or written directions, but he never emerged.

The next time I deal with a guy like that, all I have to do is pull out sanitary supplies. Stop! I have tampons!

CHAPTER FIFTY-FOUR

Stalkers, Fans, and Friends

I thought that playing in Provincetown was better for the bigger names because they drew larger crowds (resulting in more money), until I talked with one well-known performer. "I hate playing there," she confided. "The only reason I perform there is because I stay with friends who cook for me."

That was sometimes true for me, too. If I had friends in the area and friendly faces in the audience, it was always a better gig.

At a Tucson concert, a fan brought her mother and grandmother. Her grandmother said she laughed so hard that she almost lost her false teeth. Can I put that quote in my press kit?

For several years, there was a fan that came to every gig I did in Downers Grove, Illinois. She owned all of my recordings and joked that she was my stalker. She had one of those open and interested faces that performers love to look at when we're onstage. I hadn't seen her at a couple of more recent gigs so I worried if she was okay. She came to my performance there in 2013, though, saying that the timing wasn't right for recent shows. Good, I don't have to call Missing Persons. I'm not sure how that would work anyway. "She's my stalker and always comes to my Downers Grove gigs. No, I don't remember her name."

Of course, she wasn't really a stalker. Aside from a couple of inappropriate letters and emails, I haven't had that kind of issue with anyone. I did, however, get a strange gift from a fan—a puzzle where one of the pieces was a heart. Under the heart was the wrapper from a Hershey's kiss. Yeah, I get it, and no, you won't be hearing from me.

There have been a few fans who hung around the CD table a little too long, but they meant well and who doesn't mind a little flattery? As long as you're not sending me empty candy wrappers, I'm fine. Besides, musicians are lousy girlfriends. We're always gone and if there's a breakup, we write mean songs about you. I have one ex who still doesn't talk to me and we broke up in 1997.

I have a song called "Bad Idea" in which I mention someone I briefly dated. During an argument, she told me, "You can write songs about the breakup. All I can do is talk with my therapist." That's the real reason we singer-songwriters do what we do. We can't afford therapists so we write songs, then you pay us. It works well.

I joke about the therapeutic aspect of writing songs. It's really true, though. In the fall of 1996, I played a gig in a little café in Pennsylvania. The guy who booked me listened intently, and then approached me after the show. He told me that he listened with tears in his eyes, amazed at my courage in coming out. Also a songwriter, he explained that he was bipolar and had written a song about it. He was proud to be out about something that wasn't always treated positively by others.

At that same gig was a guy who sat alone at a small table. Aside from the booker, he was the only other man in the room. He listened closely, approached me at intermission and requested songs. He knew my music and not just the frequently requested tunes. He asked me to sing "No Damn Factory," a song I'd put on my *Never Assume* album years before. Even though I rarely performed it, I was very proud of it because it's about my Grandpa Anderson and my connection to him. I told the fan that I couldn't remember the words, so he pulled out the CD and opened the booklet so I could read the lyrics. I was happy to do the song for him.

Sometimes there isn't that connection with an audience. After a gig in 2000 at Whitman College in Washington State, I was invited to a party. Keenly aware that I was at least twenty years older than most of the audience, I joked about being the oldest one there. One of the students paused, turned, and addressed his friend, "Lisa's mom is coming, right?" Sure, Lisa's mom and I can talk about, oh I don't know, mom things. I decided not to go.

Audiences help me decide whether a new song is good or not. Sometimes, before performing it in a public venue, I play it for a friend or partner. One of my buddies thoughtfully commented that I should take my new song, tie it up in the woods and leave it there. After I finished laughing, I realized she was right. It was an awful song. Another time, I played "Three Bridges" for my friend Martie. She's a therapist and always zones right in on the lyrics and the emotional content. For this one, she leaned forward and sternly asked, "What is this song about?" At the time, "Three Bridges" had a vague chorus so I made it clearer and it ended up one of my more popular songs. In 1994, after I'd written "When Cats Take Over the World," I played it for my partner. Usually she was a great sounding board for new tunes. Aside from some polite giggles, she didn't laugh, and then commented that it wasn't one of my funnier songs. I decided to do it at shows anyway. I still get requests for it. If you search for it online, you'll get pages of hits, from mentions in blogs to videos where it's used as a soundtrack.

Martie and my then-partner both lived in my hometown. Many of the people in my life I met on the road. I was first introduced to Kara Barnard when she opened for me in Bloomington, Indiana. Author Bonnie Morris and I met when she offered me housing on a West Coast tour. I met Toni Armstrong Jr. at a women's music festival. Toni has been very active in women's music and culture, as publisher and editor of *HOT WIRE: The Journal of Women's Music and Culture*, as a musician and much more.

The problem with these friends, though, is that they lived all over the country. When I went through a terrible breakup (Aren't they all, really?), I only had one buddy in town who I could really count on for support. (Somehow, I'd not only lost the house, the dog and my health insurance in one divorce, but also most of our friends.) I was on the phone almost every night, ranting with someone. It was great, but not as satisfying as a good cry in someone's arms after they've fed you their mama's chicken soup.

I played a show three days after that breakup. The drive there was difficult. At one point, I was crying too hard to see the road, so

I pulled over at a rest area to calm down. At the gig that evening, I didn't feel like unburdening myself. I did my usual show except for one small thing. Instead of singing "You're her problem now," in my song "Her Problem Now," I sang, "You're *his* problem now." (My ex had left me for a man. And no, I don't think it's worse because he was male. Man, woman or giraffe, she left me.) I ripped into that lyric like it was my last bag of potato chips. I never explained the word change.

By the time I did a later gig in Ohio, I was talking a little about the breakup during my show. A very sweet guy approached me afterward and wished me well, commenting, "You're so beautiful, how could anyone leave you?" He told me about his boyfriend who was stationed in Iraq, and how much he loved him, assuring me, "You'll find someone who loves you that much." It was all I could do not to lay my head on his shoulder and sob.

Earlier in my career, I met Karen and M.B. when they were my artist liaisons at a women's music festival in Albuquerque and we quickly became friends. Karen was so sweet and M.B. teased me unmercifully. I loved it. I looked forward to staying with them when I was in Albuquerque. Their son was born on my birthday. It's been nice to see him grow up.

Speaking of parents, anyone who thinks that lesbians shouldn't be parents should talk to me. I've met many loving LGBT parents. At a show in New Mexico, I met a couple who were foster parents to three kids, all of them disabled. One child needed twenty-four-hour care, so they alternated staying up all night with him. Because of some archaic laws, they weren't able to adopt all of the children. Last I heard, they'd moved to California, where they could more easily adopt.

My brother was a sperm donor to friends, a lesbian couple. They named the baby Jamie. She's a great kid and they're wonderful parents. I wrote a song about them and others:

Raising three foster kids, two moms in Albuquerque
Little girl with two dads on the mall in DC
This is what family means to me

I've heard great stories from lots of audience members, from the drug counselor who was a former addict, to the student at the University of Wyoming who knew Matthew Shepard. I've seen tears in the eyes of fans as I sang "My Dad Loves to Sing" because it reminded them of their father who loved to sing. My song, "Beautiful," has probably gotten the biggest response of any song I've ever done:

Hey how ya doin' she says, with a quick embrace
I step back and look into an almost familiar face
Laughing, she says she lost almost fifty pounds
I can wear most any clothes now I'm not so big around
Her smile is hopeful, but I can't think of more than
I thought she was beautiful before

Body image is always a tough subject for women and so is gastric bypass surgery. I heard everything from "my cousin died from the surgery" to "it saved my life." After one show, a slender woman approached me. She was holding the hand of another woman. With tears in her eyes, she thanked me for "Beautiful," and went on to tell me that she was alive because of the surgery. Tears started down her face as she looked at the woman next her and said softly, "She never knew me when I was bigger, so I showed her a picture and she said, 'I would've loved you then, too.'"

Another time, after a noisy bar gig, I had a pleasant conversation with an audience member. Over a beer, she laughed and confided, "I look as young as I can afford," and mentioned having plastic surgery. I hadn't done "Beautiful" at the show and it didn't seem appropriate to talk about body image with this stranger in a bar. She bought the CD that featured it, though. A couple of months later, she sent me a letter, telling me that she'd listened to "Beautiful" over and over again and added, "I wish someone had told me that."

CHAPTER FIFTY-FIVE

Odd Gigs and Twilight Jesus

I've played in a variety of venues, from churches to music festivals. Some of those gigs I'd rather toss off a high bridge to crash on the rocks below, but they tend to be the most entertaining in the retelling.

There was the time I played in a large old Protestant church. Partway through my show, as I was introducing a song, a light illuminated a balcony I was facing. Over the balcony was a stained glass window featuring a giant Jesus, arms outstretched, appearing as if he was beckoning me to stop. To my audience I said matter-of-factly, "Jesus is here."

I could hear my producer scrambling around backstage, mumbling under her breath, looking for the balcony light switch (which must have been on a timer). I heard a soft "Oh!" then the light clicked off and Jesus disappeared.

I muttered something poignant like, "Thank God."

At another church, I had a fun gig, although one of the coffeehouse organizers approached me afterward, horrified that I'd used "fuck" in one of my songs. It's not my usual presentation, but it's comedy, and it's not as funny with a synonym. "I can't believe you said that on the altar of my church," she exclaimed. As far as I knew, it was a coffeehouse in a church space. I wasn't at a church service and most of my audience didn't belong to the church. I would've forgotten about the whole thing, except that I've heard through the grapevine that this person refuses to book me at another event she helps to organize, because I "use profanity."

At a bar in San Diego, the dance music bass in the room below boomed so loud I started playing music along with it, making up a song as I went. (I'm not the first to do this. Guitarist Michael Hedges once lived above a dance bar and wrote a song to the bass line in a Rolling Stones song. In the middle of his "Funky Avocado" he'd burst into the Stones tune.)

In June of 2004, I played in a small-town Midwest bar where the act before me was a drag show and after me, strippers. That's just where I'd put the folksinger.

At a house concert in a Colorado backyard, a little dog yipped in the next yard. I considered that a cue to launch into "I Miss the Dog (More Than I Miss You)." The pooch was taken inside moments later. Speaking of dogs, I once had one howl through "When Cats Take Over the World." I've also had cats stroll out in the middle of a song, stop in front of me and casually clean their privates. No one hears the song after that.

At another house concert, I had a different kind of distraction. Everyone sat on the couch and on chairs except one woman with a toddler who stretched out on the floor at my feet. It was a casual concert so at first, that didn't seem too odd. One by one, though, the audience started watching the woman on the floor because she was breast feeding. I forged gamely on, although some in the audience wouldn't have known if I was singing one of my own songs or a medley of polka hits. After the kid was done with her meal, Mom released her to toddle about the room. Most eyes were focused on the tyke. When she headed toward the fingerpicks and glass of water sitting near me, and reached out her chubby little hands, I stopped the song and asked the woman to take the child. She looked surprised, but grabbed her daughter and plopped her close by. During the next song, Mom pulled a diaper out of a nearby bag. In my head I screamed "NO" and apparently the vibe was received. After I finished singing, she carted the child and bag into the other room. (By the way, I don't have an issue with women breast feeding anywhere they damn well please—that's what that body part is for—but please sit with the rest of the audience.)

On another occasion, I played in a bar. As a group of women arrived, I thanked them for coming. One smiled and said, "You yelled at us the last time for talking." I laughingly replied that I'd kill them if they did it this time, especially during the ballads, so during a serious quiet tune they stage-whispered while everyone around them was dead silent. When the other artist on the bill did her set, they talked in a normal tone all through it. I guess she should have threatened to kill them, too. Ironically, she has a song called "I Have to Kill You Now." It's comedy. I think.

One time at a bar gig, a woman talked on her cell phone through three of my songs. I'd just finished a song when I asked her if I could have the phone. She smiled and said into the phone, "Someone wants to talk with you," then handed it to me. I said into the receiver, "Your friend is busy listening to live music." I stabbed the "end call" button and handed the phone back to the surprised woman. People at nearby tables applauded and I felt a whole lot better.

At another noisy bar gig, I had a few tables up front that were clearly having trouble hearing my music over the roar of noise from the people at the back. I told the folks closest to me that I bet I could sing a song about boogers and the noisy ones wouldn't know. I started singing about that very topic and rhymed it with "sugar." Almost no one from the back even looked up. At least I entertained myself and the front-row listeners who were trying not to snort their drinks.

Sometimes, the crowds are a little too quiet. At a recent house concert one of the hosts listened with his eyes closed. At first, I thought that was just his way of enjoying the music. However, his head started to fall forward. He yanked it back, half opened his eyes, and then his head fell backward. He repeated this so many times during the show that I had to stop looking at him or I'd erupt in giggles. At another house concert my host texted her friends through my entire show. At least the guy who was dozing off was trying to pay attention.

A private gay club in the Midwest had a different kind of crowd. It made me think of what gay bars might have been like before Stonewall, except this was in 1993. The small building had bars on the few windows and no sign out front. Only members could get in, using a key they got when they joined. My loud knock was greeted with a "Who's there?" When I answered, the door creaked open and the bartender motioned me into the dark bar that smelled of smoke and spilled beer.

There was a shabby wooden bar along one side and an old pool table on the other, a few mismatched chairs and tables set up next to it. A microphone sat on a rickety stand at one end of the room. The battered PA speakers hung from the ceiling along the wall in the middle of the room. There was a hiss coming through the speakers, but with a sound guy who'd already snapped at me once and a PA older than Moses, that was the best I was going to get. As I set up my CDs for sale, I eavesdropped on the conversation between the bartender and owner.

"Is Janet still in jail?"

"Yep."

"Have you seen Barbara since she crashed into the bar?"

"Nope."

"I heard Jackie was convicted. Where's she doing time?"

"Dunno."

It seemed like half the regular patrons were incarcerated.

The place soon filled with boisterous lesbians dressed in flannel shirts and blue jeans. I'm not sure they heard all the words through those scratchy speakers, but we had a good time. I never went back to that bar, though, just in case Barbara was still driving around.

In the early nineties, a fan named Mary asked about bringing me to her small town in Washington State. We decided on a date. When she discovered that the local folk music society was doing a show that same night, she asked me if I might be interested in opening. I'd heard great things about the main act, The Righteous Mothers, so I said yes. Mary took my press kit and CD to the folk society's next meeting. One of the members asked Mary, "Just how lesbian is she?" and then thoughtfully pointed out, "But there'll be mothers there."

"*I'm* a mother," Mary replied. She did her best to get them to book me, but to no avail. They dodged the issue by saying they didn't want an opener at all.

Mary decided to do the show on her own. Even though she'd never organized anything like that, she found a venue and got some promo, with just a couple of weeks to do it. She was careful not to schedule the show at the same time as the folk group. One of the guys from the folk organization ran sound for free.

I played to twenty-two wonderful people in a little Unitarian church. Most were gay or lesbian. They were a little subdued at first, but warmed up quickly. I had a great time. Afterward, a woman who'd sat quietly in the back approached me. "I'm the folklore bigot," she announced, and went on to tell me that she was the one who asked how lesbian I was. "I wanted you to open the show," she continued, "but the rest vetoed me." She came to my concert—I've got to give her that much credit.

Sometimes transportation is an issue. In 1994, I had a wonderful time at the Virginia Women's Music Festival, until my ride didn't show up at the appointed time. A second ride fell through when it was determined that she didn't have room for me, my giant guitar case and my suitcase. A third ride failed to show up, too. I started to panic—afraid I'd miss my flight from the Richmond airport, about a half-hour's drive away. I ended up at the festival gate, stopping every car and asking if they were going to Richmond. Two kind women in a Honda Civic said yes. We wedged the guitar case between the backseats and I squished in on one side with my suitcase. Their camping gear was smashed in around me. They got me to the airport on time.

On a later tour, when I had my own vehicle, I booked myself into a small New England coffeehouse, grateful to get a gig in that area. There's a great singer-songwriter on every corner in that region so engagements are hard to get. The sign outside said "Janie" from "New Mexico" was playing. (I've never lived in New Mexico.) My friend and I stepped into the dank church basement with scuffed tile floors. The stage area was lit by a weak set of holiday lights and a yard lamp covered in red cellophane, the dim glow lending a gloomy air. The open mike that started the evening featured some very off-key singers and a couple of poets, the last one reading an emotional piece about herpes and diarrhea, complete with sound effects. I realized that most of the small audience consisted of the open mike performers, and I was getting paid by the head. After doing the math, I discovered that I'd net less than it cost me in gas. My companion leaned over and whispered, "Do you have to stay for this?"

I gravely nodded yes. A gig is a gig. But when she suggested a hot cup of coffee in a nearby coffeehouse, it sounded like a much better idea than trying to please this crowd—if fifteen people could be called a crowd. Besides, I didn't have a song about herpes.

I walked slowly to the woman who was running things, placed my hand on my stomach and said I didn't feel too well. She studied my face and replied that I didn't look too good. The horror film lighting of the semi-dark venue actually worked in my favor. I told her I was sorry, but I had to go. She nodded sympathetically before I slouched out the door, my friend carrying my guitar and gig bag. I know I'm going to hell for all that.

I played at a venue in California that had nothing out front to identify it—no sign, no street numbers, nothing. I was told to look for the hair salon next door. Behind the blacked out windows of this storefront in a neighborhood of boarded up buildings was a venue that featured acoustic music. It clearly wasn't a legitimate business. They were careful not to publicly advertise any concerts. People found out about the shows strictly by word of mouth.

It was a great gig, with warm ambience and a full house that drank in every note. I shared the stage with several fine acoustic musicians. After the show I lingered, talking with the other performers. Just as I was getting ready to head out the door, the owner came in from outside, his eyes wide open as he trotted to the back of the venue shouting that he needed a telephone. He'd been robbed at gunpoint right out front. Apparently, the bad guys knew to look for the beauty salon, too.

Fortunately, there was no guy with a gun at an all-comedy show on the East Coast for a crowd of a hundred. My co-performers and I hardly got a laugh. We discovered later that the vast space had an echo that made it impossible to understand our words.

At a solo Seattle concert in March 1999, I wondered why they weren't laughing at the funny tunes. It slowly dawned on me—I was at an international youth hostel. Too bad I didn't know any jokes in German.

At a Texas coffeehouse, I knew I was in trouble when the booker insisted that they had an "apolitical and asexual coffeehouse." I can understand a venue that didn't want political music. I was puzzled about "asexual," though. Maybe it was something they only told the lesbian performers? Though I was tempted to sing a song where the only word was "lesbian," I dialed it back because I was opening for another performer and didn't want to mess up his gig. Fortunately, on that same tour, I played at the Texas Lesbian Conference. It was like removing your bra and pantyhose after a long day of business meetings. (Men, have a woman explain that to you.)

One evening, I had the smallest crowd I'd ever played for. In October of 1999, I showed up at the agreed upon time, but found no one in the lounge of a women's college dorm where I was supposed to perform. I sat on a couch and rehearsed, waiting for someone to show. A lone woman wandered in about a half hour later. She seemed surprised she was the only one there and commented, "There are usually four or five students at these things." We talked for a while, and then I sang a couple of songs while she read the newspaper. We ended the night watching TV for an hour on the nearby big screen. I was paid five hundred dollars for the gig. Sometimes, as long as the check doesn't bounce, I'm happy.

That same month, at another college, my listeners sat with their arms folded in front of them. A couple of them stared blankly at me like I was some TV show that wasn't too interesting, but Mom wouldn't let them change the channel. I couldn't even get them to laugh at "I wanna drive without a map / I wanna wear a jock strap" from "I Wanna Be a Straight Guy."

Later, I talked with the woman who hired me, the head of Women's Studies. When I said I thought the straight guy song had bombed, she replied, "Oh no. They liked it. We've been studying it in class because we're doing a section on male privilege."

That song is about male privilege? I just want to pee standing up.

Some of my favorite gigs were at the Antique Sandwich, in Tacoma, Washington. A comfortable place, I always had a warm crowd. The name made me laugh, though, because I'd picture some old moldy sandwich—far from the tasty food they offered.

In April of 1990, I played at a restaurant in a conservative West Virginia town. The concert was scheduled to begin at ten p.m., when the restaurant usually closed. My fans, mostly lesbians, would know when to show up. I assumed the patrons eating dinner would leave. However, a few saw the sound equipment and decided they'd stay for the show. I opened with songs that didn't reveal my sexuality. Some of the lesbians looked puzzled. I decided to do

"Dark Chocolate," a song that makes it clear I'm a lesbian. A few of the straight couples whispered to each other as the queer women grinned broadly. As I sang the next few songs, the straight couples drifted out, except one pair sitting right ahead of me. They stayed until I did "I'm Sorry," my tongue-in-cheek song-of-condolence for straight folks ("I'm sorry that you're straight / Where do I send the card?"), then left. When the door shut behind them, I cracked, "Good, they're all gone."

At a bookstore gig in Southern California, I played for a noisy and uninterested group of people who were busy reading and talking. I played "When Cats Take Over the World" and asked the kids to come up and dance. They happily obliged. I got more requests for the song, so I did it a couple more times, always with a pint-sized dance troupe. An adult requested "Amazing Grace." I only know the first verse and that would've taken thirty seconds, so I didn't do it. At one point, just to waste time, I put my guitar into an open tuning and just noodled around for fifteen minutes. I still got lukewarm applause after I stopped.

There were no dancers at a major festival a couple of years later. I worked hard to get booked at this event and after a few years, it paid off. As I stood in the darkened area next to the stage, I heard a group of festival workers talking about the night's show, due to begin soon. One of them asked who was on that night and another one gave her the list. "Oh, Jamie Anderson," said the first woman. "Let's go out to eat instead." They had no idea I was standing there. I went onstage that evening and killed, getting two standing ovations. I hope their dinner was really good…or really bad.

I was greeted at a New York show by someone I'd never met, asking if I'd seen the concert producer. When I said no, I was informed that no one had heard from her in a week. Fortunately, others took up the slack and pulled off the show. We found out later that she'd simply left town without telling anyone. She approached me at a later gig and apologized.

Sometimes, I wish people didn't show up. At a West Coast gig, a skinhead with a knife showed up early, wanting to know where all the queers were. He happened to approach a teenager who was the daughter of one of the concert organizers, and the only straight person there. He left and we called the cops. We were a little jumpy after that, but the show went off without a hitch.

Then there was the gay pride march in Boise in the early nineties where one of the protesters had a pickup truck sporting a full gun rack. He stood in the back of it, grilling hot dogs on a barbecue, a big sign on the side proclaiming that he was grilling weenies for Christ.

Jesus certainly wasn't there, but I know a church in the Midwest where he lights up every night at nine.

CHAPTER FIFTY-SIX

Mama Said Don't Talk to Strangers

I travel alone most of the time so it doesn't feel safe to talk with people I don't know. Even waitresses don't get much out of me except my order. There are exceptions, though, where someone wouldn't leave me alone or it just felt okay to talk.

I'd driven quite a few hours and was enjoying a brief break at a rest area picnic table somewhere in the Southwest. Eating a sandwich, my nose in a book, I jumped when I heard a male voice boom, "Hello."

I looked up to see an older guy, his face wrinkled in a grin. As I wondered how to get rid of him he started to ask me questions—where was I headed? Been traveling long? I answered with vague responses while studiously reading my book and hurriedly eating my lunch. Then he pointed to a camper, proudly telling me that it was his.

"Ever since my wife died, I've been traveling," he explained, a trace of sorrow in his eyes. I softened, asked him a few questions and listened to his stories. I never revealed much about myself. He wished me good luck as I got up from the table. I hope he found peace somewhere.

Another time, after playing in Lubbock, I found myself on a lightly traveled two-lane highway. The endless west Texas prairie can seem pretty lonesome and a bit scary. When I got hungry for lunch, I looked for a diner, but gave up after a half hour. There wasn't much out there but scrub brush, and I was starving. Remembering that I had some food in the ice chest, I pulled over at a rest area. Describing it as desolate would be kind. It didn't have trees, restrooms or picnic tables and the only other vehicle was a tractor-trailer with no one around it. It had a sleeper cab, so I figured the driver was napping.

I parked, got out of my truck and opened the back. I busied myself getting cheese and a Pepsi out of the cooler, and then got some crackers out of the food box. I settled on the tailgate and stared out over the wide horizon. It was kind of pretty, that wide pale blue sky streaked with white clouds. Lost in the scenery I almost didn't hear the footsteps on gravel. I turned toward the noise and saw a big, rough-looking man coming from the truck. With no traffic and no other cars at the turn-off, my stomach lurched.

"I need to wake up. Can I buy a Pepsi off you?" he asked in a friendly voice.

"It's caffeine-free. And you don't need to pay me for it." I pulled one out of the ice chest and handed it to him, hoping he didn't pick up on my nervousness or ask any questions. He simply made a few comments about having an all-night run, smiled and when I shook my head at his outstretched hand with coins, he left a pile of change on my tailgate.

At another rest area, this one in the Midwest, I again pulled off to eat lunch. In back of me was parked a new pickup truck, a gray-haired man and woman in the front seat, with a huge nice-looking fifth wheel behind it. I sat in my truck to eat and in the rearview mirror saw the man get out and approach me. Uh-oh, I thought. He motioned for me to roll down my window and against my better judgment, I did.

He told me a long story about how he and the missus had sold everything they owned and gone on the road, but their first truck broke down a few hundred miles ago. They spent all their money on the new truck and now it's not running so well either and they're almost out of fuel. He mentioned something about his wife's bad health, too. Could I give them some money for gas?

Here was a guy who's probably made more money than I have in my entire life and driving what looked like a new vehicle, and he approaches a musician in a small pickup that was several years old and asks for gas money? My emotions changed from anger to sadness as I pondered his tale—what if his story was true? Something seemed false to me, though. I shook my head no and he slowly walked away. I still feel guilty. Would it have made any difference if I had given him a twenty?

I don't usually stop for stranded motorists since, as my mother used to say, I don't know if someone's going to jump out of the bushes at me. As I was leaving Milwaukee, though, I made an exception. She was a small woman with white hair, in a prim print dress, slightly stooped with a pocketbook clutched in front of her like a shield, standing in back of an older luxury sedan. I eased my truck in front of her, parked and hopped out. In my ragged jeans, baggy T-shirt and wind-whipped hair I must have looked a sight, because her eyes opened wide and she stepped back. I offered her a ride, and she said thanks, but she'd wait. I told her I had a phone— could I call someone for her? She hesitated and replied that she wasn't sure of the number. I again offered to give her a lift and this time she consented. She smoothed her dress over her lap after getting in the seat and commented that her nephew had a garage just a few exits up. During the short drive she relaxed, telling me that her car had never just stopped like that before and Jesus must have brought me to help her out. I nodded. Whoever she believed brought me was fine with me.

We pulled up to the garage. I waited to make sure her nephew was there. She came out a minute later, and with tiny steps slowly made her way to my window and insisted I take a twenty "for gas money."

Another time, while driving in mid-Pennsylvania, I stopped for a young white woman standing by an old Datsun. All of my instincts screamed "no"—she probably had a boyfriend with a gun who'll jump out of the shrubbery—but I stopped anyway. It was clear she was alone as she explained that she had a flat and no spare. I tried to get Triple-A on my phone, but couldn't get a good signal. I looked at her almost-bald tires and asked if she had to go far and could I give her a lift?

"Oh, I'm going to Rhode Island to see my boyfriend. He works at the Kmart and I plan to surprise him just as his shift ends." How she planned to get that far on four tires with little tread, I'm not sure. I tried talking her out of it. She was firm, though, so I took her to the next exit where there was a gas station. She had little money but was carrying a credit card she was pretty sure was good. I briefly contemplated buying her a tire. I thought better of it. She really needed four tires and I didn't have much dough. She didn't have much sense. We were even. I left her there.

I once stopped to do laundry in a small town south of Jacksonville, Mississippi. As I loaded my clothes I saw an older African American woman doing the same. She smiled in my direction and I grinned back as we both started up the machines. I sat down on a bench to wait. She sat next to me and asked friendly questions, like: Where I was from? Was I married? How did my husband feel about me traveling? I didn't feel like explaining I was a lesbian, so I pretended I wasn't in a relationship. She said she'd been married for many years and with a chuckle told me, "Marriage is like a parking lot. It's easy to get into but hard to get out." Did I feel safe traveling by myself? I had to admit I didn't always; however, it was okay most of the time. She nodded and replied that she would've liked to visit some other places, but didn't have the money. Besides, it's not the same for me, she said, our differences in skin color and age acknowledged. I agreed. We talked more until our laundry was done. She waved goodbye and wished me luck as I walked out the door.

In June of 2013, I stopped at a Taco Bell for lunch. Ahead of me was a harried father and his two young sons. He clutched a bag of food in one hand while he filled a soda for one of the kids, his eyes trained on them while he admonished them to stay close. I smiled and uttered some words of sympathy. He grinned and replied, "Sometimes you're the waiter and sometimes, you're the commander-in-chief."

I once stopped to eat at a pizza place while driving in rural New England. I couldn't see the people in the next booth over, but I could hear a guy loudly telling his companions that gay people were more aggressive than heterosexuals. "You don't see men go after women the way that gays go after each other," he confidently commented as I silently hoped in his next lifetime he would be a single straight woman.

The homophobic comments seemed to never end as he nastily talked about a lesbian co-worker and told his friends that picturing two women or two men together was disgusting. The two women accompanying him murmured in agreement. I was horrified when I heard a child speak. It's bad enough to talk trash with adults, but with kids? As I left my table I looked at them and was tempted to spout something witty like "Don't you wish your penis was as big as your mouth?" I elected not to say anything. In a small town, driving a vehicle with out-of-state plates, it didn't seem safe.

A couple of hours down the road, I stopped at a fruit stand. I picked out a couple of delicious-looking apples and walked up to the cashier, placing my purse on the counter. The cashier saw the "Celebrate Diversity" button on my bag and started talking about the stupidity of funding war when there were still millions of people with AIDS. Ah, so not everyone in small-town New England was a bigot.

I'm always looking for people like me when I'm on tour. At a restaurant somewhere near the Pennsylvania turnpike, two women who seemed very friendly with each other followed me to the cash register. One of them had a gruff manner but a ready smile for her companion. I turned around, a bright smile on my face. It was then that I realized they were wearing white dresses, each with a huge crucifix around her neck. I guess I still could've said, "Hi," but was stumped at what should follow.

Even before 9/11, flying has been weird for this traveling musician. One time a security person reached into my carry-on and pulled out the heavily beaded silver hip sash of my bellydance costume. He held it up high, silently inspecting it from several angles, getting the attention of several people standing nearby. He turned toward me, eyebrows up, as I explained that I was a bellydancer. "Oh," he slowly replied, hardly blinking, as he carefully placed it back in my bag. I'm glad I don't travel with sex toys.

Strangers on planes are a whole different kettle of fish. They feel safe, somehow, to talk with, maybe because there are so many other people around us. Recently, I was on a plane with a pleasant-faced woman older than me. We talked about her grandkids and music—she'd seen my guitar and said her husband played the banjo. As we got ready to leave the plane, our conversation turned toward more general topics and I commented that the main reason there were so many problems on our planet was that there were too many people, some religions urging everyone to have many children. With an angry look in her eye she said sternly that she was Catholic and the Pope did not encourage people to have more kids and by the way, the rhythm method works. Then she added, "Besides, disease will take care of over population."

I was stunned into silence. I wondered if she would act the same if it were one of her grandbabies who got sick.

Maybe Mama was right about not talking to strangers.

CHAPTER FIFTY-SEVEN

Four Wheels and a Crystal

I did my first tour in a van owned by my (then) touring partner, Martie. It wasn't available for our next tour, in 1988, so we took my trusty 1977 Toyota pickup. Bought with income from a warehouse job, it was a beautiful dark blue with a camper shell—the older kind, with aluminum siding on the outside, and inside, seventies-era wood paneling and little side windows with my handmade curtains. There was a cassette deck. However, it was slowly dying. I retired it after I put a Meg Christian tape in it and my riding companion thanked me for the "wonderful world of underwater women's music." After that, an old portable tape player sat on the seat and worked even better, as long as the batteries were fresh.

The truck faithfully got us to our first destination, the National Women's Music Festival, in Champaign-Urbana, IL. She'd developed a little cough, though, leading me to believe that all of the cylinders weren't firing. A local mechanic confirmed that and quoted me hundreds of dollars to get it fixed. I barely had enough money for the next tank of gas. A thoughtful woman at the festival gave me a big crystal and told me it would help get my little truck down the road. So, I taped it to the top of the air cleaner with the point facing toward the front. It was a lot cheaper than a valve job.

We made it to our gigs in Syracuse and Baltimore, and then turned west. In the middle of a drive across Missouri on a hot muggy day, the window on the passenger side fell down into the door. Fortunately, there was enough sticking up that we could grab the window and pull it up. Unfortunately, it meant keeping the window up. Have I mentioned that the air-conditioning didn't work? In the dry desert air of home, open windows and a spray bottle of water sufficed. Not so much for a humid Missouri summer day and only one window. By the time we got to our concert, my clothing was sprouting rain forest flora.

That big crystal got us home, but I decided not to tempt fate any further, and in 1990, bought a three-year-old Nissan pickup. It had working air-conditioning and tape deck, so I was living in luxury. It got me through several more years of touring until it was getting a bit too close to 200,000 miles. Even though it'd been reliable, I didn't want to cruise all over the country by myself in a vehicle with that many miles. After some consultation, my partner and I bought a new Toyota pickup. I felt like a millionaire driving around in a new truck. It was a beautiful white with a matching camper shell, and had a five speed standard transmission and manual windows, the cheapest truck on the lot. I didn't care because it was mine, or rather, ours. My partner was on the paperwork, but since I was touring about six months of the year, she didn't get to see it much.

That little truck got me to every gig, even the night I was driving with my head up my arse and plowed into someone at an intersection. On a later tour, it was rear-ended in Chicago. After many miles, we sold it and bought another new truck. This truck was hit on the driver's side while I was parked in front of Dianne Davidson's house in Rochester, NY. Besides the body work, I never had to put any money into these Toyotas, aside from usual maintenance items like tires and batteries. I never fixed the side dent. It added character and I figured a truck with a dent was less likely to be broken into.

I sold the truck in 2010, just before I emigrated to Canada. I would've kept it, despite the many miles, but it wasn't on the approved list. Apparently, immigrants only drive newer cars. So, my partner and I bought my first car in thirty years, a Toyota Matrix. I wasn't touring full-time anymore so I didn't need the space offered by a truck. Also, a friend had used her Matrix to haul construction materials for her new house and if she could put a cement mixer back there, surely, a small PA and a guitar would fit.

When I fly to gigs, I usually rent a car. I always go for the least expensive model, like a Chevy Aveo. If they're out of the economy models, I move up to something bigger, like a Ford Focus. You know you're a poor folksinger when moving up means a Focus. I didn't care. As long as it got me from point A to point B, life was good. That wasn't usually the issue, though. My huge guitar flight case, nicknamed Big Bertha by a friend, didn't fit in most trunks, especially in those little cars. The problem was typically solved by placing it on the backseat. Not even that worked for one tiny compact. The door shut and even though I could hear a faint click, it didn't close all the way. I prayed to the appropriate goddess (Keepdoorshutia) and zoomed down the interstate. Fortunately, the goddess heard me and kept my guitar from flying out on I-90. Good thing, because I'm pretty sure that case could stop a speeding semi.

For a tour in Arizona, I reserved my usual economy car. When I arrived at the rental center, the agent, with a grimace on her face, told me they were out of economy cars, would I mind a substitute? Even after I said yes, she turned to the other agent and they mumbled back and forth, ending with the other one shrugging.

"We, um, have to give you a Mustang," she informed me. "Is that okay?"

Okay? My first car was 1965 midnight-blue Mustang. I loved that car. I tried not to jump up and down as I answered, "Yes."

The new Mustang looked more like a Pinto. I didn't care. It was a beautiful bright green convertible with a CD player (rare in those days) and it was all mine, at least for five days. I dragged my suitcase and huge guitar case out to the car and stood, open-mouthed, at the two doors and the tiniest backseat I'd ever seen. There was no way Bertha was going to fit. I considered traipsing back to the counter and asking for the only other vehicle they'd offered—a huge van—when a lightbulb went off over my head.

I put the top down, put one end of Bertha between the front and backseats with the other end sticking up, crammed my suitcase beside it and I was good to go. Never mind that it was late

November in the desert and I could see a sprinkling of snow on the faraway mountains. I popped a favorite CD in the player, cranked up the heat and cruised down I-10. When I pulled up in front of housing, I'm sure my hosts wondered if folksingers were suddenly getting paid a lot more.

Another time, I didn't rent a tiny car because my travel agent had a coupon and snagged me a discount on a full-sized pickup truck with a locking cover for the back. I didn't like the twelve miles per gallon. The room was really nice, though, and Bertha fit in well with room to spare. It was the only time I'd taken two gigs in one night. I had fun at the first concert, then, with an hour to get across town, headed for the next one. As I was turning left across a busy intersection, the engine quit. My hands gripped the steering wheel as I coasted into a gas station. It wouldn't start again so I called the rental company. A cheery voice assured me that someone would be out within two hours. "I don't have two hours," I responded. I phoned the conference where I was to play next and they sent someone to pick me up. While I was performing, the rental company delivered another truck and parked it in the lot outside the venue. Now that's service.

At least both trucks were in one piece. I can't say the same for a poor rental car in Washington State. On the last day I had it, a young man rear-ended me. He jumped out of his car in a panic, asked if I was okay and with a frown told me he didn't have insurance. Could we avoid calling the cops? I looked at the small dent in the back bumper and replied that I'd just tell the rental company it was a parking lot bump. He looked relieved as I told him to leave and not worry about it. It wasn't until I fueled up a couple of hours later that I realized there was a good-sized buckle on the passenger side, near the bumper. I phoned the car company, still sticking with the parking lot story, and got a terse response from a woman who informed me that I'd have to get there an hour and a half early so they could do a damage assessment and by the way, did I sign up for the extra insurance? Shit.

I nervously approached the counter at the rental place, and gave them my carefully rehearsed speech. The agent sauntered out to the car, glanced at the driver's side, walked around to the back, spied the little dent in the back, and then headed back to the office. He never saw the damage on the passenger side. "These cars are always getting dinged, don't worry about it," he assured me. "Just the other day, one of our guys backed into another car." I breathed a silent sigh of relief as he checked the "returned in original condition" box on his form. It's a good thing I had a crystal in my pocket. I hope it keeps me from hell.

CHAPTER FIFTY-EIGHT

I Don't Need a Meat Dress, Although a Nice Meal Would Be Great

Lady Gaga makes enough to keep herself in meat dresses for rest of her life. What about the rest of us? Musicians have to negotiate a price for every gig and hope it's enough to pay the loan on the new guitar. Sometimes we're asked to play for free because it's good exposure. Buy me a parka and we'll talk about frostbite.

Some people go to college to learn their profession. I dragged myself to a squealing microphone, boldly strummed a G chord and hoped no one left before the song was over. After enough open mikes and showcases, I could blaze through "Angels from Montgomery" and not have John Prine fans leave in a huff.

In the mid-eighties I formed a duo with a flute player and we made plans to play at weddings and parties. We bought a huge music book, had a few rehearsals, borrowed my dad's ancient sound system and placed an ad in the paper. (This was BCL—beforecraigslist—when we chiseled words on a stone tablet and sent it off via stegosaurus mail.) We were ready to go...except for the money part.

Where does the daughter of a musician go for advice? To Daddy, of course. He placed a steady hand on my shoulder and intoned,

"Charge a minimum of a hundred and fifty dollars, whether you're doing two songs or twenty."

Really? That was half my rent. (Remember, this was BCL. Way BCL.) I shook my head.

He smiled and added, "People will think you stink if you don't charge enough."

When the first bride and groom asked our fee I stammered, "One hundred and fifty dollars." I almost added, "Although we're flexible," but as I opened my mouth they smiled and went on discussing what songs they wanted. It was the same with other couples. My partner and I learned that if we respected ourselves enough to charge a fair fee, then they would have respect for us.

Thanks to support from my (then) partner Dakota and others, I started touring in the late eighties. When Dakota first proposed this, I said no because I thought she was offering me charity and I'm a proud working-class woman who's always earned my own way. It took a few weeks for me to mull over the idea. What really cinched it for me was something Dakota said, "You don't want to wake up when you're eighty and say, 'I wish I'd tried that.'"

Even though Dakota was paying most of my bills in the beginning, I still had to worry about money. Public concerts were a different animal than private parties, so I often worked for a percentage of the door. There were a couple of nights when I played for the bartender and two of her friends, but mostly, I had good crowds, thanks to an extensive women's music network. These days I play in a variety of venues, and while I prefer to get a guarantee (an amount I receive no matter how many people are there), I still sometimes work for the door. If I lose money one night, I hope to make it up in subsequent concerts.

Sometimes my producers were able to get grants or other funding to pay for my concerts. At Winona State in Minnesota in April 2000, a student wrote a grant and gave a presentation for a campus board. They asked if I was worth $750. She listed my accomplishments and in the end, got the funding. When she told me about all that, I thanked her and asked what Student Activities was paying Live (a popular band) to come to campus. When she replied that she thought it was around $60,000, I joked about being the discount entertainer.

I play for free when it fits my schedule and it's an organization I really want to support. If I sent them a monetary donation out of my meager musician's earnings, it wouldn't be enough to buy a box of paper clips. But I can do a concert for them and raise much more.

Do accountants and teachers get asked to work for free as often as musicians? I'll bet they don't get emails like I do. "Sure, we're paying everyone else, including the sound guy who wants a five-hundred-dollar minimum (because after all, he has to haul in all that heavy equipment), but you love what you do, right?" If I said I hated it, would you pay me something?

Most of the time I do get paid. However, I'm amazed at the lack of fairness at some concerts. I was the featured performer at one gig although the bass player got more money. At another concert, the venue owner charged me three-fifty for a sandwich even though my total take for the evening was twelve dollars. Normally, I'd have some sympathy for his side of the story, but the guy didn't even put up posters about my show and yes, I'd sent him some. At a gig in Wisconsin, the producer handed me the ninety-one dollars I'd made that night, boasting, "Not bad for two hours of work!" How did she think I got there? What I spent for equipment? How long it took me to write and rehearse the songs? If she'd wanted me to write the songs while I was up there, it would've been a far different show.

While music and teaching are my bread and butter, I'm a writer too. I started getting paid for it about ten years ago when the editor at *Acoustic Guitar* asked me to pen a few articles and a book chapter about songwriting. Over the years, I've also had the pleasure of writing for other magazines and websites.

For a few months, I blogged for a major website. I appreciated that they paid me, but it was barely enough to buy a doughnut and a double-double at Timmy's. (Translation for non-Canadians— that's Tim Horton's, a Dunkin' Donut-like place with coffee that some folks find positively heavenly with double cream and double sugar. There's a good reason we have free health care.) I found myself rushing through each post so I wouldn't spend much time and get more than minimum wage. My work suffered so I don't write for them anymore. It's not that the others pay me a lot—I've just whittled it down to the ones I really want to support. As long as teaching and performing are my main source of income, I can choose to do that. For everything else, as long as you're a nonprofit I can afford to support, or if you pay me a decent income, I'm there. I'll even do "Wedding Song" if you request it, although that particular song will cost you a lot of money.

CHAPTER FIFTY-NINE

If I Stand Close Will It Rub Off?

I've met a few famous people in my travels. Sometimes, calm comes over me and I freak out later, like my grand meeting with Melissa Etheridge. It's not always like that.

One summer when I was playing in Provincetown, I was walking down the main street with Suzanne Westenhoefer. Crossing a small side street, we passed in front of a car stopped for traffic. Suzanne grinned at the driver, slapped the hood with her hand and called out, "Hey, Janis Ian!"

Janis Ian? One of the best songwriters on the planet? A guitar player who I've idolized for years? The one who penned "At Seventeen" that came out when I was seventeen and I still cried when I heard it? THAT Janis Ian?

As Suzanne leaned into the car to have a chatty conversation, I stepped back and thrust my shaking hands into my pockets. I'd seen Janis in concert a few years before. After she ripped through a very impressive electric guitar solo, I yelled, "Eric Clapton, eat your heart out." She smiled in return. Those were the only words that came to mind as I watched them talk. I was afraid I'd blurt it out again, like some church lady taken by the spirit and speaking in tongues. Suzanne and Janis talked for a minute then Janis waved and said she'd better get going.

As Suzanne and I headed back down the street she turned to me and offered, "She's a songwriter who's put out some albums." Suzanne had never seen me stunned into silence.

I already knew Suzanne and while she's now one of the best-known lesbian comics around, I met her when only her mama knew who she was. She was booked at a small women's music festival as was I. Among the Birkenstock-shod crowd, she seemed a little out of place with her big blond hair, makeup and chic clothes.

"They're going to hate me," she whispered to me backstage.

"Nah," I assured her, and I was right. As they say in the comedy world, she killed.

In 1993 Tim O'Brien was in my band. Well, not exactly a regular member. He was an instructor at a music camp I attended. For open mike, we could ask any teacher to join us. Standing onstage, looking over at him holding his mandolin, I forgot what song I was playing. My hands had formed chords so I just went with that, managing to squeeze out a decent version of Mary Chapin Carpenter's "I Feel Lucky." (At the end, where she sings about Lyle Lovett putting his hand on her knee, I changed it to k.d. lang. Because I could.) Those of you who know folk and bluegrass might be freaking out at that story, while the rest of you are mumbling, "Who?" He's a Grammy winner who's played with Kathy Mattea, his own band Hot Rize and his sister, Molly. In the folk/bluegrass world, he's Lady Gaga, or at least, a better dressed male version who plays guitar and mandolin.

One year at the Kerrville folk festival, I played one of my funny tunes, "All of Me," at a crowded campfire. One guy had a laugh louder than the others. I looked in his direction and saw Paul, of Peter, Paul and Mary. In my press kit, can I include, "'Hahahahaha,'—Paul Stookey?" (Maybe it was Peter Yarrow. I get all those white guys with guitars mixed up.)

A poster from an album I co-produced, *A Family of Friends*, was in the Susan Sarandon movie, *The Client*. When you watch this 1994 movie, look at the artwork on Reggie Love's (played by Sarandon) office wall and you'll see the brightly colored print. I first saw the film in a crowded Northampton, MA, theater and couldn't resist yelling out, "That's my poster!" during the first scene where it appeared. A few people shushed me. One time I rented the movie just to see the poster again. I have this fantasy that Sarandon was so taken with it that she took it home. (When this book is made into a movie, she's going to play me, right?)

In 1996, at the National Women's Music Festival, I was a little nervous about meeting Ronnie Gilbert. I knew her from her work with Holly Near and her history with The Weavers. I was the emcee that night so I went to her dressing room to introduce myself. She reached out and warmly shook my hand, then referred me to her manager for the questions I had about her intro. It was a great pleasure to introduce this wonderful performer. My intro was so good that her manager called me a week or two after the festival to thank me. It came from the heart, how could I not do it well?

At that same festival, I also got to meet and introduce Linda Tillery. She's a big woman with a powerful voice that I've heard on albums and at various festivals throughout the years. When the stage manager told me that Linda wanted to approve my intro, I thought, Uh-oh. I tapped lightly on her dressing room door and entered after I heard a soft "Come in." I was dressed in a sequined bellydance costume and hurriedly assured her that I wouldn't be wearing it when I introduced her. She grinned and said I looked nice. Reaching for my long beaded earrings, she gently touched them and said they were beautiful. I relaxed and read her the intro. She asked me to change a couple of things. As I walked out, she thanked me for checking in with her.

At that same festival was a performer who treated me much differently. She asked to meet with me earlier in the day. Strolling in late and wearing dark shades (indoors) the whole time, she acted like she'd rather be getting a root canal. She was very exact about how she was to be introduced. That night, just before her set, she stood backstage and loudly complained about the smoke machine being used the previous act's performance, whining about how it was going to be bad for her voice. The stage manager assured her that the fog wasn't harmful and anyway, there'd be enough time between sets for it all to evaporate. It didn't erase her frown. Later, when I introduced her, I totally screwed up the joke she wanted me to tell. I was horrified because no matter how someone treats me, I always try to be professional. My subconscious had other ideas. As the audience applauded she pushed past me with a grimace like

I had done her a giant disservice. She didn't talk to me the rest of the festival.

At another festival, I was pleased to introduce The Butchies. I told the audience they made me press my thighs together. They passed me as I made my way offstage. I heard one of them say to another, "Did we approve that?" Her bandmate giggled and said, "I liked it."

In June of 2004, at the White River Folk Festival in Indiana, I was excited to see that singer and dulcimer player Jean Ritchie was on the bill. She is to Appalachian music as Chuck Berry is to classic rock. Someone had given me a tape of hers twenty years ago and I about wore the damn thing out. I loved her original tunes about her coal mining family and the traditional folk songs she'd learned as a child. She was probably in her eighties then, but her voice was strong, and she offered a very entertaining set with stories to accompany each song. I approached her later and said what a thrill it was to see her live.

She leaned closer, eyes sparkling and joked, "Well, just barely."

At the same folk festival, I heard a great set by John McCutcheon and Tom Chapin. In his set, Tom included a couple of his brother Harry's songs. The audience joyfully sang along. The next morning, as I was checking out of my hotel room, the tall guy next to me looked at my T-shirt that said "Local 1000" (my union).

He smiled and exclaimed, "Ah Local 1000," and reached out to shake my hand. My much smaller hand was almost lost in his firm grip. Tom Chapin! I remembered that he was a member of the same union, making it so much easier to talk with him. I gushed about his set the night before and he seemed genuinely pleased that I'd enjoyed it.

I once passed Pat Benatar on a staircase at a music industry party. I know, it's not much, but I had it in my press kit for years. Frankly, I was more excited about meeting Jean Ritchie.

The first time I was booked for a women's music festival, I strolled into my room to find my roommate relaxing on her bed, reading a mystery. It was all I could do not to blurt out, "Alix Dobkin!" Instead, I kept my cool. It wasn't hard because Alix is far from a diva. Over the years, I've run into her at many events. It's always good to see her.

Another time I stayed with my friend Toni Armstrong Jr. in Chicago. Also there was Kay Gardner. I knew Kay from her work in spiritual and healing women's music, but we'd only met a time or two. I reined in my usual weird humor, censoring myself because, after all, there was Kay Gardner. We decided to see a Drew Barrymore film, *Bad Girls*. Drew's character often wore dresses with a tight bodice and revealing lots of cleavage. When she'd appear on screen, Kay would wiggle her eyebrows and say, "Ooh, luscious wench!" It cracked me up every time.

One morning at the National Women's Music Festival in 1997, I woke up early. Nervous about my main stage gig that night, I couldn't get back to sleep, so I got dressed and walked downstairs to one of the lounges. The sun was just starting to peek over the horizon, a few rays slipping into the almost-quiet building. As I entered the performer care area, I heard a familiar melody. Kay was seated alone at the piano, playing something from her *A Rainbow Path* recording. It was so beautiful and just the thing I needed. I lay on a couch nearby and closed my eyes as she finished the song and started another. The music carried me like a calming dream.

In 1992, a group of us recorded "A Family of Friends," a song that Sue Fink and I had written to be the title cut of a compilation of women's music. When it came time to record my little solo part, I had to do it with my eyes closed. If I opened them, I'd see Deidre McCalla, Sharon Washington (Washington Sisters), Sue, June Millington, Jean Millington, Margie Adam, Robin Flower, Libby McLaren (The Roches), Helen Hooke (Deadly Nightshade), and others. I managed to finish without singing notes unknown to humankind. When we rehearsed the group parts, we sang in a circle around the mike, Deidre to one side of me and Margie across from me. At the end of the day, when we were almost done, some wanted to record yet one more harmony part. Libby turned to her partner Robin and pleaded, "Honey, you know I love to sing." Robin smiled, nodded and agreed to stay just a bit longer. I love to sing, too, especially with a bunch like that.

I once did a women's music festival where the set after me was a trio of women pianists—Liz Story, Margie Adam and Barbara Higbie. They took turns doing solo pieces as I watched from the wings, enthralled. I knew Liz and Barbara's work from their recordings on Windham Hill and it was my first time to hear them together live. While Margie was onstage, Barbara slid in to the seat next to me, put her hand gently on my knee and leaned over, whispering, "I love your voice."

"Uh, blubbub…thanks."

Later on, Liz complimented me, too. I answered with a simple but more mature, "Thank you."

Not long after that, I flew to Chicago. Next to me on the flight was a member of sixties pop group The Association. He'd seen my guitar case, and told me he was a performer too. After that, it became hard to get a word in edgewise, although I didn't mind much—how often do you get to talk with a member of a big-name band? He rattled on about their gigs, and then confided that two of the original members couldn't tour with them anymore. One had a serious drug problem and the other was "too fat" to fit in an airline seat.

Our flight was delayed and many of us missed our connecting flights. Twenty or thirty of us patiently stood in a line at the airline counter, trying to get other planes. My flying companion stood at the back of the line and shouted to the harried airline employee, "I've got to get a flight out *now* or I'll be late to my sound check!" Yeah, Big Name Musician, go to the front of the line.

After another flight, I waited in the baggage claim area. A buzzer went off and the belt started to move. My suitcase came out soon. I waited as the belt slowly brought it to me. At the same time, I kept an eye on the separate area where oversized luggage came in. It was there that my guitar would show up. As I reached for my suitcase, I heard a thud and saw that my guitar had also arrived. I grabbed my suitcase, and then turned to walk toward my guitar. A tall guy in a dark uniform was lifting it off the belt. It was clear he wasn't with an airline and my first thought was that this jerk was stealing my precious guitar. I flew across the long expanse of floor like my feet were on fire, and yelled out, "Hey, that's mine!"

He looked startled and carefully put it down. I pointed to my name on the outside of the case, and said, "I'm Jamie Anderson."

"Oh. I'm sorry, ma'am. I'm Patti LaBelle's driver and I thought this was with her."

Patti LaBelle was on my flight? Why is it that I never get to sit next to musicians like that? I'll bet she never fired someone from her band because he was too fat.

The National March on Washington (for gay, lesbian, bi and transgendered rights) in 1993 was a feast of celebrities. Unfortunately, most of them were keeping me from doing my set on time. Originally, I was supposed to perform after Jesse Jackson's speech and just before the march kicked off. However, the stage manager kept pushing my performance back to accommodate other acts. It was a hot day, but I found some shade so it was actually nice for a while to lounge backstage and watch people such as Phil Donahue strolling around. When he got onstage I could hear him give his speech that ended with getting thousands of people to chant, "Get over it!" in response to those who had a problem with LGBT folks.

I heard Barney Frank speak. Several music acts played after him and still, I wasn't onstage. The thirty or so people I'd asked to sing with me were getting antsy. A few of them had to be at the other stage blocks away in a short time and couldn't wait much longer. Finally, the stage manager lined us up on the ramp leading to the stage. My heart pounded as I prepared to perform for several hundred thousand, the largest audience of my career. Just as we were about to step onstage, the manager rushed forward and said to wait because there was one more act that needed to go on ahead of us.

It was like someone else's voice came out of me when I firmly said, "No." I explained that originally, my set time was a couple hours earlier and we were tired of waiting. Sandra Washington, one of my singers, stepped forward to back me up as the others nodded.

The stage manager sighed and motioned us onstage, muttering something into his walkie-talkie about "The Divas" having to wait. At the time, I thought they were some drag queen group, but I found out later that we'd displaced Brenda Russell, Eartha Kitt, Martha Walsh and, I think, Mary Wells. They probably don't remember me—Janis Ian, either. Maybe it's better.

CHAPTER SIXTY

I'm a Songwriter and I Play One on TV

It started in 2006 with an email from a fan: "They played your song on *Good Morning America*. Congrats!" Surely she had me confused with Shawn Colvin or someone. I checked it out anyway and I'll be damned if they hadn't played my "Potato Chips" because, as everyone knew, it was National Potato Chip Day.

I wasn't sure how those things worked, but I was pretty sure that a big TV show like that should have a sent me a check. I asked a few musician friends and found that indeed, they screwed up. Musicians who get airplay on TV shows get paid. A lot. Again, I consulted my network of musicians and one kind soul came up with the contact information for the music supervisor at the network. This is not something you can just Google, so I owe her a case of chocolate.

I left a voice mail and the supervisor called me back right away. "Those guys in the production room make choices at four a.m. before our office opens," she confided. "We'd be happy to license it. What's your fee?"

Should I quote just enough to buy the chicken enchilada plate from my favorite Mexican place? Or enough to purchase the BMW with leather seats and a custom paint job?

I told her I needed to consult with my attorney and I'd call her back.

I don't have an attorney.

I did, however, find a legal organization that does pro bono work for artists. A very nice lawyer looked over the contract and told me it was a fair and standard agreement, but advising about fees was outside of his expertise. So, I went back to my network of musician friends. One friend's band had airplay on a cable program and another, on a news show. There are different levels of payment for shows that might run again, versus programs that only run once, like sports and news. It also depended on time slot, network, and how many cups of coffee the music supervisor had consumed. I picked an amount that was a good deal more than the cost of that enchilada plate, but way under the price of the BMW. I rehearsed my confident pitch. I was ready.

On tour at the time, I called the music supervisor from the bedroom of my housing. Sitting on the little single bed, I took a deep breath, and quoted a fee.

"Sure," she answered too quickly.

Damn. I should've gone closer to the BMW level. Ah well, it would buy a new computer and since I'd been hearing my current one's death rattle for over a year, that was a good thing.

While I had her on the phone, I extolled the virtues of my other songs. Several thousand dollars (yes, it can be that much) for a few seconds of airplay on *Grey's Anatomy* would be a great thing. Unfortunately, she was in charge of news and sports mostly, and none of my folk songs were going to be quite right for football or that story about the pope's visit. (I do have a song where I sing "Hallelujah" a lot, but somehow, I don't think the lyrics about two girls falling in love at church camp would work.) However, she promised to get my songs to the person responsible. I sent a packet of CDs with suggestions for shows. Surely, the programs with queer characters would need one of my LGBT songs.

I never heard anything else from them, despite a few phone calls and emails. My brief moment of fame will be that thirty seconds of music behind shots of potato chip bags rolling off a production line.

Getting airplay on that show was a total accident, but when I first wrote the song, I did try to get Frito-Lay interested in it. Through diligent library research, I found the ad agency responsible and phoned them. I left a polite message on their voice mail. I never got a response. There goes another chance to buy that BMW. (Actually, what I really want is a new Toyota pickup. I am such a lesbian.)

It's one of the few songs I'd license for a commercial because I wrote it quickly and didn't care much about it, beyond having fun singing it. It bothers me that younger generations think that Carly Simon's "Anticipation" was just a ketchup commercial. I don't want people to remember "Dark Chocolate" because Hershey's used it.

"Potato Chips" is famous in other ways. In 2006, I heard from a women's rugby team in Dublin that used it as their theme song. They wanted to know when I was doing a European tour. Not until *Grey's Anatomy* picks up one of my songs. It's the only way I could afford airfare.

It pays to be lucky. A few years before, I ended up on nationwide TV without even trying. I was onstage at the 1993 National March on Washington for LGBT Rights, playing for a few hundred thousand people. A huge platform crowded with enormous cameras sat to my left. A clip of me singing my song "No Closet" was on CNN at the top of the hour almost all day. Guess I'm out to everyone now.

Over the years I've been on several cable TV shows, the kind that only the lone guy on shift at the all-night doughnut place sees. Quality varied since they're mostly done by volunteers. Thank God these were done before the advent of YouTube or I'd have to retire. I still live under the threat that one of those shows will make its way online.

I teach bellydance and one of my classes was once profiled on a local news show. My butt made more appearances than the rest of me.

True TV fame might continue to elude me, but if you happen to work for one of the networks, call me. There's a rugby team in Ireland who needs to hear me in concert.

CHAPTER SIXTY-ONE

I Could Be Bonnie Raitt Up There and No One Would Know It

If the audience can't hear me well, it doesn't matter who I am, so getting a good sound system and technician is very important.

After slogging through a too-long sound check at a gig in Baltimore, the sound guy groused, "You've just never worked with such great equipment before." I was tempted to answer, "It sounds like you've never *seen* sound equipment before." Nothing I did would convince him that my guitar does not usually scream like a jet at O'Hare and my voice sound like something from an ancient boom box.

I once played at a New York technical college where the sound equipment was run by a computer that automatically adjusted everything. That would have been fine had my guitar not quavered like the soundtrack of a lousy science fiction flick. I ended up sitting on the edge of the stage in that huge theater and singing without amplification because the students didn't know how to adjust the computer. That night someone got an F in live concert sound.

I had a gig in Ohio where the sound equipment was locked in a cabinet for which no one had the key. I still did the gig, but only the folks in the first few rows could really hear me.

At more than one college performance I've been offered a podium with one tiny mike. Just try to hike that guitar up close to the mike and get your voice amplified too. Clearly, I need to do more yoga.

I once sang into a mike the sound guy told me had been used by a punk band where the lead singer had pushed it into a certain orifice. I started carrying my own mike after that.

At a Midwestern gay bar, the owner was driving a new pickup and bragged that she also had a BMW. She complained about the cost of the sound system. Cry me a river.

There are the good stories, too, like when someone brings in their band's battered twenty-year-old Peavey and still makes me sound great. Or the college kid who looked twelve who carted in what seemed to be enough equipment to amplify a heavy metal band with two drum sets. My side player and I looked at each other with dread—sure we were in for a long and painful show. Instead, we got crisp and realistic sound. When we complimented the sound guy he just shrugged.

At the New Daisy Theater on Beale Street in Memphis, I was prepared for a tough time because their posters showed that they featured mostly rock bands. For a place like that, I'd sometimes find technicians who barely had enough hearing left for simple conversations, much less the subtleties of an acoustic guitar and solo voice. The sound guy and lighting tech both had that unwashed rock dude look—rumpled T-shirt, unkempt long hair and faded baggy jeans, but they certainly didn't fit the rest of the stereotype. The sound was wonderful, the lighting tasteful, and my requests were treated respectfully. At intermission, as I sat in the green room, the sound guy stuck his head in to apologize for a small mistake. "No problem," I assured him. I wish I could have sound like that at every gig. Maybe they felt as good about me. I'm sure I was easier than their recent Courtney Love show.

At a gig in Oregon, the sound and light guy had some fun with my songs. During "Menstrual Tango" he turned a red light on me. For the third chorus, he turned on a disco ball. For another song, when I sang "hot flash," (Are you sensing a theme here?) he flashed the lights. I was laughing so hard I had to stop the song.

Some sound problems are my fault like the time I used a guitar cord that was too short and during a dramatic rock star hip thrust, accidently pulled it out of the amplifier. Or one year at the National Women's Music Festival where I strapped on an electric guitar, feeling very Joan Jett, and then paused as I puzzled over the lack of volume. One of my bandmates leapt forward to flip the switch to "on." (Note to self: folksingers shouldn't play electric guitars unless they know how to turn them on.) Then, there were the many occasions when I've forgotten to plug in my guitar, usually at the start of a show when I really wanted to impress a crowd.

Some of my favorite gigs have been house concerts where there's no microphone at all. Having all that modern technology sometimes only complicates things. Maybe I should just pound on a rock with a mammoth bone. Think anyone would come to that show?

CHAPTER SIXTY-TWO

Openers and the Fine Art of Admiration

"You'll like them," I was guaranteed, "they do a lot of funny songs like you do."

I'm flexible when it comes to my opening acts so for this West Coast gig, funny or not, and without checking out their music, I said I was fine with them. I figure that if an opener is really good, it'll challenge me to do my best. I get to be entertained, too. And if it's the other way around, well, I've got something to write about.

The act mentioned above certainly did some unusual songs, including one about snot. As they said from stage, they sang about it because no one else did. Yeah, and there's a good reason for that. They had a few friends in the audience who laughed loudly. Everyone else looked puzzled. With their mugging, they probably would've been better off at a kid's birthday party.

At a college gig in another town, my opener was a young woman who assured the audience that her new album was so good she couldn't stop listening to it. Yeah, and I can't resist gazing at my reflection, but I try not to say that into a microphone.

Once I shared the stage with a duo that did a song about menstruation. When one of my own songs is called "Menstrual

Tango," I can't possibly have an argument with that. There's more to the story, though. I was booked for the performance because they loved that song. Flatter me any time. Offer me a gig on top of that and I'm yours.

I sang a few of my songs and ended with "Menstrual Tango." The duo was on next. Their first song started with an A minor chord, then an E…hey, that sounds like the opening to the song I'd just played. In fact, a lot of the chord structure and part of the melody was identical. The lyrics, however, wandered around like a lost child in a crowded grocery store. The vocalist would deliver a line with eyes wide open and a huge grin—so we'd know it was a funny line. The topic? You guessed it.

I tried not to groan. In fact, I wasn't sure what to do. Should I laugh? Smile politely? Stare off into space? Hope someone puts a few shots of tequila next to me?

There's borrowing and there's stealing. If you're going to do the former, at least credit the original, and if you're going to do the latter, at least do it well. They did neither.

I've had several openers who didn't know how to tell time. Just before one show, I asked how long one opening act planned to perform. "Thirty minutes," she answered. At the twenty-five-minute mark, I started reviewing my set list. At thirty minutes she started a lengthy intro to the next song. I crossed off one song from my set list. Thirty-five minutes, and she was up there blabbing away about her dog, then beginning another song. I crossed another song off my set list. Forty minutes…forty-five minutes… fifty minutes later she finally finished. I'd crossed five songs off my set list. If I'd been the producer of that show, I would've gotten out the big hook. They were paying me the big bucks. In their shoes, I would've wanted my money's worth.

At a house concert on the West Coast, a young singer-songwriter did a short set before mine. Every song had the same tempo, the same types of chords and the same angst-ridden words about relationships. Her set came perilously close to sounding like one long song. I felt my eyes shut and my head drop. If I'd been in a darkened theater a few rows back, I probably would've been okay as long as someone elbowed me in time for my set. However, there were only twenty people there. You've got to start somewhere. I hope that with experience she got better.

Early in my career, my first album barely under my belt, I played at a college. I was surprised to find that my opener was a singer-songwriter who recorded for a well-known independent label. I could hear her in the green room before the concert, singing every song in her set. After the show, I sat at my sales table talking with fans and selling albums. Almost no one was at her table. She sold only one of her LPs, and then quietly left. If she'd done a better show, she probably would have sold more. I felt bad for her. I've been in that place before.

My opening act at a Nevada concert was a chorus that sang everything in unison except one song, where harmony was attempted. Either that or they'd simply wandered off the melody. At any rate, I sat in front with a smile plastered on my face. It's hard to sing in front of a crowd and no matter how they sounded, I wanted to support their efforts.

I once did a show with the Indianapolis Women's Chorus—a group that not only sang on-key, but also knew how to put on a really fun concert. Instead of dividing up the night into two even-length sets like most of my choral gigs, the program interspersed my songs throughout the evening. The evening was orchestrated like a symphony, with each movement about a different topic. They sang a song about loving big thighs, and then I sang my song about body image, "All of Me." I played "Menstrual Tango," then they sang a tango while I did a tango with the choral director. (We'd had one lesson. She looked dashing in her tuxedo. And no, she wasn't gay.) They donned cat ears and performed my "When Cats Take Over the World" with me. The night ended with a big patriotic number. The audience joined in on kazoos as two women bearing flags marched in with me following, twirling the baton.

I've also been an opener many times.

In September of 1995, I opened for a singer-songwriter at a little New England coffeehouse. There were only twenty or so audience members, most whom were fans of mine. Only two people had come to hear the main act. My fans were lesbians who were thrilled to have an out lesbian play in their small town. They loved my songs, were quick to laugh at the funny tunes, and bought lots of recordings afterward. Disappointed that I was only playing a half hour, they still listened politely to the main performer. Almost every one of his low-key songs used a similar picking style, with melodies that barely moved from a few notes. After he played, the coffeehouse booker rushed over to him, gushed about how great his work was and enthusiastically told him that she'd book him again.

As I was packing up, the booker approached me and commented anxiously, "I hope you don't think this is rude," then asked if I did a "straighter" show. I only did two songs that mentioned my sexuality and they were pretty innocent. I told her it was clear that the majority of the audience wanted to hear those songs. She fretted about how her regular audience would receive me. They weren't there that night, though. This could've been her opportunity to expand her audience base since I would bet good chocolate that the lesbians who heard me that night would bring their friends next time. Perhaps she should've asked the main act to do a "gayer" show, given the crowd that night. She never booked me again.

I've loved Cris Williamson's work for a long time, so I'm always happy to open for her. At one gig, as I waited offstage to play, she reached around me in a quick hug and whispered that my voice just got better and better. Just then the emcee introduced me. As I rushed up there, it was all I could do not to blurt out, "Cris likes my voice!"

Another time, I opened for her at the Iron Horse in Northampton, Mass. I walked onstage, strapped on my guitar and just as I reached for my pick, the strap let loose and my cherished six-string dropped like a sack of lead. I caught it a split second before it hit the ground. Why is it that my reflexes are good when it comes to a falling guitar, but I was picked last for every team in grade school? (In high school I was able to skip that indignity. As an incoming freshman, I was given the choice of taking PE or music. Yeah, let me think about that.) I calmly reconnected the strap and started my first song. Beginning the evening with hysterical crying probably wouldn't have been good. Not long after that, I bought a new strap.

In May of 1995, I was thrilled to open for Suzanne Westenhoefer in a refurbished movie theater in Atlanta. The big marquee out front featured my name as well as hers. It truly is exciting to see your name in lights.

After a short sound check, I wandered around backstage until I found a dressing room. Mirrors surrounded by lights lined one side. A large bucket of ice with several bottles of water stood on the counter. I relaxed into one of the chairs, put my feet up and opened a bottle of chilled water. Minutes later the stage manager charged in and exclaimed, "That's for Ms. Westenhoefer! This isn't your dressing room!"

"Where is my dressing room?" I replied, trying to hide my irritation.

He pointed up a steep spiral staircase.

I'm legally blind in one eye. Distances and I don't get along. (You should see me parallel park. On second thought…no.) There was no way I was going to balance my guitar case and heavy purse as I negotiated those stairs. I left the guitar case at the bottom and trudged to the top. Three long flights up was a tiny airless room holding nothing except a couple of hard plastic chairs. I don't need that kind of climb outside of a gym, so I elected to sit in the theater with the audience before the show. The chairs were cushioned, and I didn't have to worry about getting a nosebleed.

Opening for a comic, I knew better than to do any songs about death. It was a big crowd—four hundred people and I got a lot of laughs, so at the break I hightailed it out to the CD table, practicing witty repartee in my head—"You loved my set? Well, I loved your clapping!" Most audience members rushed past me, though, like I was a disheveled guy at an intersection with a sign that said "Forget food. I need beer."

I sold one CD.

I had drinks with Suzanne and a few others after the show. She told me what I already knew—that she didn't care if I drank "her" water. She was probably just grateful that I didn't do any songs about snot.

CHAPTER SIXTY-THREE

Staying With Ghosts

I once played at a New England coffeehouse. I arrived at my housing, a nondescript brick ranch, before the gig. Robert opened the door, extended his hand and cheerfully beckoned me in.

The living room looked better suited for an elderly aunt, not a fifty-year-old straight guy. The carved tables sported delicate porcelain figurines, the worn chairs had lace doilies on the arms and much of the house was done in pink. He lived alone and talked about his girlfriend, so I'm sure he wasn't gay. The decor made more sense when he explained that he'd lived with his mother until she died a year or two before.

His mother's presence was even more apparent in the room where I was to sleep. A flowered robe still hung on a hook on the back of the door, her slippers laid out neatly next to the bed. A closet was so stuffed with women's clothing that it didn't shut properly. The dusty nightstand held reading glasses, a bottle of pills and an old lamp. The adjoining bathroom featured a counter crammed with perfume, lilac-scented lotion, hairspray, brush and comb, the latter two sprouting short strands of gray hair. A portable plastic seat squatted in the shower stall.

My heart ached for this man who obviously had a hard time letting his mother go.

At least this wasn't like the story another musician told me. She also stayed in the room of a recently deceased relative. His yellowed dentures were still on the shelf in the bed's headboard.

On another tour I stayed with a woman who'd recently lost her partner of many years. I knew her lover had spent her last months at home. Judging by the hospital-type bed table, plastic pitcher and other items found in my room, I wondered if this was her sick bed.

My host gave me a tour of the rest of the large house. Her stooped shoulders and slow step made her look like she'd rather be stretched out on the couch watching some numbing TV program. She warned me to watch my step—"The animals are still upset, I guess, so they've been peeing all over the floor." I was sure to keep my shoes on the whole time I was there.

I guess her friends thought it'd cheer her up to have a guest, but really, I just felt in the way. She clearly wasn't done mourning and here she was dealing with this cheery stranger who wore shoes, even with her pajamas.

Still, that wasn't as strange as the almost empty house I was given in another city, this time in the South. My hosts had recently purchased it with plans to renovate. Most of the rooms were completely devoid of furniture, although my quarters had a bed. The kitchen had no dishes, utensils or food. There was a stack of bedpans in one bathroom and an odd-looking pulley contraption hanging from the ceiling in another. One of the owners explained that it had been a nursing home before they bought it; then she headed to the place where they currently lived, leaving me alone.

I could swear there were unhappy spirits in that house. If I fell asleep would I be awakened by the creaking of that weird pulley thing in the empty bathroom? I called one of my best friends to tell her I was creeped out. She advised, "If it doesn't feel right, you shouldn't stay." See, that's why I choose friends far smarter than me. I called my hosts and they moved me to a place with furniture. And no bedpans.

CHAPTER SIXTY-FOUR

Wasn't That a Red Light?

When you've toured for more than twenty years, most of it by car, there's bound to be mishaps. No humans or animals were hurt in the course of these stories. There's a lot of bent metal and bruised egos, though.

A few years ago, I was driving across Ohio on I-80. Construction had closed one lane, slowing everyone down to an almost-stop. I glanced in my rearview mirror and saw a semi bearing down on my little truck. Heart racing, I quickly looked to the lane on my right—it was blocked off with orange cones. I considered jerking my steering wheel to the left and stomping on the gas, because the car in that lane had just moved. I didn't move fast enough. I heard the screech of brakes as I braced myself for the crunch of metal, but heard only the hiss of air brakes. The semi had come to stop just inches from the car in the lane to the left of me.

Even after traffic started to move, I sat in my lane, stunned. Jerked back to reality by the honking of a horn, I drove like a robot until I could pull off the road and stop. I dropped my head to the steering wheel, arms folded around me. I didn't just cry, I wailed.

Another time, on a busy L.A. freeway, I was doing what everyone else in five lanes was doing and trying not to get run over in the process. One lane over and about five car-lengths ahead, I watched in horror as a semi's brake lights snapped on. The whole back of the truck rocked to the left, then to the right. Time slowed as I planned where I would go when it toppled. Superman must've been driving the semi, because that enormous truck rocked back to the middle, stayed there, and continued to zip down the interstate. I wonder if the driver was tempted to pull over and cry.

A few years later, after playing a disappointing gig in the Midwest, I was gratefully heading back to comfortable housing in Chicago. My mouth watered as I thought of the thick sandwich I'd have in my hand as I sat with my feet up in front of a favorite TV show.

While I was sitting at a stoplight on Lakeshore Drive, however, a cab driver had other plans for me when he slammed into the SUV four cars back. It started a chain reaction that ended with the tailgate of my truck mashed into a V. I was so pissed I jumped out of my truck in the middle of traffic, left the door hanging open and stomped back to look at the damage. A cop who'd been directing traffic at the intersection pointed at my purse on the seat and admonished, "Lady, this is Chicago!"

I dutifully got back in my truck and pulled off to the side.

The cop turned out to be a youngster who was part of a volunteer force that only directed traffic. "Since you can all drive your vehicles," he soberly informed us, "you'll have to drive to the police station. I can't call someone to come out here."

Two of us were from out of town. We were dependent on the vague directions he gave us because this was way before GPSs or online maps. Construction had closed one of the streets. After driving in circles, I found expensive parking and walked into the station.

The other drivers were there, but no cabbie. Fortunately, one of them had noted his license, called from the station lobby and angrily informed the dispatcher about their inept and cowardly driver. It was a good hour before the cabbie strolled in, a glassy look in his eyes. His hands shook as he picked up the pen to fill in the forms. I found out later that the cab company had let their insurance lapse. No wonder, given the fine gentleman they'd hired to drive one of their cars. I could've sued them, but as the old saying goes, you can't get blood out of a cab company. I elected to let my insurance pay for it. My agent said it'd be better to get the work done after I got home so I drove the rest of that tour with a dented rear end.

I had a gig in a small bar in the Southwest in 1994. The woman who offered me housing rode with me in my truck. She clutched the dashboard every time I pressed the brake. She warned me about every danger until I was close to pulling over and making her ride in the back.

I stopped at a light. I didn't expect another one just a short block beyond. I cruised through the intersection going about thirty mph and T-boned a truck going the other way. In a shaky voice my passenger thoughtfully pointed out, "I think that was a red light."

I felt about two feet tall as I jumped out of the truck and ran over to the guy I hit. "Are you okay?" I asked.

He nodded yes but didn't say anything. We pulled out of the intersection while someone called the police. After a couple of minutes, the guy ambled over to me and said, "I'm sorry I was short with you."

Huh? Dude, I ran into you!

We talked more while waiting for the cops. He'd just made the last payment on his truck the day before. Just make me disappear, Universe.

There was only a small dent above one of his wheels, but it might have bent the axle so he was towed away. My little pickup had a smashed front grille, a buckled hood and a missing headlight. "Are you still going to the bar?" my nervous riding companion asked.

"Sure," I answered confidently, like I was some master mechanic who could just look at my truck and know it wouldn't be crawling sideways to the gig. Besides, I'm a touring musician! I'd like to see a mail carrier continue her route after that.

I jumped behind the wheel, started it up and drove slowly to the gig. The truck didn't rattle, grind or overheat, so I figured it was okay. I shouldn't have bothered driving there. I've had better gigs. Maybe I was too distracted by my poor mangled truck parked just outside.

I had a tour to finish, with little spare time or money. I cautiously drove during the day and bummed rides for my gigs at night. The truck was fixed after I got home.

My next vehicle will have a special sensor for uninsured drunken cab drivers and distracted semi drivers. And a cattle prod for me, so I won't miss any more lights.

CHAPTER SIXTY-FIVE

If It Doesn't Have a Label, Don't Eat It

Not long ago, I was in one city for a month, teaching and doing performances. Instead of getting an expensive hotel room, I did some house-sitting. I loved it. I had a place to myself where I could buy groceries, do my own cooking and watch *America's Got Talent* without being embarrassed.

It was July in the South and there's nothing I love better than a tall glass of ice-cold club soda with a slice of lemon. I bought the soda and the fruit. I didn't think to buy ice cubes. Not only was there no ice at the house, but even if I wanted to make some there was no room in their tiny freezer. I supposed I could eat something in there to make room for cubes—they told me to help myself—but it was full of unmarked containers and plastic bags of frozen white liquid. Fortunately, when they gave me a tour of the house I was told the bags held breast milk.

Think I'll leave those alone.

Club soda without ice wasn't so bad. I felt very European drinking it and I swear it helped my French lessons. *Parlez-vous français? Oui, surtout quand je bois du soda sans glace.* If that's not right, blame Google Translate. The only phrase I can remember on my own is *Voulez-vous coucher avec moi* and I'm pretty sure it has nothing to do with club soda.

Before I go on, let me tell you that if you put it in front of me and tell me it's food, I'll chow down like I haven't had a meal for weeks. Bonus points if it includes chocolate, sautéed onions or melted cheese...not in the same dish.

Sometimes I'm told to eat anything I want in the kitchen. I'm not sure what to do, though, when there's nothing in the fridge except a bottle of water and a row of condiments, some dating back several years. If I were an archaeologist, it'd be great. For a hungry musician, not so great. This is precisely why I usually travel with food.

In the mid-nineties, I had a Midwestern gig where someone picked me up at the airport and then took me to the house I'd have to myself for three days. I asked where I could find a grocery store or a restaurant, but my ride wasn't from the neighborhood and didn't know. I didn't have a cell phone or a GPS. I was told that the owner said I could explore the kitchen and eat whatever was there. I found one frozen entrée and a box of cereal.

That night at the gig, I met the owner of the house. I thanked her for the housing and then asked if she had a pantry that maybe I'd missed. She knitted her eyebrows, pursed her lips and commented, "Well, there's Rice Krispies...and wine."

Thanks to all the kind souls who've offered me refuge and a hot meal while on the road. If I'm scheduled to stay with you, don't worry, just know that I prefer milk with my Rice Krispies. And please label the frozen breast milk.

CHAPTER SIXTY-SIX

Just Bake a File in the Cake, or at Least, an Extra Key

In April of 1991, it seemed like I heard Bette Midler singing "From a Distance" everywhere I went. From a distance, my housing in Chicago looked good. I met the woman who lived there, unloaded my truck and got a key. She was giving me her cozy apartment for a few days and wouldn't be around.

Friends wanted to take me out to dinner. I decided not to drag my purse along, so I shoved some cash in my pocket along with the key and took off in their car. After having a grand time, they dropped me off at the apartment and sped off. I strolled up to the door, put in the key and...nothing. It wouldn't turn. I tried the other lock. Same thing. I did that a few times like I thought some lock fairy was going visit me and magically make it all work.

Now what? All I had was the wrong key and about a dollar in change since I'd spent most of my money on dinner.

Hands sweaty and breathing a little too fast, I wandered about the strange neighborhood. After a mile or so, I found a bar with a pay phone. Several old men hunched over drinks sat at a scratched and well-used bar. I think they were speaking Polish.

I was the only woman, the only one under seventy and probably the only one who didn't speak Polish. They stared at me as I stood in front of the phone, trying to remember the number on my phone card. I started pressing numbers, hoping muscle memory would kick in, and was relieved to hear the automated voice welcoming me to the phone system and telling me to please dial the number I wished to call.

I called home, catching my girlfriend who gave me my friend Toni's number. Toni lived in Chicago and happened to answer the phone—something I've rarely known her to do. She gets a lot of calls and voice mail is her friend. Surely the pay phone number that came up in caller ID wasn't one she recognized. For whatever reason she picked up and I owe her my firstborn. (I'm beyond child bearing and I doubt she wants kids. It's the thought that counts.)

I asked if she knew the number of my host. Although Toni knew a lot of women in town, she didn't know this one well enough to have her number. However, she had the number of someone who knew her girlfriend. We each made a couple of phone calls and tracked her down.

In the middle of all this, one of the men at the bar angrily jabbed his finger at the carefully lettered sign above the phone that stated, "Limit calls to five minutes." My crazy-eyed look probably scared him. He turned around.

I walked several blocks back to my accommodations and met my apologetic host. She gave me the right key.

The opposite happened in Baltimore. I woke up the morning after my gig. My host had already left for work. I made myself breakfast, packed and headed to the front door. It had a locked deadbolt—the kind that needed a key for the inside, too. I had no key. I tried the back door, but had the same problem.

I wasn't sure when my host would be home and I had just a few hours to get to my next gig. Fortunately, I had her work number. Too bad she wasn't answering. I left a voice mail and waited. (There was no Internet then.)

I considered breaking a window, yelling for help or sobbing hysterically. None of them seemed like a good choice so I waited… and waited…and waited. Finally, at lunchtime, she came in and said a little too casually, "Sorry about not leaving you a key."

If you ever end up in prison, pray that I'm not your roommate. You'll have no chance of escaping, although I'm thinking it might help if you knew Polish.

CHAPTER SIXTY-SEVEN

Danny DeVito and the Latest in Princess Wear

It's 2012 and since I'm currently sitting in the Newark airport, it seems fitting that I talk about flying. Every touring musician has their favorite road stories and some of mine are about the people I see on flights and in airports.

(A pigeon just strutted by, pecking at stray crumbs. Inside the airport. I love Newark.)

On my flight a few days ago, I sat next to a pleasant guy with a warm Kentucky drawl. He didn't blink when I said something about my wife. (Yes, we're legally married. How civilized of Canada. Eh?) We chatted about our jobs and our trips. I was headed to Florida gigs and he was going to Las Vegas to gamble. He stumbled when it came time to refer to my partner. He grinned and said, "Partner, er, wife, friend, um…"

I can't blame the guy. We don't know what to call each other, either. It was kind of him to try to find the right word. So much for that stereotype about Southerners being bigoted jerks.

(There's that pigeon again. Guess he came back for dessert.)

A few years ago, I sat next to a Danny DeVito look-alike. He sported a bright print shirt unbuttoned several inches down, revealing several gold chains across a chest matted with thick black hair. After a brief introduction, he sprang into a monologue about his life as a professional bridge player and his beautiful statuesque blond girlfriend. Nothing I did could deter the chatter about his exciting job and his gorgeous babe. I rummaged through my bag, pulled out my book and opened it in my lap. I stared at my book. I frowned and pointedly looked away. I did everything short of shouting, "Dude, I don't care!" Fortunately, it was a short trip. At the gate an impeccably dressed leggy blonde rushed forward, wrapped her arms around him and murmured something into his neck.

Professional bridge players must make a lot more money than I thought.

(Okay, I've got to interject some more—right next to me is a little girl and her dad. She is dressed completely in bright pink. Her sparkly top has a picture of a Disney princess, her little pink carry-on features Snow White, and on top of Dad's luggage is a pink pillow with another Disney princess. Completing the ensemble are matching pink pants and a petite pink flowered hat. What, no tiara? She just opened her suitcase and it's filled with cartoon DVDs and junk food. Her clean princess clothing must be in her father's suitcase.)

Another time, I flew from Salt Lake City to Boise. Sitting next to me was a young woman in a prim flowered dress. With a friendly smile, she said hello. I said hi back and busied myself with a book. She said she was heading home after visiting relatives and asked why I was going to Boise. I just wanted to relax and read, but my mama raised me to be polite so I gave a short answer—"I'm a musician and I'm performing there"—then went back to my book.

"That's nice," she said pleasantly. "Where?"

I thought, okay, babe, you want to talk with me? I'll be honest. "At the gay pride rally downtown."

After a couple of long seconds she warmly responded, "Oh how interesting."

In the end, we had an enjoyable conversation about LGBT pride. Her questions were respectful and a far cry from the rude

"Which one is the man?" kind of inquiries we sometimes get. I told her about Stonewall and about some of my own experiences.

As the plane was touching down, she said she could understand the struggles of my people because she was Mormon and her people have faced discrimination, too. I opened my mouth to argue, but she had got it right on some level. I pictured her at the next church potluck, telling them about the really nice lesbian she met on a plane.

CHAPTER SIXTY-EIGHT

Music, Migraines and Me

I'm lying on the floor of the church where I'm supposed to perform. There's a rowdy party in my head where everyone has a metal chisel that pounds on my skull. My stomach has joined the fiesta, rumbling and threatening to do something ugly.

There are forty people in the next room who are expecting me to play.

I'm not sure why this particular migraine started—maybe because I napped in the car on the way there, my head at an odd angle. Maybe it was something I ate. Maybe the driver we accidentally cut off at the light put an evil spell on me. Hard to say, except I've gotten migraines since I was nine years old, and I'm not the only one in my family who gets them. Maybe it's welded into my DNA.

So there I am, stretched out on the floor in the church office because there's no couch and standing up makes the room spin. While I've played through all sorts of cut fingers, tendinitis, allergies and sleep deprivation, I can't make it work now. There's a parade of concerned people lightly tapping on the door and tiptoeing in…my sweet partner who rubs my shoulders, the worried event producer with a bottle of water and a plethora of folks offering everything from Percocet to Valium. It's amazing the drugs that people pull out of their purses and pockets. Too bad we're law-abiding citizens. All we need are a few ladies of the night and illegal gambling and we'll raise more money for this church than they've ever seen in their lives.

But no, that's not such a good idea.

I'm also getting a running commentary about what's happening out there. One audience member is doing her drag king routine. Another one is warbling a tune a cappella and still another is telling some jokes. The reports get more and more desperate. I keep thinking the headache is leaving so I'm murmuring encouraging words about getting up soon.

As time goes on, I hear the door to the parking lot click open and shut several times.

The pain in my head finally subsides to a dull rumble and I can stand without careening. I tell the producer I can do a short set. If I don't walk too quickly and keep my head upright, I can sing without losing my dinner.

What's left of the audience sits politely, their eyebrows furrowed in concern. I put them at ease immediately, joking that, "The good thing about a migraine is that it can't kill you. The bad thing about a migraine is that it can't kill you." I thanked them for waiting and then did a set of songs and comedy. If I turned my head too quickly, the room blurred, but other than that, it went well and toward the end I almost forgot about the clanging in my head.

I offered to return at another time to do a show for free. I never heard back from the event organizer, though. Maybe he was afraid he'd have to have paramedics standing by.

The first time something like that happened was on one of my early tours with my friend Martie. We got up onstage in a Washington D.C. restaurant and started our show. Every time a waitress passed by with a fragrant plate of food, my stomach did a flip-flop in time to the jackhammer in my brain. After a few songs, I looked at Martie and asked off mike, "Can you finish the set alone?" She nodded sympathetically. I crept offstage. The audience thought it was part of the show.

A few years ago, I played for Charlotte's Web in Rockford, Illinois, one of my favorite venues. The evening started with a meal at the Chinese restaurant down the street. Afterward, my friend Kara and I played to an enthusiastic crowd that was everything an entertainer could ask for. Feeling great at the end of the night, I said goodbye to Kara and headed to my hotel. Sometime in the middle of the night, a racket in my head ratcheted up to a brain cell-destroying level. I swallowed medication and went back to sleep. I woke up a couple hours later with the same pain and took more drugs, but the migraine persisted. I had a teaching gig that night, a few hours away. I canceled it. Fortunately, it was a small class so I only disappointed four people. I slept until checkout time.

I returned to that venue recently and once again had a wonderful time. I ate at the same restaurant and like before, I woke up with a headache. Fortunately, the drugs killed it, and I could go on to my next gig.

No more MSG-laced Chinese food for me.

I was scheduled to play at a festival in 2009. Wanting to give them some notice, I told the artist liaison early in the day that I was sick. I was taking some drugs and going back to bed so all should be well in time for my evening performance. She called back and said they'd need to know by two that afternoon so they'd have time to replace me. Yikes. Pressure like that can sometimes make a headache worse. I called forth a calming energy, took more drugs and had a long hot shower. Fortunately, that fixed me right up.

I've found some relief with bio feedback, better eating, regular exercise and really good drugs. While I can't argue with the health benefits of a good diet and being in shape, I don't like taking the drugs. They're expensive, sometimes hard to get and have weird side effects.

I've also tried acupuncture, massage, a multitude of herbs and whining. Whining helps a little. And a good massage is more than worth its weight in migraine meds.

Lots of well-meaning folks have suggestions for relief but really, taking the herb feverfew or getting a gentle foot massage is like shooting BBs at Godzilla. And for those folks who think it's a hangover or just a little headache…you may find yourself in one of my satirical songs. If I'm really pissed, I'll include your name and phone number.

I'm migraine-free for ninety-nine percent of my performances. If Godzilla breaks into my head, he'd better watch out. I'm armed with migraine meds and I'm not afraid to use them.

CHAPTER SIXTY-NINE

M&Ms Are My SuperPower

I get through long drives with great road tunes or intriguing talk radio. Conversations can also help. Since I tour alone, that means I'm talking to myself or my GPS, Marcia. She's got a sexy voice (I love how she admonishes me with reCALculating) but really, what gets me to the next gig is food.

M&Ms are the perfect road food because no matter how hot it gets, they stay self-contained. Chocolate bars, not so much. More often than not, they melt into pieces of art that require a yoga position to remove from my food bag. Oh, the sacrifice one makes for Good Chocolate.

I don't measure trips by miles (or clicks or bad billboards), but by M&Ms. I can make a small bag last an hour if I'm going about seventy mph on an interstate. It can be an issue if I'm pulled over. "But, officer, I was only going thirty M&Ms per hour."

If you listen to my music it's clear where my passions reside. I have one song about chocolate, one about potato chips, one inspired by cheesecake and one called "Dark Chocolate."

Occasionally, I get food gifts from fans. Often, it's chocolate. No complaint there. One enterprising fan gave me a gift bag of chocolate, potato chips, cheesecake and pork rinds—the last item because I used to tell the story onstage about sharing housing with a pig. Recently, I got a basket of dark chocolate, lotion, a towel and a photo of Rachel Maddow because they're mentioned in "Menopause Mambo" and well, Rachel couldn't be there in person.

I need to write a song about lasagna and salad so I can get a good meal.

During one tour I got caught in an ice storm. Fortunately, I found a motel, but there was no restaurant nearby. I didn't bring my usual food box, so I was stuck with what I found in the vending machine and leftovers from my last restaurant meal. It's amazing how far you can stretch a box of biscuits and several bottles of root beer. Three meals, it turns out, but never, ever, dunk a biscuit in root beer.

A few years ago after one long day of driving, I collapsed in a motel in a tiny Midwestern town. The only restaurant was across the street. It featured bright orange vinyl booths and a menu where almost everything was smothered in canned gravy. I was encouraged by the fact that they had a salad bar, so that's what I ordered.

I scooped brown-edged iceberg lettuce and watery carrot shreds onto my plate. There were two dressing choices—lumpy light brown (Thousand Island?) or bright orange (French?). I slopped some of the latter on top. I skipped the other salads that were swimming in mayonnaise (I swear one piece of macaroni moved of its own accord) and the orange (Are you sensing a theme?) gelatin dotted with canned pineapple. I contemplated sprinting for the door and checking out the motel vending machine, but they'd know where to find me. Anyone who eats that much gravy is bound to own guns, so you definitely don't want to piss them off.

As I pushed the weary vegetables around on my plate the waitress slumped by and said, "Honey, you can eat all you want."

I simply smiled and thought, This *is* all I want.

That meal stayed with me, but I wasn't so lucky another time. In April of 2004, my stomach started clenching up on the long drive to a gig. After nearly doubling over with pain, I stopped at a rest area and curled up in the front seat of my truck. I considered calling my producer and telling her I wasn't going to make it. We musicians are like the post office, though, so I forced myself into an upright position, got behind the wheel and made my way to the gig.

My voice was ragged from the end of a cold so my audience probably figured my pasty color was from that. I struggled through the show, judiciously timing my breaks. I even stayed to sign albums. Fortunately I had no gigs for a few days, so I holed up in housing—an apartment I had to myself—and ate only plain yogurt and drank gallons of water.

An hour after coming home from that tour, my partner of seven years broke up with me. If you want to know the story just listen to my plethora of breakup songs. While you're at it, check out the food songs, too, and tell Frito-Lay they need me for their next marketing campaign. That fat check could buy a lot of M&Ms. No orange ones, please.

CHAPTER SEVENTY

Walking With the Dead and
Dancing With the Living

After the first tour I did alone in 1990, I came home and found that I'd gained eight pounds. I'm not a slave to a scale. I haven't even owned one most of my life. But, I couldn't afford a whole new wardrobe. I also had mysterious pains in my back and right leg. Maybe the long drives—my record was sixteen hours in one day—and bacon and eggs every morning were a bad idea?

My chiropractor gently suggested that walking would alleviate the pain. I figured out on my own that fried food every morning would eventually cause my arteries to slap shut, and my bank account to dwindle. Dragging my guitar to and from my truck was not going to be enough exercise. Since I considered my chiropractor right up there next to Ghandi when it came to wisdom, I decided to follow her advice. Anywhere I was, if I had an hour or two free, I'd walk. My housing hosts would often point me to beautiful wooded trails, a reservoir ringed with a walking path or just a neighborhood with light traffic. My favorite places, though, were graveyards. Some people get the oogies walking through them, but I enjoy the quiet, and on hot days, the shade. Why should dead people be the only ones who get to use these beautiful places? (I live between two major cemeteries now. I joke that it's great—the neighbors are really quiet because most of them are deceased.) I love to look at the headstones. Some have funny inscriptions or a story almost told, like whole families spanning several generations. Some are heartbreaking, like the little stones carved with cherubs that mark where the babies are buried.

I once stayed at a bed-and-breakfast in rural Vermont. I took the dirt road that ran by the house and walked for a long time, the ground crunching under my feet on a beautiful, crisp day in late fall, bare trees reaching for a blustery sky. As I rounded a curve, I saw a small cemetery in what seemed like the middle of nowhere. There was no church or other building nearby, just these worn granite headstones with barely readable names and dates, some going back to the early 1800s. When I returned, I asked my host about it and she said there were little plots like that all over the area. This particular one probably was near the family's house at one time.

I found other ways to exercise. For a while, I belonged to the Y and discovered that my membership there got me into other Y's all over the country, either for a discount or for free. They ranged from cramped, dingy buildings with a few worn weight machines, to bright, spacious ones with lots of equipment.

Hotel exercise rooms were always a grand adventure. It didn't matter if it was a Super 8 or a Hilton, I never knew what I would find. It could be a cheap grimy elliptical machine made by cave people (and believe me, those stone steps offer a great workout), or a well-outfitted gym with clean mats and a TV that got something beyond three shopping channels. The American Host in Hart, MI, has a trail behind it that goes through a nice wooded area, all the way into the small downtown. No graveyard, though.

Recently, I stayed in one place for a whole month. The Y there was really nice so I asked about buying a one month pass. (I no longer belong to one at home.) I'm not sure exactly how this happened, but they gave me a free pass for the entire month. Not only did I get to use their gym, but I went to Zumba classes, too.

I love Zumba, from the great polyrhythmic Latin-style music to the cool dance moves. I've found a few classes while on tour. They've really been fun, except for that one in southern Florida where the music was so loud I could feel the bass pounding in my chest. I persevered, stuffing tissue pieces in my ears.

For several years, I looked for bellydance classes while on the road. One of my favorites was a class in Washington State, near Portland. The teacher apologized because they were perfecting choreography for a show. I told her I didn't care, as long as they didn't mind me stumbling along. I picked it up fairly easily and before long, was sailing along with the rest of them. Afterward, the instructor asked if I was sure I didn't want to move there and join their troupe?

Once, instead of taking a bellydance class, I taught one. My buddy Kara owned a small music store in Nashville, Indiana. She moved a couple of instrument racks out of the middle of the floor, giving us room to stretch out. There were still instruments lining the walls, though, so I hoped that none of my students threw up their hands and took out a guitar or two, a real danger since they were all beginners. Fortunately, the two-thousand-dollar guitars were too high to be damaged by a casual arm fling. I opted to stay away from the veils that day.

My absolute favorite teacher in the world was my first one in Tucson, Kathryn Ferguson. She was one of the early originators of the American cabaret style and is such a beautiful dancer. Even after I moved, I'd catch a class or two when I was back for a concert. She always warmly welcomed me, announcing to the class that I was a big star. Only to my mama, but I never corrected her.

If you ever have trouble finding me, look for the nearest graveyard. I'll be hanging out with the dead folks even though they don't dance. At least, I hope they don't.

CHAPTER SEVENTY-ONE

Radio Stardom

It used to be that a musician had to get airplay to successfully tour and sell recordings. When I did my first tour in the late eighties that was the case. Too bad most stations weren't clamoring for lesbian folksingers. The wonderful exceptions were the plethora of women's and LGBT programs that were supportive of my music. The others took a little convincing and eventually, I also had a good group of folk DJs who were gracious about playing my songs, even if "Menstrual Tango" made a few of them twitch.

All of these programs were on public radio. You have to be twenty and look good in tight pants to get airplay on mainstream radio.

I sought out interview opportunities whenever I was playing in a town that had a strong public radio station. These are not the people with huge budgets and celebrity DJs. We're talking small six-channel boards that only worked when the mice stopped chewing through the wires. And since most of the DJs were volunteers, I encountered everything from professionals who'd read my press kit and asked astute questions, to the ones who could barely remember my name.

At one college station sometime in the 1990s, the perky host parked me in front of a mike, then climbed on a nearby table, plopped into a cross-legged position, reached over to flip the lever to put us live on the air and inquired, "Well?" She said little after that and even walked out of the room for a while as I interviewed myself. At another college station, the DJ asked a couple of questions that I answered, then she paused, scratched her head and asked, "What do you wear onstage?"

"Clothing."

Next question.

In 1997, I was on a popular folk show in Washington State. The DJ referred to the "taboo subject matter" of my songs. I guess that was code for "lesbian." Either that or he objected to the stellar cat barf imitation I do in "When Cats Take Over the World." (When we recorded the song, it was actually done by backup singer Linda Severt. My cats would like to take credit for my training, but it was really Linda. No one hacks up a hair ball like her.)

I loved listening to public radio, too, even if I wasn't the featured guest, and it got me through some long drives. I always looked around on the left end of the dial to catch the local bluegrass show or one of my favorite NPR shows. What a thrill it was to hear *Car Talk* play my music. They did it four times—twice for the song "Drive All Night." I didn't have the heart to tell them it's not really about driving.

One time, late at night in California, I found a station that was broadcasting in a language I didn't recognize. When I heard them say a small town in northern Arizona, I figured it might be Navajo. I didn't understand the words, but the music was cool. One early morning, as I zoomed out of Chicago, I found a gospel station. I love the energy of gospel—how it simmers in the beginning and builds up to a huge and joyous ending. The DJ was into the spirit, too, and sounded as upbeat as the songs. I listened to it until it was out of range.

In May of 2013, I tuned into an Asheville, NC, public radio station as I passed through town. I thought I heard the DJ say that coming up next was "Francophone Friday." I married into a Francophone family so I thought, How cool, then, Is there a Francophone community in North Carolina? When the DJ announced it again, I realized he was saying "Frank on Friday."

It was a regular show featuring music by Frank Zappa—only on public radio and only in Asheville.

I got a taste of the other side when I deejayed at KXCI, my local community radio station in Tucson, for six years in the nineties. It was great to be behind a mike when I wasn't touring and I loved discovering all that great indie music in our library. I didn't care that it was a volunteer position because it was so much fun and a great way to support all musicians, regardless of whether or not Sony dumped millions into their careers. I especially liked that we were required to play at least one local artist per hour. Tucson has a great variety of wonderful musicians, from mariachi to alt rock.

Our board was from an old dance DJ setup. Some of its wires were connected with duct tape. On chilly days, the tower on a nearby mountain would sometimes stop working because of ice. During one early morning shift in the winter, I got a call from a listener who politely inquired, "Did you know you've been off the air for an hour?"

Oops.

I was good at choosing the music and I'm a decent announcer. I can freak out about the technical stuff, though. We may not have had an elaborate setup, but all those dials and lights might as well have been the cockpit of a 747. It took every ounce of concentration from my tiny musician's brain to remember which knobs and levers needed to be turned. For my first shift by myself, I often forgot to breathe. Afterward, I felt like I'd consumed a case of Red Bull. I got better after that. I still had moments of terror, though, when one of the cranky CD players refused to work or when I couldn't find the next song and the one currently playing was ending in five...four... three...two...NOW seconds.

When I wasn't panicking I was a pretty good DJ. After a particularly good show, the music director liked to poke his head in the studio and exclaim, "Great show! We're going to triple your salary."

We played just about everything except opera. When I was home and off tour, I subbed for anyone who couldn't do their shift. My knowledge of the music library was pretty extensive, so I could do a variety of programs. The Morning Meditation Show was tough, though. Try playing ethereal instrumental music at six a.m. I'm sure there was dead air a few times as I fought to wake up enough to cue the next song.

One Sunday evening I was hosting the women's show, which was easy for me. Fifteen minutes before the end, the DJ for the next show hadn't come in. Minutes went by and I started playing the last song. The music librarian brought down a crate of LPs and said, "The DJ for the African Music Show can't make it."

I knew nothing about African music.

I arbitrarily chose an album and cued up the longest cut. While it was playing, I pulled out another LP, picked a song at random and played it next. Crossing my fingers that listeners wouldn't be reaching for the "off" button, I continued for the rest of the show. After it was done, I wiped my brow and thanked the Universe that I wouldn't have to do that again.

I hosted the show for three weeks.

People often asked if I played my own songs and the answer was rarely, and only if requested. During one shift, a listener phoned and asked if I was the artist who did that song about sleeping on sidewalks. I replied that I was. ("Sidewalks" is a song about a homeless woman that was written by Michelle Marquand and appeared on my first release, *Closer to Home*.) The caller told me that until last month, she had been homeless, and would I play that song for her? You bet I did.

Once people found out that I was a DJ, some of my interviews on the road changed. At one tiny station in Texas, the host interviewed me and then asked if I would like to program one of her sets. I had such a great time that she wondered if I could make some announcements, so I did those, too. Then she said she'd forgotten something at home and Martin Sexton was coming in. Would I mind interviewing him? I hardly knew his music, but I said, "Sure." He probably appreciated that I didn't ask him questions about his clothing, like that college DJ did to me a few years prior.

In 2012, I had the pleasure of being on *Canadian Spaces*, a folk show hosted by Chopper McKinnon on CKCU in Ottawa. He'd started the program in 1980, making it the longest running folk show in Canada. With his gentle manner, white hair and beard, and overalls, he seemed like someone straight out of the sixties. We talked a bit and he played a couple of my CD cuts as Chris White co-hosted. Just before I left, I pulled out a recording for the library and warned Chopper that one of the songs had a four-letter word, but the rest were okay for airplay. I gave it to Chris who dutifully took a pen and on the CD cover, drew a careful line through that song. A week or two after that, Chopper pulled out the disc and thought that Chris had underlined the song, so he put it on the air. After a minute or so, someone rushed into the studio and put on another song. We lost Chopper in 2013. He can play whatever he wants now.

CHAPTER SEVENTY-TWO

Waiting for the Phone to Ring

Some people think I just wait for the phone to ring or for that email to arrive and, voilá, I have a gig. Maybe if you're Sheryl Crow. For Jamie Anderson, as well as thousands of other indie performers, it means contacting venue after venue, over and over again because the squeaky wheel gets the gig—hopefully, the squeaky wheel that also has an entertaining show.

When I was performing full-time and off the road between tours, I spent about thirty hours a week pestering, uh, contacting, venues and promoting gigs. I actually had to schedule time to play the guitar and to write. I'm not complaining. If this was what I needed to do to make a living playing music, show me the venue contact list and let me go to it. And I wish there was that one venue list. There were a couple of directories, but venue information changed so frequently, they were often out of date. It took a lot of research to find places to play. I'd scan other performers' tour schedules, collect information from fans, and check local newspapers. With the advent of the Internet, that job was made easier. It can still be time consuming, though.

I did have a booking agent a couple of times in my career. One got me some great bookings with two other funny songwriters, but another one that was booking me as a solo quit after a few months, telling me that her partner bugged her about getting a "better" job, even if it was at McDonald's. It's pretty bad when flipping burgers pays better than booking a folk performer.

I'm like a dog with a bone. There are venues I'm still contacting after twenty-plus years, because eventually, they'll come around. For me, the latte is always half-full.

There's a well-known folk coffeehouse in New England where I really wanted to play. Favorite musicians like Cheryl Wheeler and Patty Larkin had performed there. What could be better than to stand where they stood? In the early nineties, I sent the venue audition material several times.

If only I'd get a response. My material probably got lost. With a place like that, they're faced with an avalanche of inquiries from eager musicians and agents. It's easy to weed out the metal bands and other inappropriate acts, and after that, what are you left with? A slew of singer-songwriters, banjo-wielding traditional folk artists, Celtic bands, acoustic blues groups and many others. It's a struggle for those of us on the other side to rise to the top. What can help is a referral from a better-known artist, for them to hear you wow them at another venue, or sometimes it's just plain luck. I think I might have fallen into the latter category with this particular coffeehouse. After a few years, they finally booked me, for a showcase that included two other performers. It's not a big place and splitting the door income three ways might give me just enough for a large latte and a quarter tank of gas. It could lead to my own gig, though, and I could put this venue on the "places played" part of my press kit. It was definitely a coffeehouse that people recognized even if they didn't live in the town, and would give me some cred.

It felt comfortable standing on the small stage, looking out over the crowd seated at café tables, cups of coffee in front of them. To my left was a row of small high windows where I could see pairs of feet strolling by. I'd worked that hard to get booked in a basement, and you know? It wasn't bad. A lot of folk and women's coffeehouses are in basements. In big cities, sometimes that's all there is, and I figure as long as you don't get a free sewer rat with your mocha, you're okay.

Each of the three of us took our turns singing a song, going around about four times. I remained upbeat through the other musicians' offerings. It wasn't hard because they were very good. During one song, I slapped out the time with my hands on my thighs. Halfway through the tune, the singer-songwriter turned around with a scowl on his face and pointedly looked at me. All right, dude, I'll stop. I was in time and not that loud, but apparently, I was not the band he ordered.

It was a decent enough gig. It never led to my own show, though, and clearly, I'll never find work as a percussionist.

Another booking I really tried hard to get was at a big festival. I carefully followed their audition directions every year. I made sure to let them know my touring schedule so they could hear me live. I just wish one of the bookers hadn't come to a gig where I wasn't exactly on fire. I don't know if I'd lost my edge that night, or if the entire audience had just come from a funeral. At any rate, the booker left early. But like that proverbial dog, I never gave up and after fourteen years, I got an email that made me whoop with joy. They wanted me! From the way the booker described the gig, it was clear she thought they'd booked me before. I wasn't going to correct her. A good gig is a good gig.

Festivals are plum gigs. You get to play for a lot of people at once and usually it results in other concerts in the region and some merchandise sales. (We don't just sell CDs. One indie performer I know had a whole clothing line, including socks.) They're hard to get, though, since like that well-known coffeehouse, they are overwhelmed with audition material. A self-booking musician gets used to the rejections. Heck, I'm happy to get them so I can cross them off my "to be pestered" list. I don't, however, love all of the form letters. Suggesting to me that I try their open mike first is great for a new performer, but not if I've played there before. That's what I got in a recent letter, from a festival where I'd headlined several times. Just say "not this year."

My phone is ringing. I gotta go.

CHAPTER SEVENTY-THREE

Through Rain, Through Sleet,
Through Smoking Monitors

It was 1998 and I'd been booked at a big folk festival in Texas. I looked out from backstage and frowned at the black clouds hanging low in the sky. The act currently performing was huddled under cover as the rain blew in toward them. I was next. It was an important gig and short of a tornado, I was determined to perform. Just call me Dorothy.

As lightning repeatedly flashed, I reconsidered. I turned to the festival organizer and shouted (to be heard over the rat-a-tat-tat of hail), "You're going to shut down the stage, right?"

He smiled, shook his head and yelled back, "We never stop the festival."

I turned to Dave Nachmanoff, my side player, leaned close and mumbled, "I think we're going to die out there."

The sound techs scrambled around to set us up as far under the stage cover as they could. A mist still reached us, making my guitar strings feel sticky, but it was nothing compared to the vats of water sloshing down on the audience. We started our first song facing rows of empty wet chairs topped by an angry gray-and-black sky. The chairs closest to us had a short row of lumpy colored plastic.

After we finished the song, a couple of arms shot out from the shapes and we heard a muffled, "Yay Jamie! Yay Dave!" Then the body parts would retract, like a line of turtles pulling into their shells.

The water continued to stream down until it turned to a light sprinkle halfway through our set. It stopped as we did the last two songs. We saw heads and legs appear from under the row of colorful rain ponchos and tarps in the front row. We also noticed a few people a hundred or so yards away, huddled under craft vendors' tents. We didn't just get a paycheck for this gig, we got to live another day. Bonus.

Later that same year, I played in Syracuse. Under a blackening sky, I made the drive. A radio DJ mentioned a tornado warning. Remembering that Midwest gig where the producer laughed at my apprehension about a tornado, I straightened my shoulders and thought, so what? I wasn't going to let a little bad weather ruin my gig. By the time I arrived, huge claps of thunder and umbrella-breaking rain had taken over. Feigning nonchalance, I quickly carried my stuff into the small café and did a sound check. Fifteen minutes before the start of the show, the fire alarm started screaming. No one smelled smoke or saw any flames, so we stayed put, fingers in our ears. It beat going outside, where we'd need a boat. Ten minutes later, the alarm quieted and I did the show, in spite of the still-current tornado warning. Twenty people showed up to hear me. I wasn't going to disappoint them.

In March of 1993, I played in Orlando. My gig the night before, in St. Augustine, had been canceled because of a tornado. Orlando had high winds and hadn't fared any better. A lot of the city was still without electricity. Still, one hundred hardy souls ventured out around the downed trees and power lines, and came to the show, bless their hearts. It was one of my best gigs on that tour.

Outdoor festivals have great weather stories. There was one in New England where there was frost on the ground in the early morning. At the time I lived in Arizona and anything colder than sixty degrees was winter to me. Thankfully, the moisture that fell from the sky was only rain, but at those temperatures, it might as well have been snow.

The stage was rescheduled several times to accommodate the tumultuous weather. When the clouds parted long enough for a show, I realized that I had a hard time strumming my guitar with fingers stiff from cold. My friend, Sue Fink, shared the set with me. I'd do a song, and then rush off the stage to be wrapped in a blanket. A kind stage tech would hand me a hot cup of water to hold while Sue did her song. Then it was her turn to dart offstage and take my place. We went back and forth like that for our whole show.

Pools of water had collected on the stage. I was told not to touch the mike stands. I tried not to think about my guitar with metal strings, plugged into an amp. I was fine until the monitor speaker in front of me started sparking, then smoking. It was oddly appropriate at first, given that I was in the middle of "Dark Chocolate." However, I prefer to die peacefully in my sleep when I'm a hundred and five, not at thirty-two in a stage fire, so I said casually into the mike, "I think the monitor is smoking." I strummed a chord and paused, stepping back as three of the stage crew frantically moved the speaker and swept water off the stage. I hoped they were wearing rubber-soled boots.

We finished the set.

Now I understand why rock bands use smoke machines, although I'm not sure a folksinger needs quite that much excitement.

In 2002 I was onstage with several other performers at a festival in southern Florida when suddenly the sky opened up. The audience rushed for the stage, the only covered spot within a hundred yards. As we stood there, elbow to elbow in that tiny space, I thought someone should continue entertaining, so I grabbed my mandolin. I jumped into the first upbeat song that came into my mind, inviting them to sing along. Half-hearted smiles greeted me. I was in the wrong part of the country to do a song called "Hurricane," especially during a thunderstorm.

Oops.

One summer, I played at nine festivals. It rained at almost every one. It got to where I was joking with festival organizers not to book me.

Years ago, at the Michigan Womyn's Music Festival, I sat in the audience as Robin Flower's band ripped through a lightning-fast bluegrass song while bolts of real lightning shot across the sky. Just to my left the stories-high sound tower swayed slightly in the wind. A crew ran up to each side of the stage and put tarps over the speaker stacks as rain started to pummel us. Audience members shrieked as they covered their heads and ran from the area. I stayed put. Robin is one of my favorite performers and there was no way I was missing her. The fact that I was in the middle of field during a raging storm didn't faze me. Much.

They had to quit soon, though. The potential to die always trumps live music, even if it's damn good bluegrass.

CHAPTER SEVENTY-FOUR

Three Bridges

I'm sitting in downtown Tempe, Arizona, the town where I grew up. It's a warm fall day in the desert in Tempe Beach Park, a funny name for a piece of irrigated greenery with a playground, but it's on the banks of the Salt River. When I was growing up, the river was dry most of the year. Now they've made part of it a lake. It's strange to see it surrounded by rock and sparse desert brush.

Children are yelling to each other—some in Spanish, some in English—as they run across the brownish-green grass under a clear blue sky. A mom calls out, "Be careful!" A ballpark is in front of me on the far side and circled by a wall made with smooth river stones that also supports the road that used to lead to the Ash Avenue Bridge. Most of the old bridge is gone now, and I can't walk on the road because it's surrounded by a fence and locked with several padlocks.

I wrote a song about this place and although I sing about the three bridges you could see from here, it was really a metaphor for the choices I've made. Fitting, too, that they are bridges and I've crossed so many of them in my life. Sometimes I chose the sturdy bridge with the safe sidewalks, and sometimes, the one that was closed, with piles of rubble and jagged rebar.

The song is a true story about taking a walk on the closed Ash Avenue Bridge, years ago, when I was a kid. I was there with friends, as well as my dad. In fact, he was the one leading the way. Instead of retracing our steps and coming back on that bridge, we returned on the still-active railway bridge, not realizing then that if the train came, there'd be nowhere to go. Just minutes after crossing that bridge, we heard a train whistle. I had nightmares all that night about speeding locomotives.

I got the desire to play music from Dad and maybe his sense of daring. From my mom, too—in 2013, at the age of seventy-five, she jumped out of an airplane (a tandem jump, but still) and in 2014, she went zip lining above a wild animal park. Why else would I set off across the country alone, driving thousands of miles, just to step up onstage and sing for a roomful of strangers? Again and again, I heard from people I met at gigs, "I could never do what you do." Sure you could, if you loved writing and playing music as much as I do. Besides, it's a lot safer than zipping over lions and tigers.

I joke that I don't tour anymore. I just book gigs to finance trips I want to make. I enjoy the hell out of those performances. There's nothing more satisfying than hearing applause when you've done a good job. I could never be an accountant. No one claps when you balance the books.

Thanks to all of you who have enriched my life and made my work possible—from the expertly produced shows, to the comfortable beds, to your mama's homemade cookies, to the sweet letters about how much you enjoyed a song. I'm even grateful for the dirty sheets and lousy sound equipment because it taught me to ask for what I need, and still let me play my music for all of you. As long as someone wants to hear me, I'm there. I'm especially interested in hearing from you if you live in Hawaii, but Burnt Corn, Alabama might work, too. And if you're Melissa Etheridge, I can always clear my schedule for a tour with you. I promise not to drink your water.

Bella Books, Inc.

Women. Books. Even Better Together.

P.O. Box 10543
Tallahassee, FL 32302

Phone: 800-729-4992
www.bellabooks.com